IMAGES
of America

CALAVERAS BIG TREES

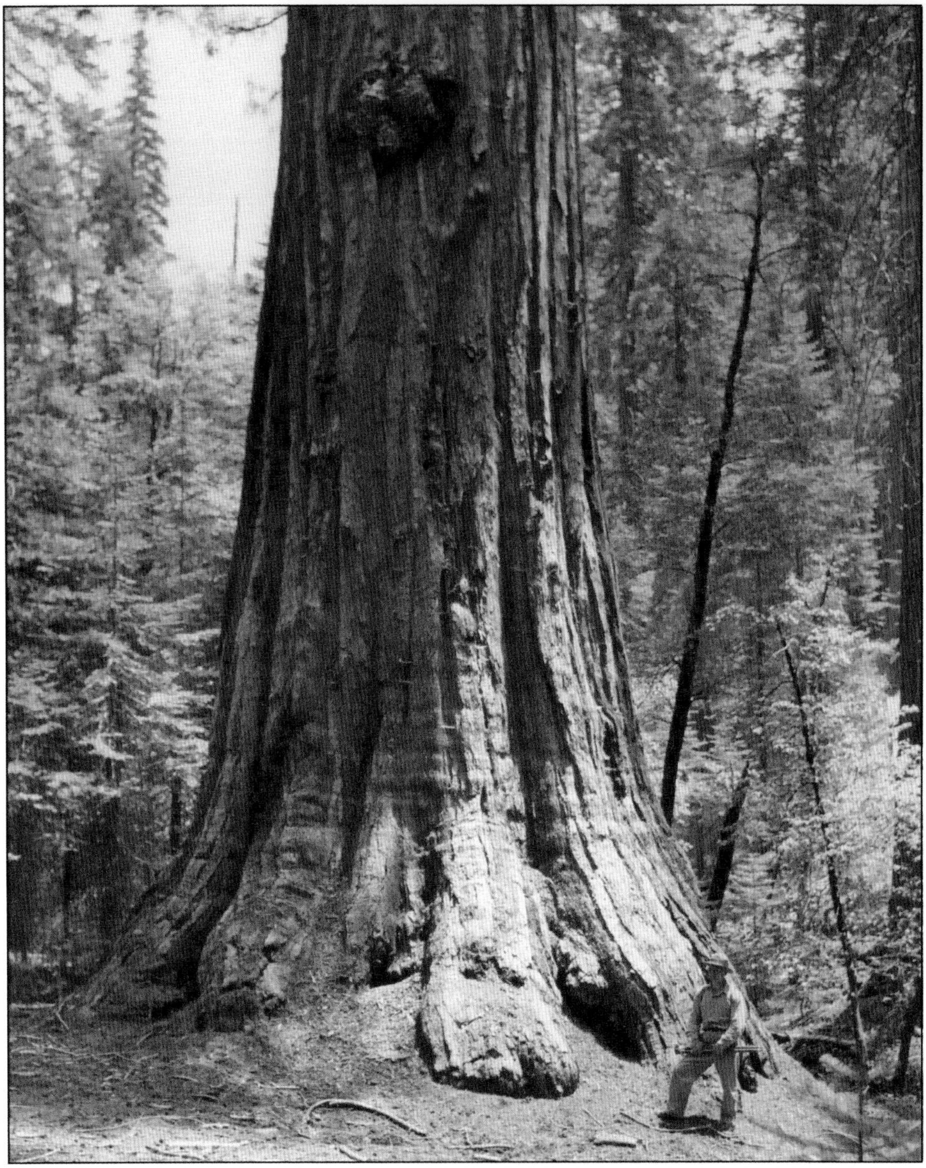

Sequoiadendron giganteum is the scientific name for the big trees of Calaveras County, although most people call them giant sequoia. Growing only along the western slope of California's Sierra Nevada range, giant sequoias are conifers, or cone-bearing seed plants. They are known as redwoods because of the reddish color of their bark and heartwood. Only two other redwood species exist worldwide: the California coast redwoods (*Sequoia sempevirens)* and China's dawn redwood (*Metasequoia glyptostroboides*). The coast redwoods are the tallest living trees on earth. Giant sequoias have the distinction of being the largest because of their mass, as evidenced in this photograph. (Calaveras Big Trees State Park.)

ON THE COVER: The Calaveras Big Trees became a tourist destination shortly after their discovery in 1852. These visitors encircle one of the giant trees in the late 1880s. Tourists often engaged in seeing how many people it would take to surround the massive trunk of a giant sequoia in the North Grove. (Old Timer's Museum, Murphys, California.)

IMAGES
of America

CALAVERAS BIG TREES

Carol A. Kramer
Calaveras Big Trees Association

ARCADIA
PUBLISHING

ISBN 978-0-7385-8118-7

Published by Arcadia Publishing
Charleston, South Carolina

Printed in the United States of America

Library of Congress Control Number: 2010924216

For all general information contact Arcadia Publishing at:
Telephone 843-853-2070
Fax 843-853-0044
E-mail sales@arcadiapublishing.com
For customer service and orders:
Toll-Free 1-888-313-2665

Visit us on the Internet at www.arcadiapublishing.com

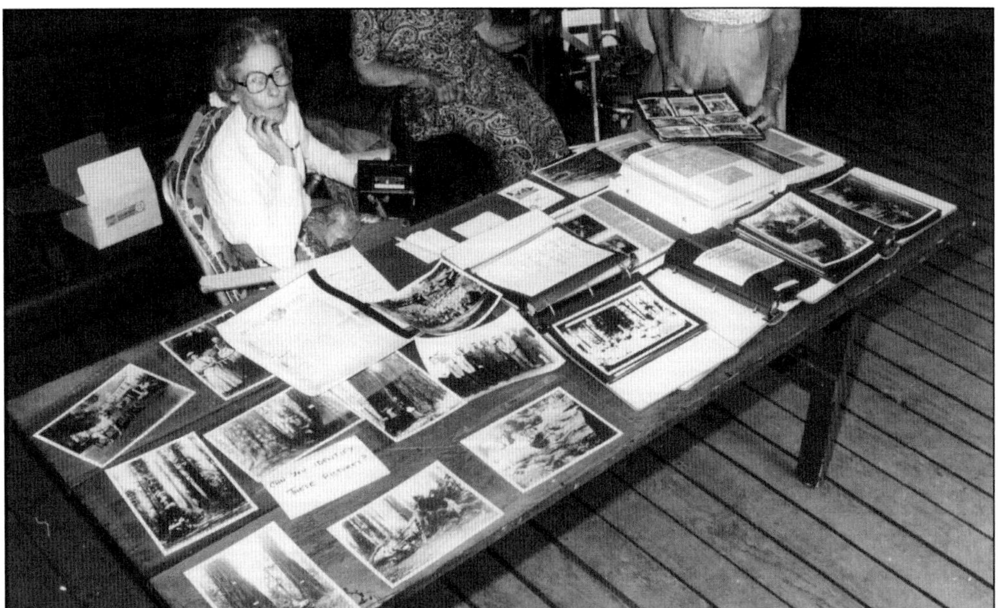

The late Frances E. Bishop staffs the history table at Calaveras Big Trees State Park's 50th anniversary celebration in this 1981 photograph. Bishop attended the park's dedication in 1931. A tireless researcher and historian for the Calaveras Big Trees Association, Bishop researched and documented the park's complicated and fascinating history. Her materials, donated to the park upon her death in 1987, provided a wonderful resource for this book. (Calaveras Big Trees State Park.)

Contents

ACKNOWLEDGMENTS

This book became a reality with assistance from many people, beginning with the board of directors and president Marcy Crawford of the Calaveras Big Trees Association (CBTA), who entrusted me with the history of their beloved "Big Trees." Support from Calaveras Big Trees State Park (CBTSP) superintendent Gary Olson and California State Parks Sector superintendent Vince Sereno also was important to this project.

I want to single out CBTA board members Steve Stocking and Bruce Thomsen for helping gather photographs and reviewing text. Bruce, a former regional interpretive specialist for California State Parks, was an invaluable resource. Thanks to CBTSP interpreter Wendy Harrison, who previously cataloged the park's historical photographs, for sharing her extensive knowledge of park history.

Thanks to Thonni Morikawa, curator at Columbia State Historic Park, for providing access to the CBTSP archives and for sharing her expertise on women's period clothing.

The following individuals assisted with accessing historical photographs while also offering camaraderie: Michael Wurtz, University of the Pacific Library; Patricia Keats, The Society of California Pioneers; Margaret Sweet, Ely-Winton Historical Society; and William Maxwell, Bank of Stockton.

I also want to recognize archivist Shannon Van Zant, Calaveras County Archives; Dr. Robert A. Buchanan, volunteer for the Old Timer's Museum; and Karen Nicholson, Calaveras County Historical Society. Photographs from these collections were vital to telling the park's story.

These acknowledgements would be incomplete without recognizing the late Frances E. Bishop. A dogged researcher and official historian of the Calaveras Big Trees Association, she left the park her research materials, historical photographs, and an unpublished manuscript. Her contribution to this project is incalculable.

Finally, I want to thank my husband, Robert, and my son, Christopher, for their support and encouragement.

The images in this volume appear courtesy of:
Bank of Stockton Historical Photo Collection (BOS)
Calaveras Big Trees State Park Archives (CBTSP)
Calaveras County Archives (CCA)
Calaveras County Historical Society (CCHS)
Library of Congress, Prints and Photographs Division (LOC)
Old Timer's Museum, Murphys, California (OTM)
Robert N. Dennis Collection of Stereoscopic Views at the New York Public Library (NYPL)
Society of California Pioneers, Lawrence and Houseworth Albums, Titles: 664-*Mammoth Grove Hotel*; 667-*Section of the Big Tree and House*; 669-*Interior of the Stump House*; 694-*Mother of the Forest*; 697-*Abraham Lincoln*; 703-*General View of the Mammoth Grove and Hotel*. Gift of Florence V. Flinn (SCP)

INTRODUCTION

The Big Tree . . . is Nature's forest masterpiece,
and as far as I know, the greatest of all living things.

—John Muir

On July 5, 1931, the famous North Calaveras Grove of giant sequoias was officially dedicated as Calaveras Big Trees State Park. It was a long time in coming and only a partial victory. The nearby and much larger South Grove of giant sequoias was in the hands of a lumber company and would remain so for another 23 years before joining the safe embrace of the California state park system.

But on that summer day, the hundreds of people gathered were happy to celebrate the preservation of the well-loved grove of Big Trees, among nature's most magnificent wonders and one of California's earliest tourist attractions.

Giant sequoias are the largest living trees on earth. They can achieve 300 feet in height, making them as tall as the dome of the U.S. Capitol building or the Statue of Liberty. Yet it is not their height alone that overwhelms the senses. Many are between 20 and 30 feet in diameter at their base with a circumference approaching 100 feet, and sometimes more.

Explorers, hunters, and immigrants traversing the rugged terrain of the Sierra Nevada in the 1830s were the first non-native people to spot the mammoth trees, most likely southern groves near Yosemite. Early reports of "some trees extremely large," spread by word of mouth or in obscure published reports, were considered fanciful tales.

By the late 1840s, all eyes were focused on the search for gold and the prospect of overnight wealth. Stories of big trees were of no interest to men seeking the next big strike in the California foothills.

Augustus T. Dowd was not the first to visit the Calaveras Big Tree Grove, yet he is the one credited with its discovery. A hunter for the Union Water Company, Dowd likely had heard none of these stories when he headed into the woods in the spring of 1852. He was simply doing his job, hunting game to feed the workers building ditches, flumes, and canals near Murphys, a thriving mining camp. He was chasing down a wounded grizzly when the sight of two enormous trees stopped him in his tracks. He could scarcely believe his eyes. Later known as the Sentinels, one still stands today, with the other fallen at its feet.

Dowd was further amazed when he stepped around these and spotted a tree even more gigantic. The Discovery Tree is estimated to have been about 300 feet tall and 32 feet in diameter at its base. More unbelievable still, he realized he was at the edge of an entire grove of 100 gargantuan trees.

Because tall tales told around the campfire were typical for an evening's entertainment among the miners and workers, Dowd's dinner companions laughed and made fun of his story. Not willing to let it drop, Dowd used a ruse a few days later to lead a small group of men the 15 miles or so back to the grove.

Upon their return to Murphys, the men shared the story of their adventure. Word of the big tree soon spread throughout the area, with an early report published in the Sonora newspaper in June 1852. Other newspapers soon reported the finding and sent reporters to verify its veracity. Within six months, the big tree story had circled the globe.

Yet many people in the middle of the 19th century found it hard to believe that trees of such monumental size existed. To the rest of the country in the decade before the Civil War, California was still a world away, the wild and unexplored West. Many simply scoffed at the nonsense of such tales.

It was not long, however, before some hardy adventurers began trekking to the grove to see the big tree with their own eyes. Among the early visitors were William H. Hanford, president of the Union Water Company, and Joseph M. Lapham of Murphys. Hanford quickly saw an opportunity to make his fortune by stripping the bark from the tree for a worldwide exhibition.

Lapham conceived of another way to make his fortune. Rather than cart bits of the tree around the country, he sought to bring tourists to the grove to see the big trees for themselves. Lapham staked a claim and built a cottage for visitors in 1853, thus opening one of California's first and longest running tourist attractions.

By late 1858, the Big Trees Ranch and Mammoth Tree Grove Hotel were in the hands of James L. Sperry and John Perry, hoteliers from nearby Murphys. Sperry owned the big trees, with a series of partners, for the next 42 years. In the late 1890s, as he was getting on in years, Sperry put the word out he wanted to sell.

Fearing that the wondrous beauty of the grove would fall to the lumberman's ax, the first organized effort to preserve the big tree grove was launched. Despite intervention from such luminaries of the day as John Muir, and even passage of a bill in Congress, the sale took place in 1900. Amid much hew and cry, Robert B. Whiteside, a wealthy timber man and mine owner from Duluth, Minnesota, bought both the North and South Groves from Sperry for $100,000.

Whiteside maintained the groves as tourist attractions until 1926, when news leaked that he was contemplating selling both groves and their valuable sugar pine timberland to lumber companies. Despite a rejuvenated preservation effort led by the newly created Calaveras Grove Association, Whiteside sold the South Grove and other land holdings in the area to the Pickering Lumber Company in 1927 for $1,804,400.

The ensuing outrage then helped secure the fate of the North Grove. A $6 million bond issue was approved by California voters in November 1928 to acquire land for the state park system. Thus the state contributed half the $275,000 needed to purchase the North Grove from Whiteside. This time, the Calaveras Grove Association succeeded in raising the remaining $137,500, with major assistance from the Save the Redwoods League and thousands of individual contributors.

On June 24, 1931, the deed for the North Grove was transferred to the state of California. Just 12 days later, the grand celebration of this newest state park was held under the canopy of the big trees. California governor James Rolph Jr. gave the dedicatory address. Local businessman Désiré Fricot, a leader of the preservation movement, thanked the countless contributors and urged diligent efforts to add the South Grove to the new park.

In 1948, the Pickering Lumber Company built a railway for logging the sugar pines closely intertwined with the giant sequoias in the South Grove, threatening the area's ecosystem. The Calaveras Grove Association, with help from the Save the Redwoods League and a large grant from the Rockefeller Foundation, raised $2.8 million to purchase the grove in April 1954. The formal dedication was not held until September 9, 1967.

Today this jewel of the California State Parks hosts 250,000 visitors each year from around the world. They are able to walk the quiet trails among these giants of nature and marvel at the area's immense beauty because of the countless individuals in the past and present who worked tirelessly to ensure that the park would be here for people to enjoy for generations to come.

One

Native Americans

The giant sequoias growing along the western slope of the Sierra Nevada are the last vestiges of a long-ago age. The oldest fossils indicate that ancestors of modern day redwoods thrived in the northern hemisphere as long as 175 million years ago. By the 1850s, however, only a few groves of the magnificent trees remained. Native American tribes of Miwok (or Me-Wuk) and Washoe were well aware of the towering giants preserved in small groves. The Calaveras big trees are along a traditional border region between the Central Sierra Miwok and the Washoe of Lake Tahoe and Carson Valley. In summer, the Washoe would cross the mountains following game and seeking trade with other tribes. Miwok traditionally summered at the higher, cooler altitudes of the big trees and moved to lower elevations before the snows came.

Evidence of Native American activity can be found in Calaveras Big Trees State Park. Within the park boundaries are several Miwok grinding rocks. The Miwok used large boulder outcroppings to pound acorns into meal, a staple of their diet. They created indentations in the rock that are still visible today. Living in the mountains, these tribes had mostly been spared the changes brought by the Spaniards as they moved north through what is now California. The discovery of gold in the Sierra Nevada in 1848 changed everything.

Hundreds of thousands of people headed west seeking their fortunes. The gold discovery and mass migration led directly to statehood for the territory in 1850. Although some immigrants arrived by sea, most traveled the overland route known as the Emigrant Trail, used from the early 1840s until the intercontinental railroad was completed in 1869. This route, with its many branches, brought immigrants through Washoe territory over the Sierra Nevada directly to the mining camps. The Miwok had the misfortune of living in the heart of the mother lode. Their way of life was altered forever and their people nearly destroyed. The miners introduced disease, moved onto their lands, took their water, and hunted their game. By 1910, fewer than 700 Miwok were counted in the census, compared to an estimated 11,000 in the late 1700s.

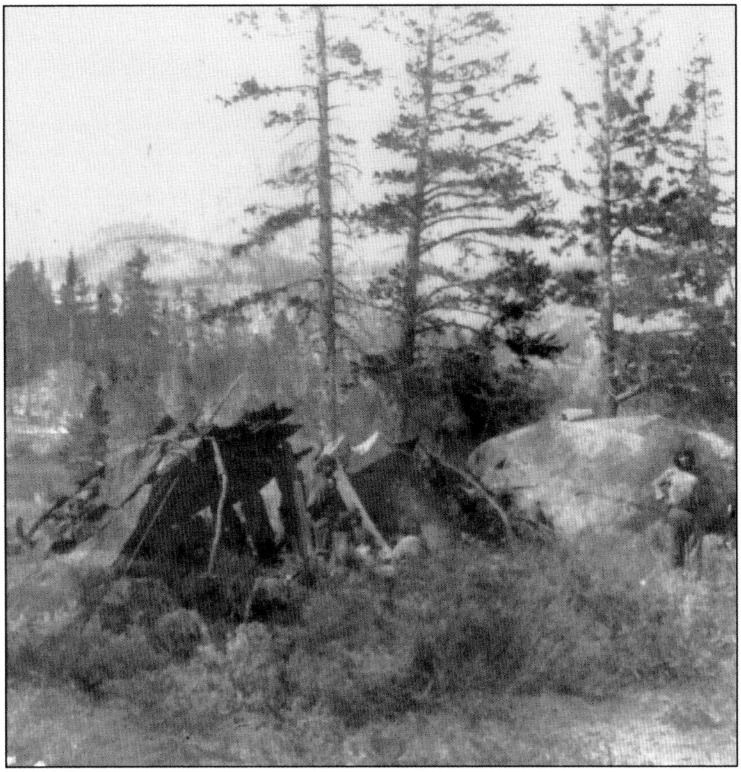

The Miwok Indians of the Central Sierra set up small temporary camps in the mountains, as depicted in this 1866 photograph. To escape the summer heat of lower elevations, they moved to encampments at higher, cooler altitudes, usually returning to long-established locations. (LOC, Lawrence and Houseworth Collection.)

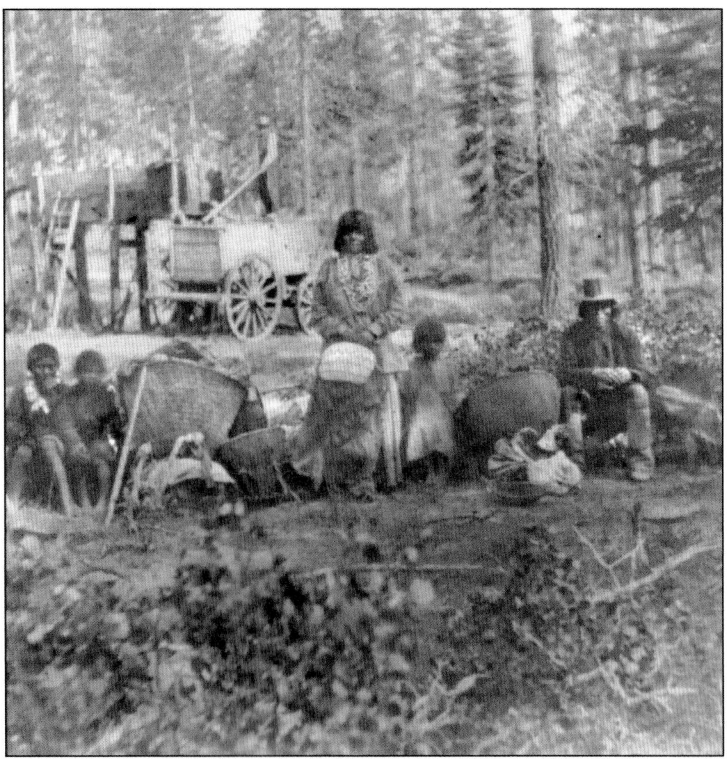

This 1866 photograph shows a Washoe chief's family at Lake Tahoe. From their spring gathering spot at Lake Tahoe, the Washoe would travel over the Sierra to present-day Alpine and Calaveras Counties to hunt and trade with the Miwok and other tribes. (LOC, Lawrence and Houseworth Collection.)

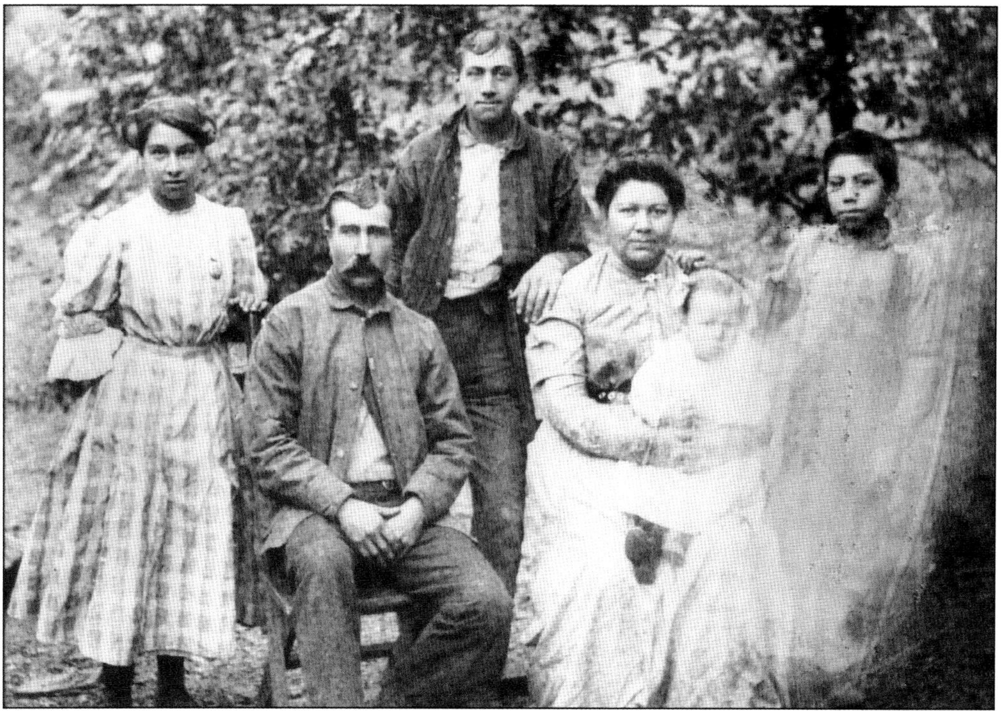

The Oak Hollow campground area in Big Trees Park was once a Miwok living site. George Hunter, from Nova Scotia, married Matilda Full, a Miwok born there around 1830. Pictured here is Matilda's daughter, Emma Hunter Shrum, seated holding her youngest son, James Edward, in about 1906. Seated beside Emma is her husband, Joseph Noah Shrum. They are surrounded by their children, Clara, Joseph Henry (center), and George Albert (right). (CCA.)

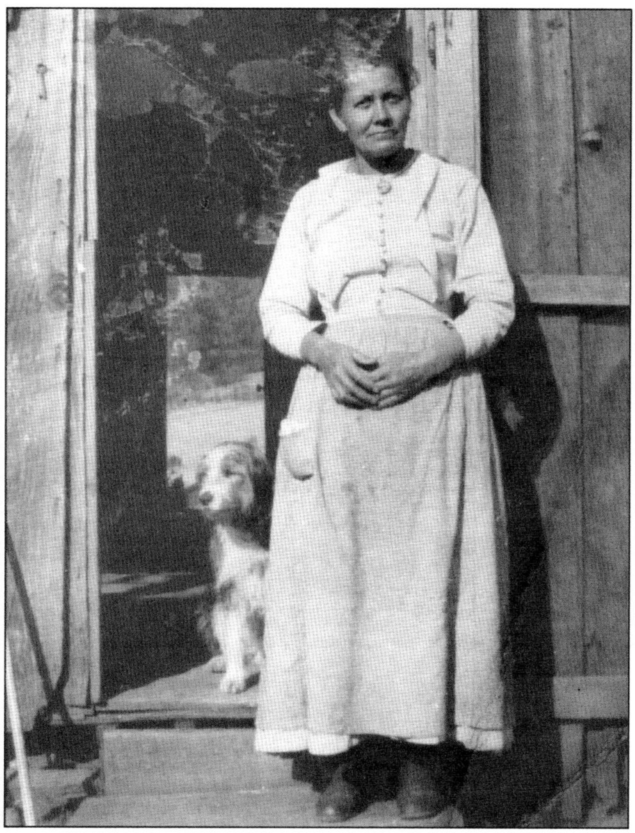

Nettie Hunter, another of Matilda and George Hunter's 10 children, is shown here in the early 1900s in Dorrington, not far from the big trees. Hunter children born in the big trees include Anna and James in the 1860s and Grace in the 1870s. Matilda, affectionately known as Tilda, died in 1914. (CCA.)

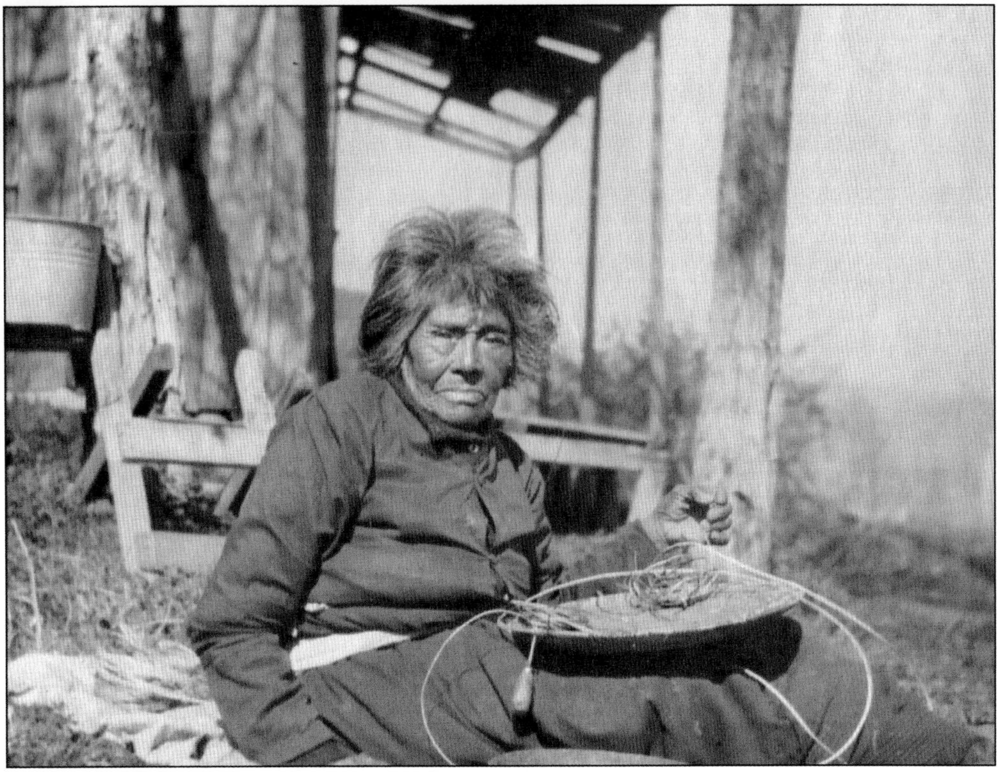

Susie of Wallis Gulch near Dorrington was known as the "Last of the Washoe Basket Makers" when this photograph was taken in the early 1900s. The Washoe created tightly woven, intricate baskets for holding water and cooking, and others for sifting nuts and seeds or even for holding babies. They became famous for their basketry skills, and their baskets were highly prized. (CCA.)

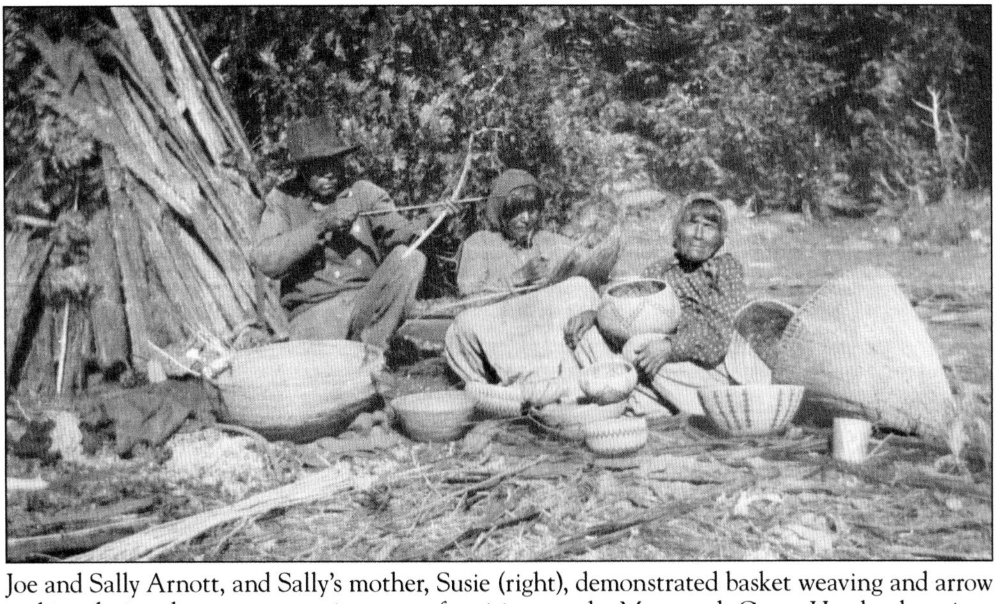

Joe and Sally Arnott, and Sally's mother, Susie (right), demonstrated basket weaving and arrow making during the summer tourist season for visitors to the Mammoth Grove Hotel at least into the 1920s, when this photograph was taken. (CCA.)

Two

Discovery and Exploitation of the Big Trees

Although not the first to explore the giant sequoia grove in Calaveras County, Augustus T. Dowd was credited with its discovery in June 1852. A few hardy souls made the dusty trip 15 miles up the mountain from Murphys to gaze in wonder at the stately giants that first summer. For one visitor, Col. William H. Hanford, thoughts turned quickly to moneymaking and speculation. The president of the Union Water Company in Murphys schemed to exhibit the Discovery Tree for profit. In May 1853, Hanford's crew stripped 50 feet of bark from the Discovery Tree, and then felled the giant. It took five men 22 days to bring the colossus down. Because no saw in existence was big enough, pump augers 10 feet in length were used to repeatedly drill through the tree. The auger marks are visible to this day on the Chip of the Old Block next to the Discovery Stump. Balanced by its perfect symmetry, the tree remained upright. With the persuasion of wedges driven into the auger-made breech, the tree thunderously crashed to the ground on June 27, 1853.

In July 1853, Joseph Lapham and his brother, William, each staked 160-acre land claims in the grove. They wasted no time building a cottage to accommodate visitors. Plagued by money troubles, the Laphams took on a series of partners. Joseph eventually sold his interest to "Billie," who with partner Samuel Smith made a number of improvements to their tourist attraction in 1854. They planed the top of the big tree stump smooth for dancing parties and created a summerhouse using cedar boughs for siding and roofing. A saloon and two-lane bowling alley were constructed upon the prostrate remainder of the Discovery Tree. They also built a two-story frame hotel within 20 feet of the stump. For $1,000, Billie became a co-conspirator in the grove's exploitation. That was the price George L. Trask paid to remove 116 feet of bark from the Mother of the Forest tree for exhibition in New York and London. Other less destructive schemes plagued the grove for years to come.

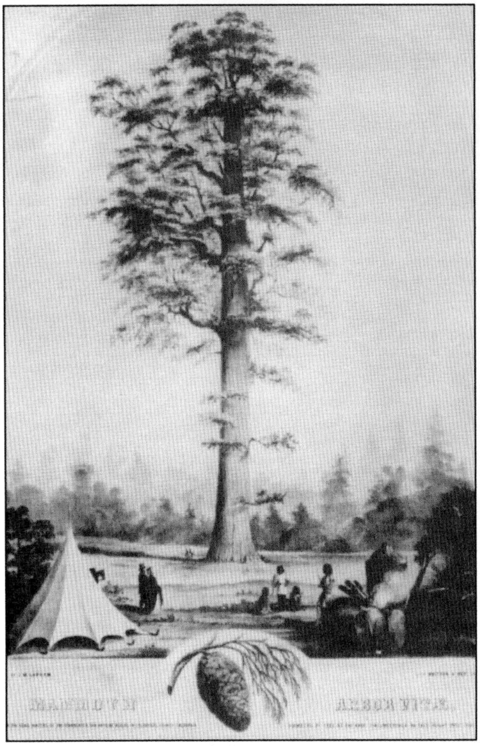

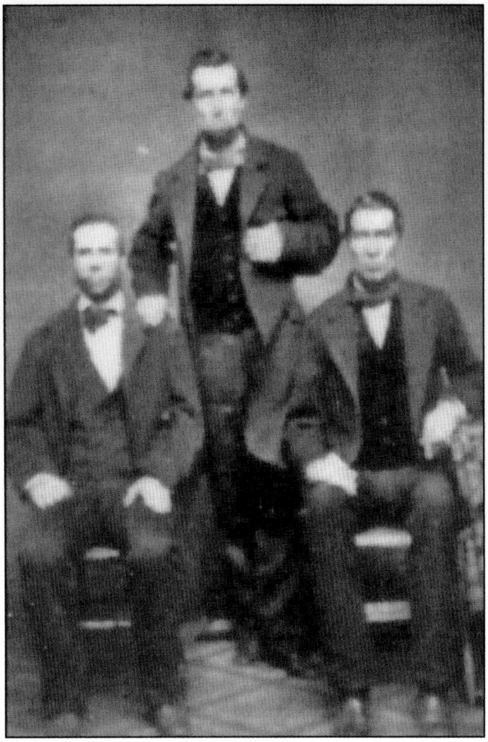

The sketch above of the Discovery Tree was made in 1854 by Joseph Lapham, the first owner of the Calaveras Grove. It reads: "Standing at the head waters of the Stanislaus and San Antoine Rivers in Calaveras County, California. Diameter 34 feet at the base. Circumference 96 feet. Height 290 FT. 3,000 years old." W. H. Hanford publicized his exhibition with this poster. Charles A. Curtis (seated, right) pictured with his brothers, helped cut down Dowd's Discovery Tree. It took 22 days to bring the massive tree to earth. The *New York Times* reported on August 10, 1853, "The mammoth tree in Calaveras County, the greatest and most wonderful production of the vegetable kingdom ever known, has been sacrilegiously cut down for speculative purposes." (Left, CBTSP; right, CCHS.)

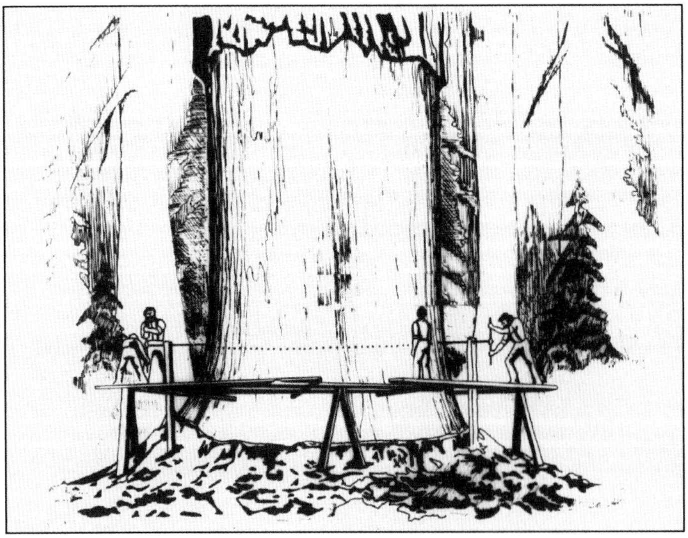

A platform was built around the base of the Discovery Tree for the workmen to drill the pump augers through the massive trunk. There was no saw in existence big enough to cut through the tree. They used the tools at hand and their ingenuity to weld long extensions onto chisels and the augers typically used to bore out wooden pipes for transporting water to miners and ranchers. (CBTSP.)

This handbill from 1853 advertises Hanford's exhibition of the Discovery Tree in San Francisco. This description of the tree inflated the height to 350 feet. Regular admission was 50¢. Each evening, cotillion parties were invited to dance in the "Old Giant" for $3 a couple. (CBTSP.)

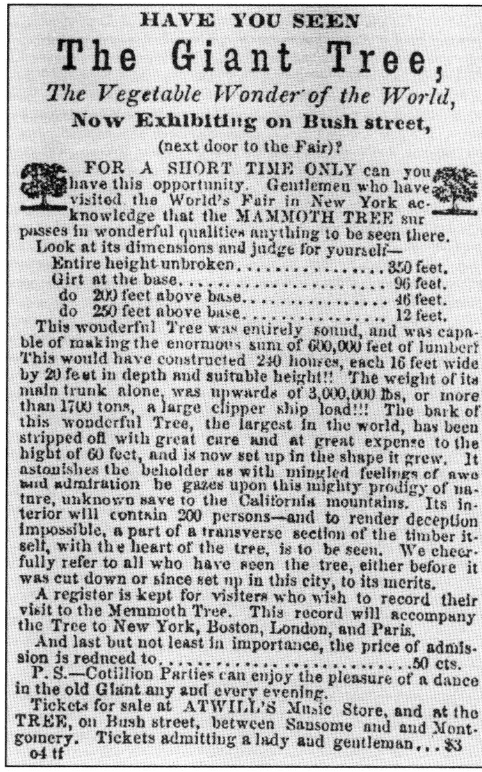

HAVE YOU SEEN

The Giant Tree,

The Vegetable Wonder of the World,

Now Exhibiting on Bush street,

(next door to the Fair)?

FOR A SHORT TIME ONLY can you have this opportunity. Gentlemen who have visited the World's Fair in New York acknowledge that the MAMMOTH TREE surpasses in wonderful qualities anything to be seen there.

Look at its dimensions and judge for yourself—

Entire height unbroken................350 feet.
Girt at the base........................96 feet.
do 200 feet above base................46 feet.
do 250 feet above base................12 feet.

This wonderful Tree was entirely sound, and was capable of making the enormous sum of 600,000 feet of lumber? This would have constructed 240 houses, each 16 feet wide by 20 feet in depth and suitable height!! The weight of its main trunk alone, was upwards of 3,000,000 lbs, or more than 1700 tons, a large clipper ship load!!! The bark of this wonderful Tree, the largest in the world, has been stripped off with great care and at great expense to the hight of 60 feet, and is now set up in the shape it grew. It astonishes the beholder as with mingled feelings of awe and admiration he gazes upon this mighty prodigy of nature, unknown save to the California mountains. Its interior will contain 200 persons—and to render deception impossible, a part of a transverse section of the timber itself, with the heart of the tree, is to be seen. We cheerfully refer to all who have seen the tree, either before it was cut down or since set up in this city, to its merits.

A register is kept for visiters who wish to record their visit to the Mammoth Tree. This record will accompany the Tree to New York, Boston, London, and Paris.

And last but not least in importance, the price of admission is reduced to..............................50 cts.

P. S.—Cotillion Parties can enjoy the pleasure of a dance in the old Giant any and every evening.

Tickets for sale at ATWILL'S Music Store, and at the TREE, on Bush street, between Sansome and and Montgomery. Tickets admitting a lady and gentleman...$3

o4 tf

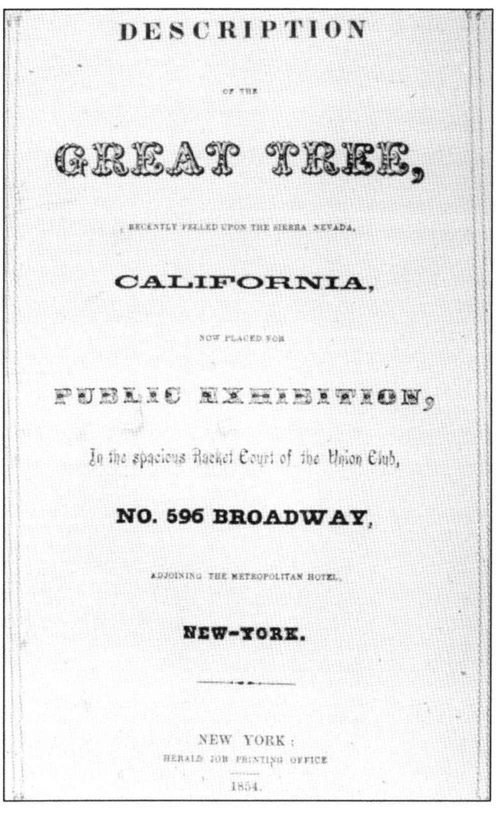

DESCRIPTION

OF THE

GREAT TREE,

RECENTLY FELLED UPON THE SIERRA NEVADA,

CALIFORNIA,

NOW PLACED FOR

PUBLIC EXHIBITION,

In the spacious Racket Court of the Union Club,

NO. 596 BROADWAY,

ADJOINING THE METROPOLITAN HOTEL,

NEW-YORK.

NEW YORK:

HERALD JOB PRINTING OFFICE

1854.

From San Francisco, the exhibit, which now included a slab from the trunk, was sent by clipper ship to New York. Unable to secure a place in P. T. Barnum's Crystal Palace, Hanford opened a competing exhibit at the Union Club on Broadway in 1854. Barnum discredited the exhibit and few came to see it. It was a financial disaster. Before the exhibit could go on to Paris, it was destroyed by fire. (CBTSP.)

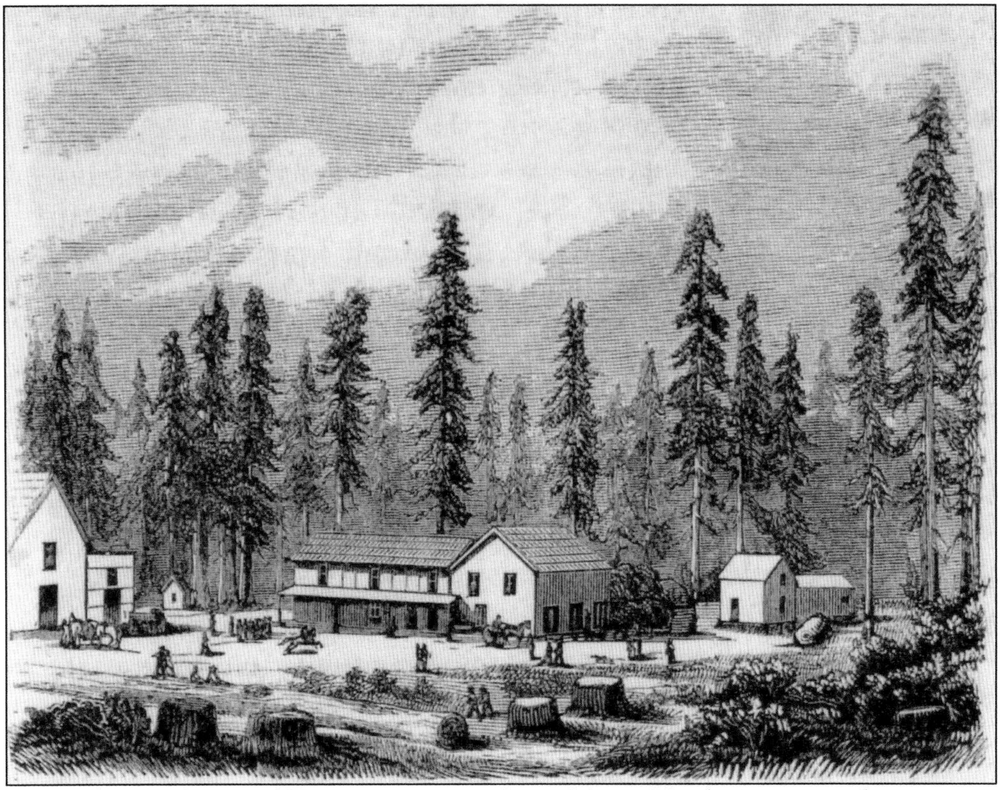

Artist Thomas Ayers and Yosemite promoter James Mason Hutchings were early visitors to the big trees. Ayers's 1854 sketch shows Lapham's Big Tree Cottage (center) in front of the Big Tree Stump, the saloon and bowling alley (right), and a barn (left). In 1855, Ayers accompanied Hutchings as he led the second tourist party into the Yosemite Valley. The cottage reportedly burned down in 1864. (CBTSP.)

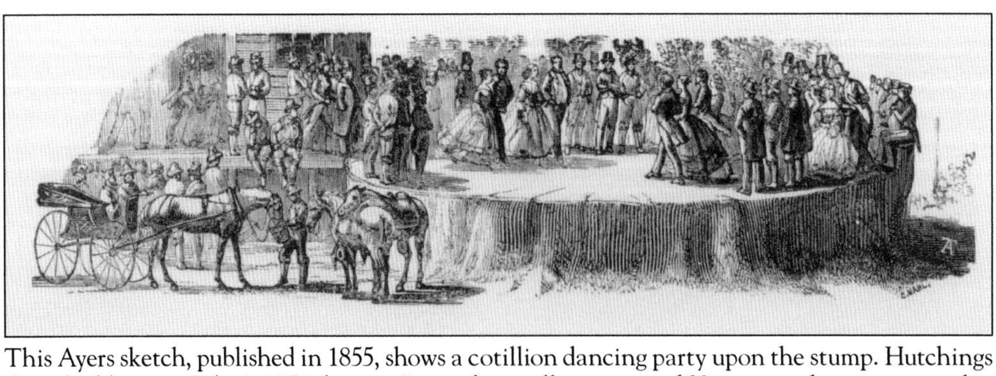

This Ayers sketch, published in 1855, shows a cotillion dancing party upon the stump. Hutchings described how on July 4, 1854, he was "one of a cotillion party of 32 persons dancing upon this stump; in addition to which the musicians and onlookers numbered 17, making a total of 49 occupants on the surface at one time!" (CBTSP.)

This photograph purportedly shows the Mother of the Forest tree before its bark was stripped for exhibition by George Trask during 1854. A portion of the scaffolding workmen erected to remove the bark is visible in the undated photograph below. (CBTSP.)

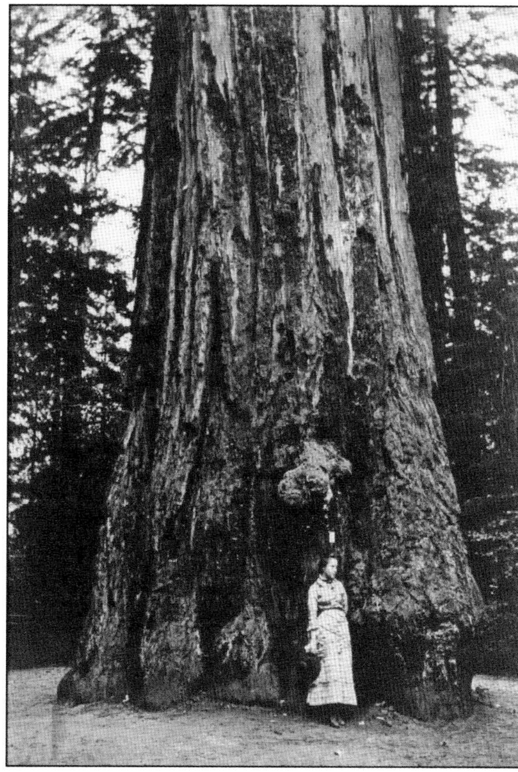

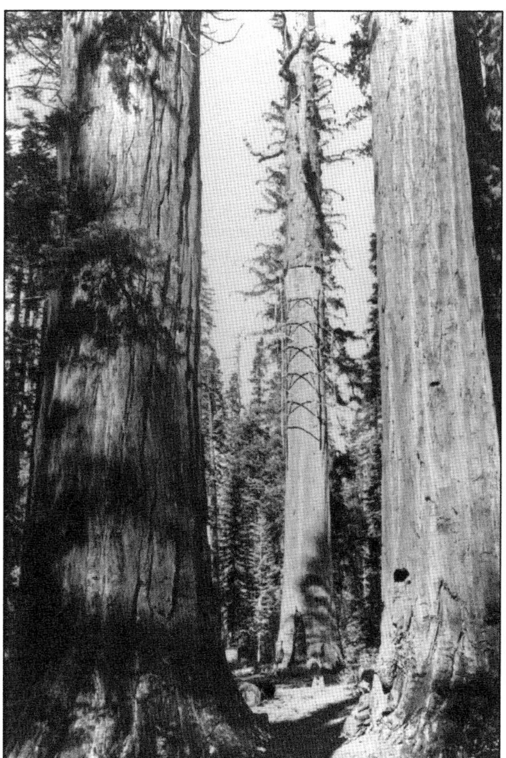

John Muir wrote of this travesty: "Another [tree], one of the finest in the grove, more than 300 feet high, was skinned alive to a height of 116 feet from the ground and the bark sent to London to show how fine and big that Calaveras tree was—as sensible a scheme as skinning our great men would be to prove their greatness. This grand tree is of course dead, a ghastly disfigured ruin." (CBTSP.)

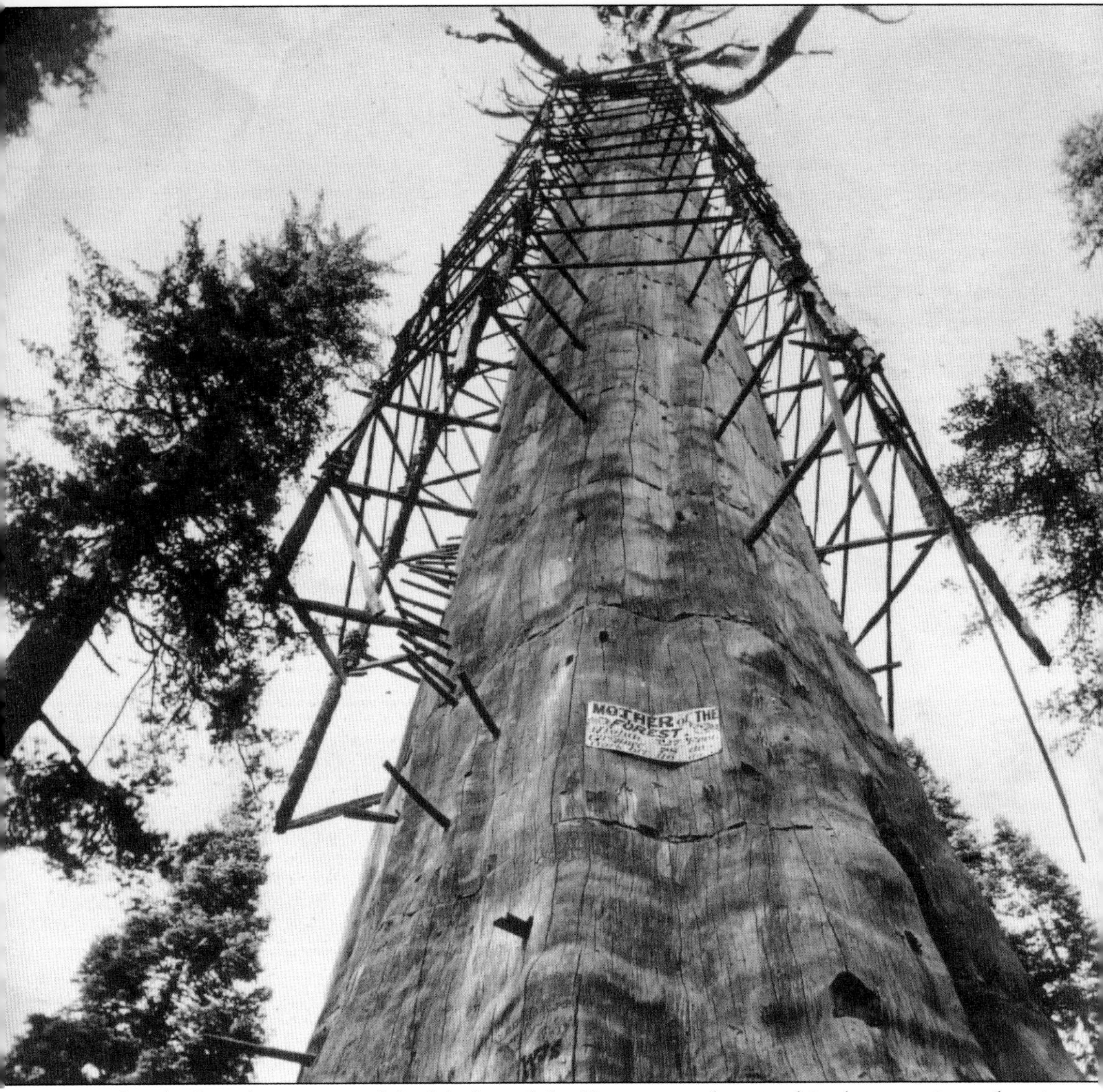

The absolute desecration of the Mother of the Forest is evident in this close-up view taken in the 1860s. The pegs and scaffolding remained on the upper portion of the tree for many years. Trask's exhibit opened at New York's Crystal Palace on July 4, 1855, to skepticism. A reporter for the *New York Times* wrote on August 9, 1855, "We have no assurance, from seeing this clothed skeleton, that the tree was actually so large. We fear it is manufactured." Trask wrote a strongly worded rebuke in the following day's paper. Later he produced, and the paper printed, a letter from a Boston businessman assuring the exhibit's authenticity. (SCP, #694.)

This handbill is for the exhibition of the Mother of the Forest's bark at the Crystal Palace in London. It was on display from 1857 until 1866, when it was destroyed by fire. (This item is reproduced by permission of the Huntington Library, San Marino, California.)

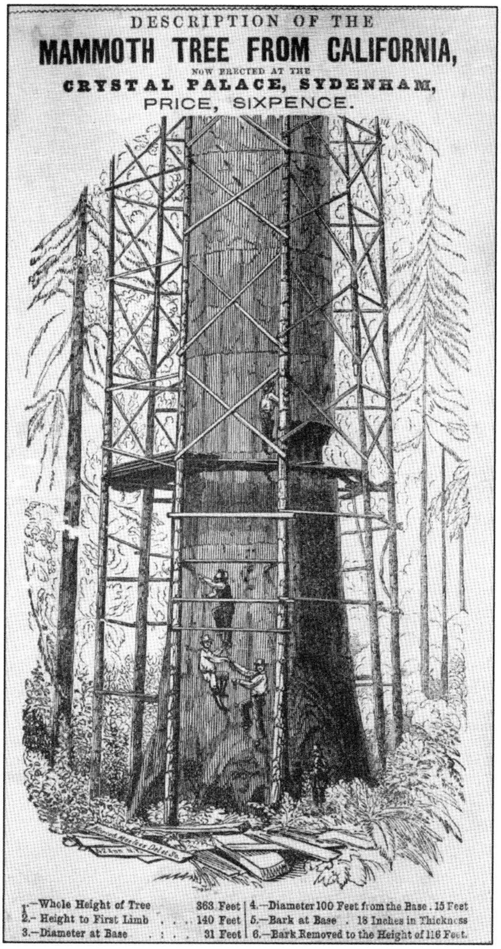

Stereoviews such as this were viewed through a stereoscope that gave the images a 3-D effect. From the mid-1800s through the 1920s, they were the most popular form of commercial photography. This stereoview of Chip of the Old Block taken before 1870 clearly shows the marks left by the augers used to cut it down. The "v" shape on the bottom was likely created by the workmen to guide the direction of the fall. (LOC.)

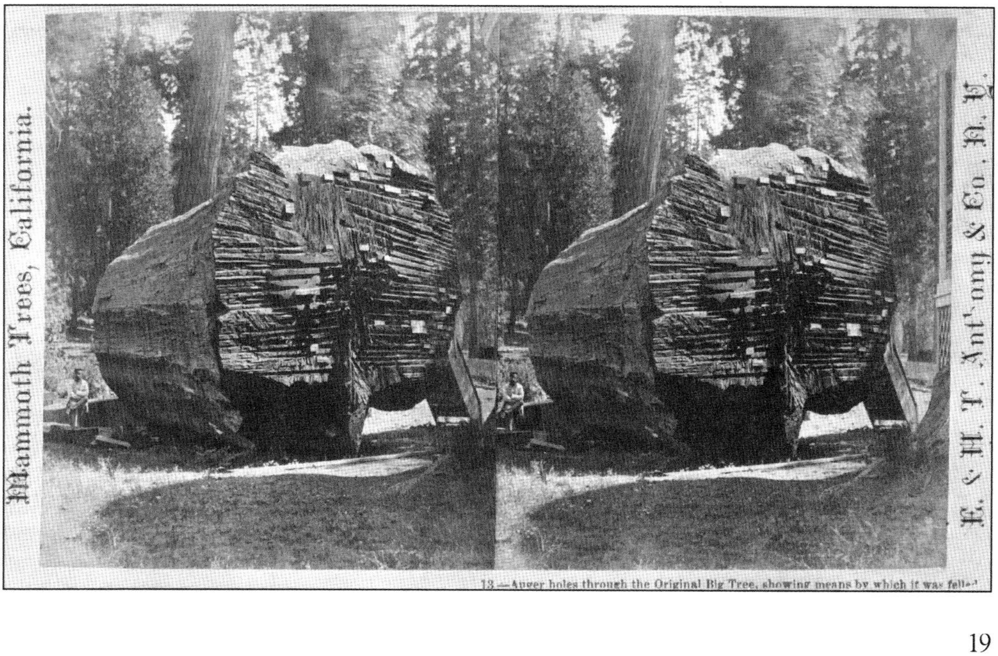

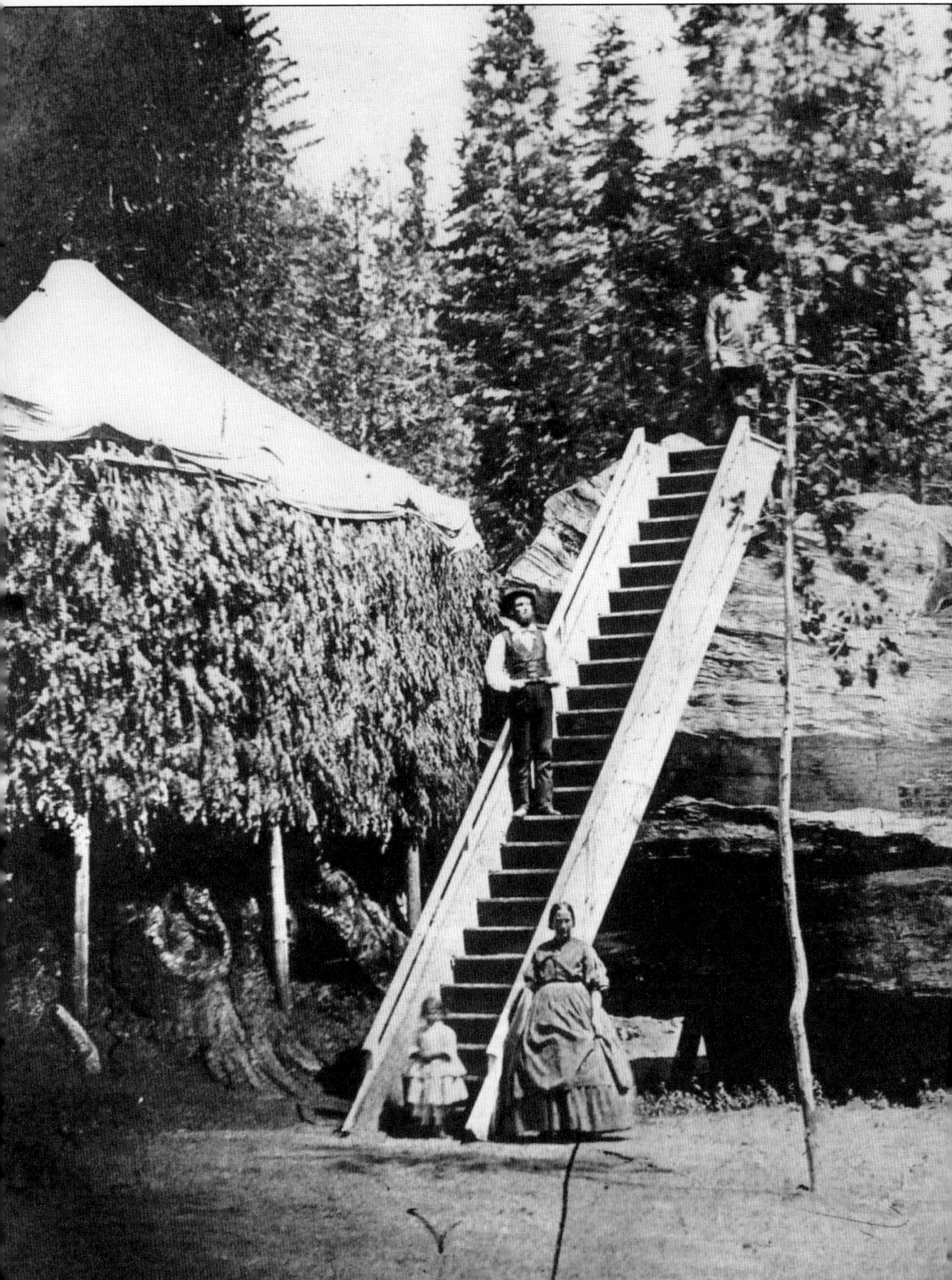

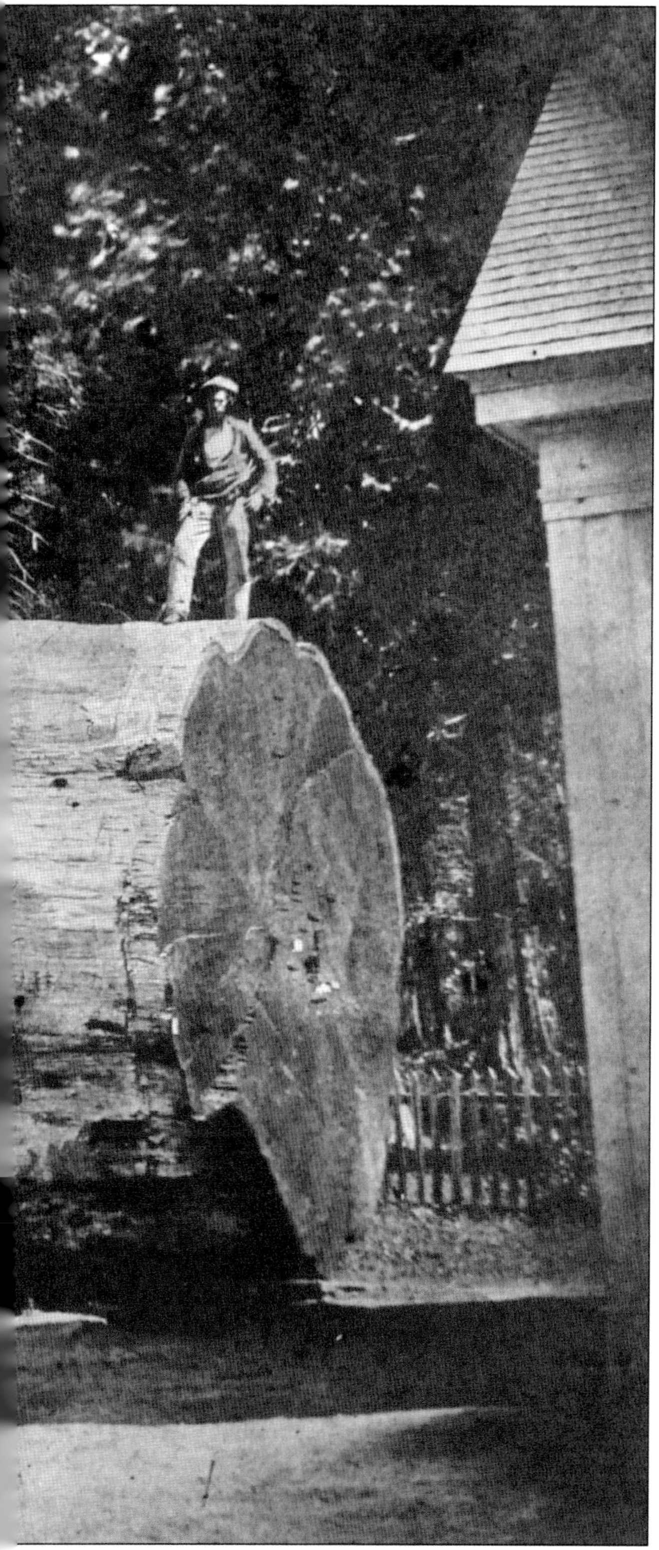

Lapham's summerhouse of cedar boughs covers the Discovery Stump in this 1859 photograph. Just visible at right is the saloon built on the prostrate tree. The stump, popular for dancing, also hosted concerts, lectures, weddings, religious meetings, and theatrical performances. In 1858, John Heckendorn set up his print shop on the stump, publishing a few issues of the *Big Tree Bulletin and Murphys Advertiser* before going out of business. In the 1880s, the stump even served as a schoolhouse. The man halfway up the ladder is believed to be Dr. A. S. Haynes, who became owner of the grove in 1857. The woman has been identified as Eliza Perry, whose husband, John, and his partner, James L. Sperry, acquired the grove in 1858. (OTM.)

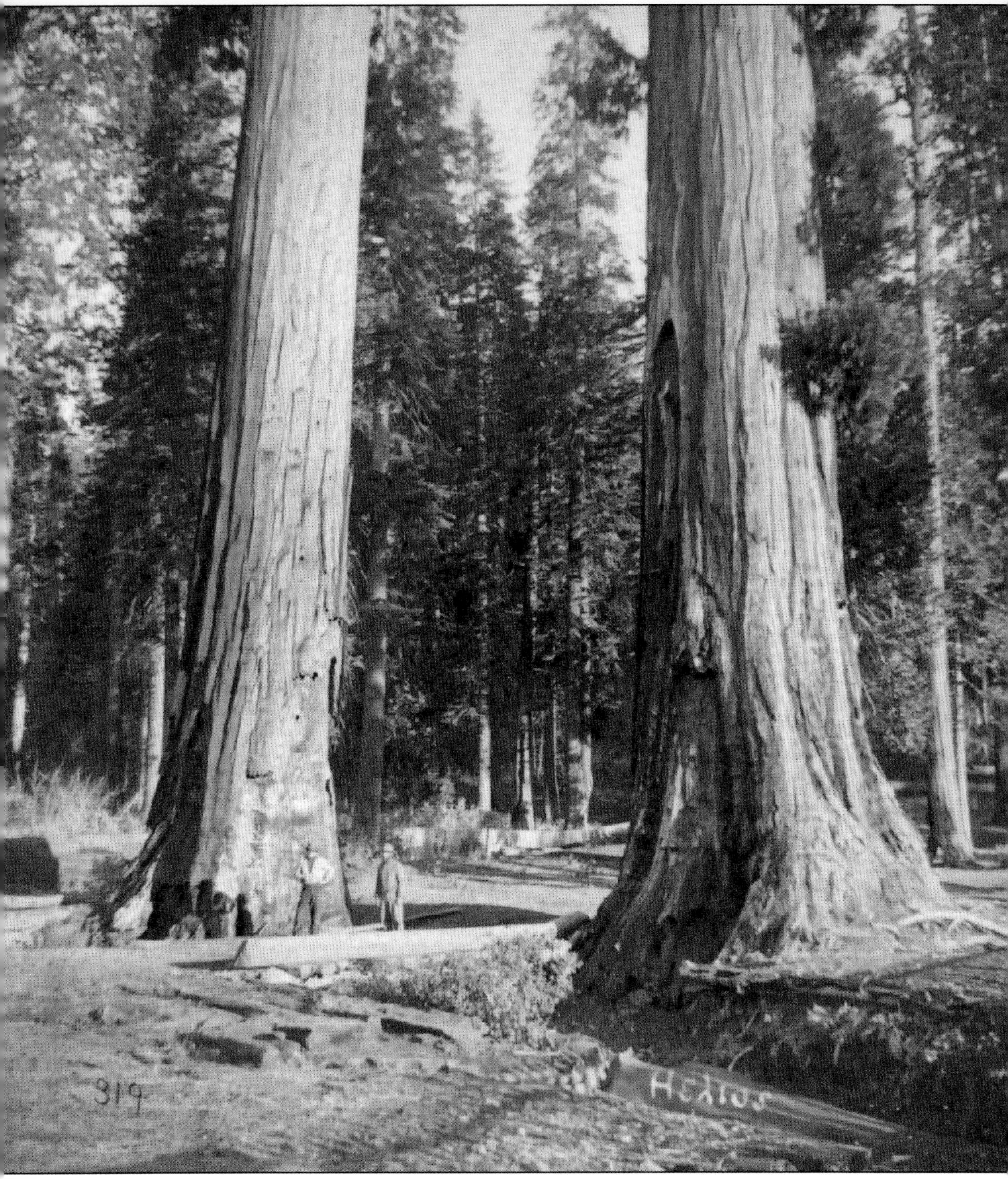

The Sentinel Trees, captured by famed photographer Eadweard Muybridge in 1868, marked the entrance to the North Grove of big trees for more than 70 years. The road from Murphys passed between the trees until the one on the left in this image fell in 1919. (NYPL.)

Three

The Sperry Years

In September 1854, Dr. A. Smith Haynes became Billie Lapham's final partner in the big tree grove, and by 1855 they had added a wing to the hotel. Unfortunately, Billie's young wife, Nancy, was seriously ill with tuberculosis, forcing them to sell their interest in the grove and move to Murphys. As sole owner, Haynes embarked on a series of improvements in July 1857 with $3,000 borrowed from James L. Sperry and John Perry, proprietors of the successful Sperry and Perry Hotel in Murphys. The financial panic of 1857 cut travel to the grove, and miners were leaving for the newest strikes. Business suffered, and Haynes failed to pay his taxes. He lost the Mammoth Tree Grove Ranch at a sheriff's sale on December 26, 1857, to George Fisher for $137.07. In October 1858, Fisher sold the grove to Sperry, Perry, and Smith Mitchell for $550, a tidy profit.

By this time, it appears that the much larger South Grove of big trees had been discovered on the other side of the Stanislaus River, although the exact date is unknown. Famed publisher and Yosemite hotelier James Mason Hutchings staked a claim in the South Grove in 1861, but a planned hotel never materialized. Haynes continued to run the renamed Mammoth Grove Hotel for the new owners. Business picked up, and in July 1860, more than 250 guests registered at the hotel. In September, Sperry and Perry bought Mitchell out for $3,500 and paid Haynes $1,000 to secure their full ownership. The experienced hoteliers set about upgrading the property into a world-class resort. A luxurious three-story hotel with accommodations for 60 guests was built in time for the 1861 tourist season, and they added a wooden pavilion over the big tree stump. The hotel was about 600 yards from the stump, where the visitor parking lot is today. Also around this time, Sperry and Perry acquired the South Grove. Over the course of the next 42 years, the Mammoth Tree Ranch remained a popular tourist destination. The one constant during that time was James L. Sperry.

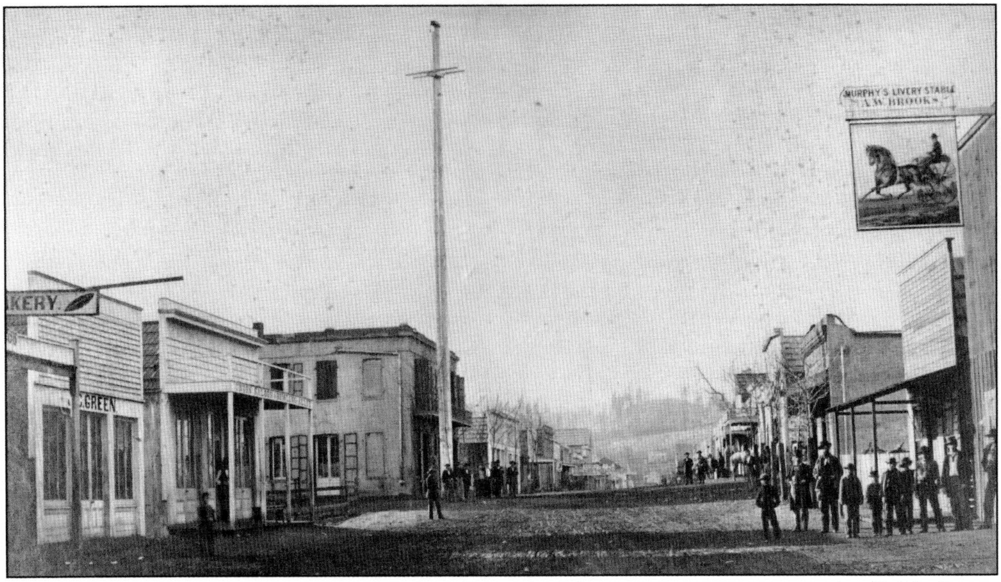

Sperry and Perry opened their Murphys hotel in 1856. The two-story stone structure (left), shown in 1861, was severely damaged in a fire that nearly destroyed Murphys in 1859. One of the finest hotels outside of San Francisco, it hosted many famous people of the day. The liberty pole in front was a show of support for the Union in the Civil War. (CCA.)

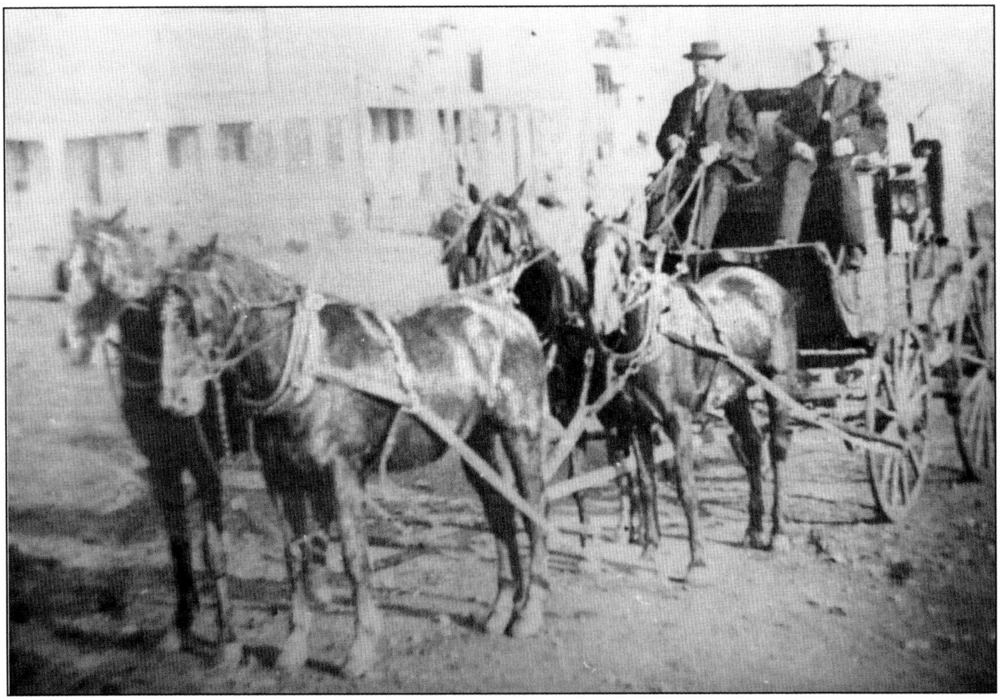

After a long journey from San Francisco, travelers to the big trees stayed at the Sperry and Perry Hotel overnight before an early morning stage ride to the grove. Col. Decatur F. Loveless handles the reins in this 1860 photograph with Sperry (right). Loveless was Haynes' barkeeper before buying and independently operating the saloon and bowling alley. (CBTSP.)

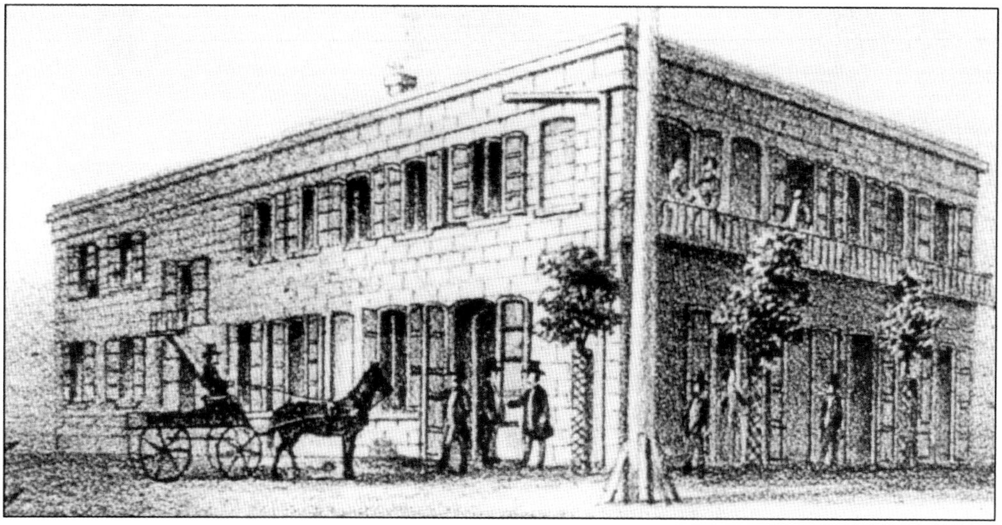

This Edward Vischer sketch, published in 1862, illustrates the hotel's stone construction. Now known as the Murphys Hotel, it is one of the oldest hotels operating in California. A California Historical Landmark, the hotel also is listed on the National Register of Historic Places. (CBTSP.)

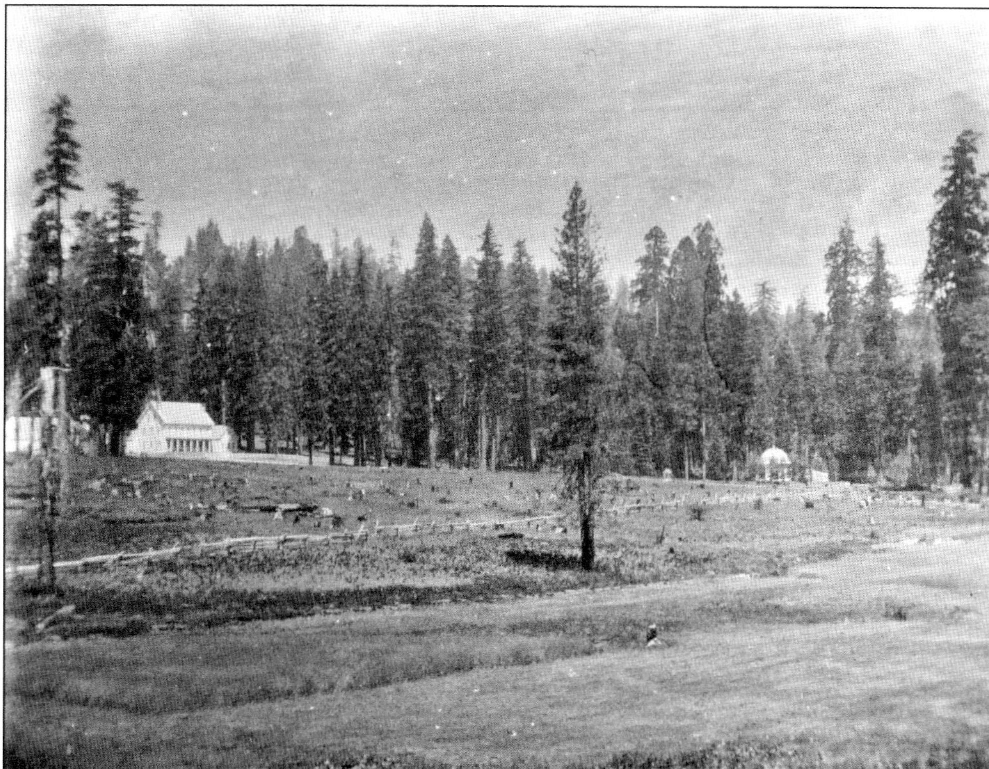

This was likely the first view travelers had of the newly built Mammoth Grove Hotel. The road curved around the meadow up to the Sentinels. Pine trees at the edge of the forest were felled for 40 to 60 yards by the Laphams, and Sperry removed more to accommodate the new hotel. The meadow areas were used to grow oat and barley to feed the teams bringing the tourists. (SCP, #703.)

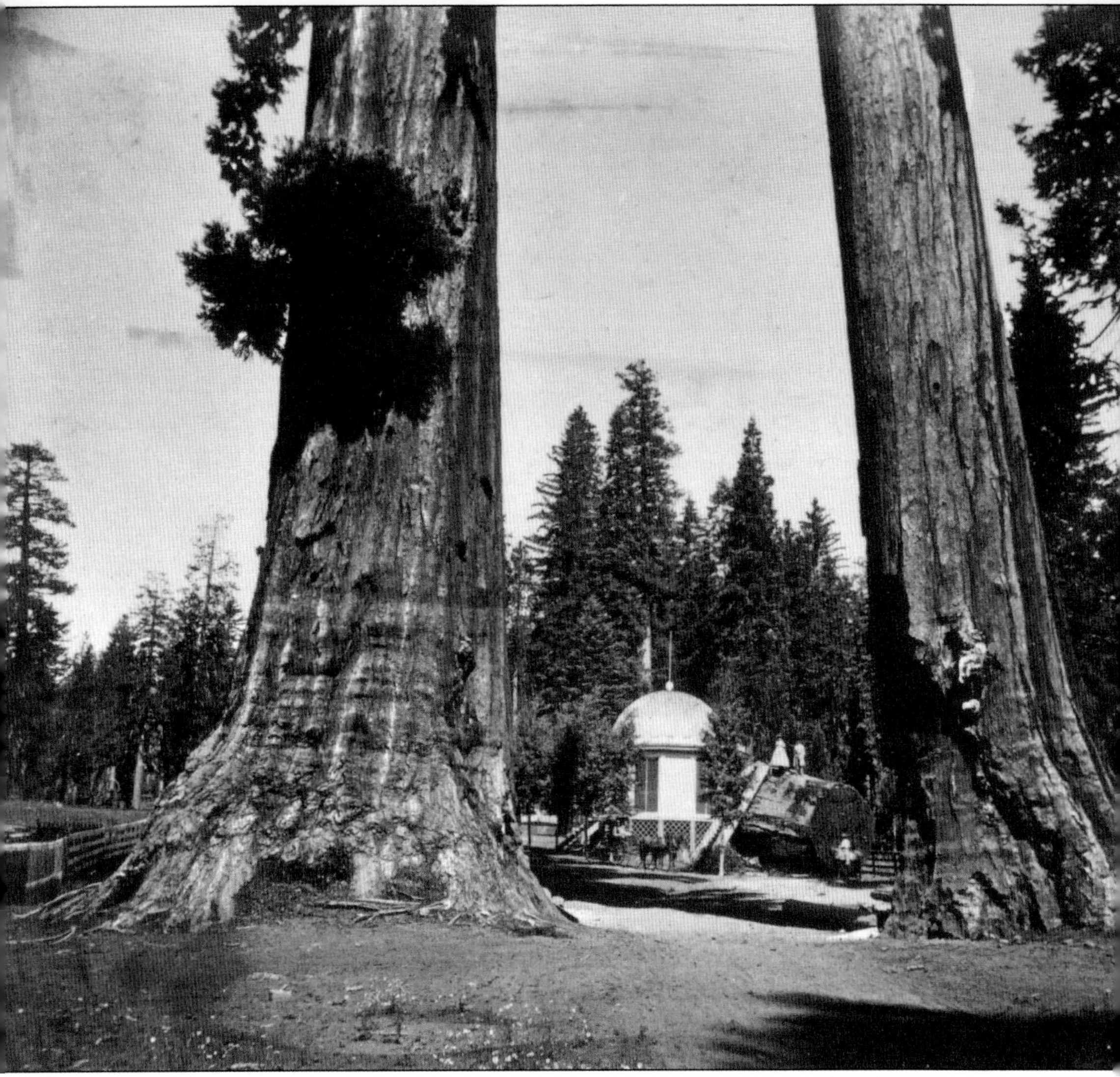

The road to the Big Trees Ranch passed between the Sentinels. Immediately to the right stood the pavilion on the Discovery Stump and the Chip of the Old Block, and behind the Sentinel on the right stood the saloon and bowling alley, until they were crushed by snow during the winter of 1861–1862. (SCP, #667.)

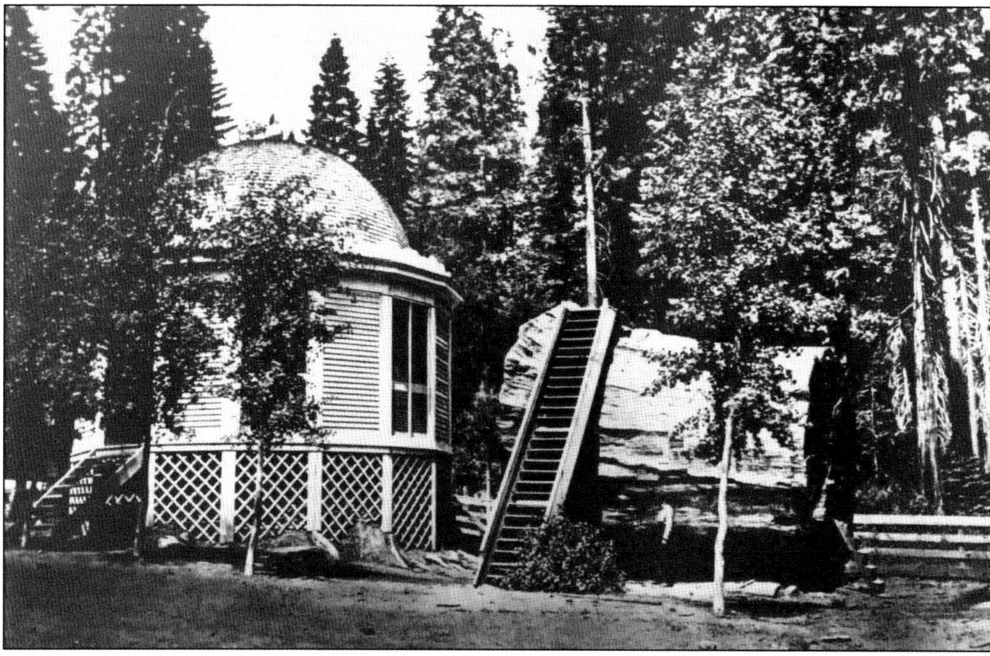

Now covered with a wooden pavilion, the Discovery Stump, shown here in the late 1860s, continued to be a popular dancing spot for grove visitors. The fate of the original Big Tree Cottage Hotel just above the stump is unknown. It reportedly burned down in 1864, yet it does not appear in photographs and sketches made in the early 1860s. (CBTSP.)

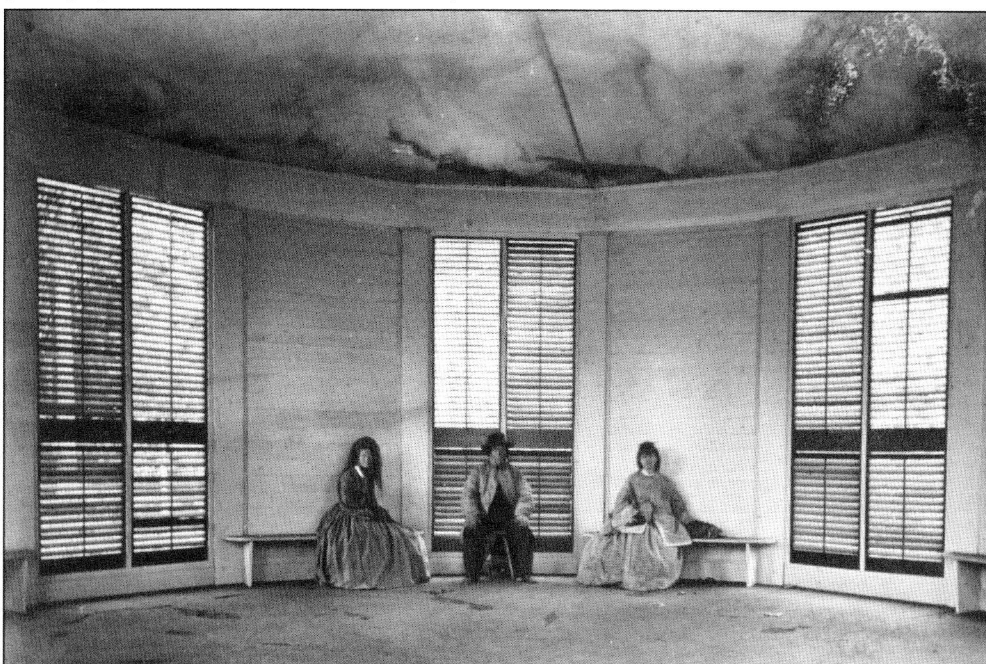

The spacious interior of the pavilion, shown here in 1861, featured built-in benches where visitors could rest after a stroll through the grove. The structure was also referred to as the Stump House. (SCP, #669.)

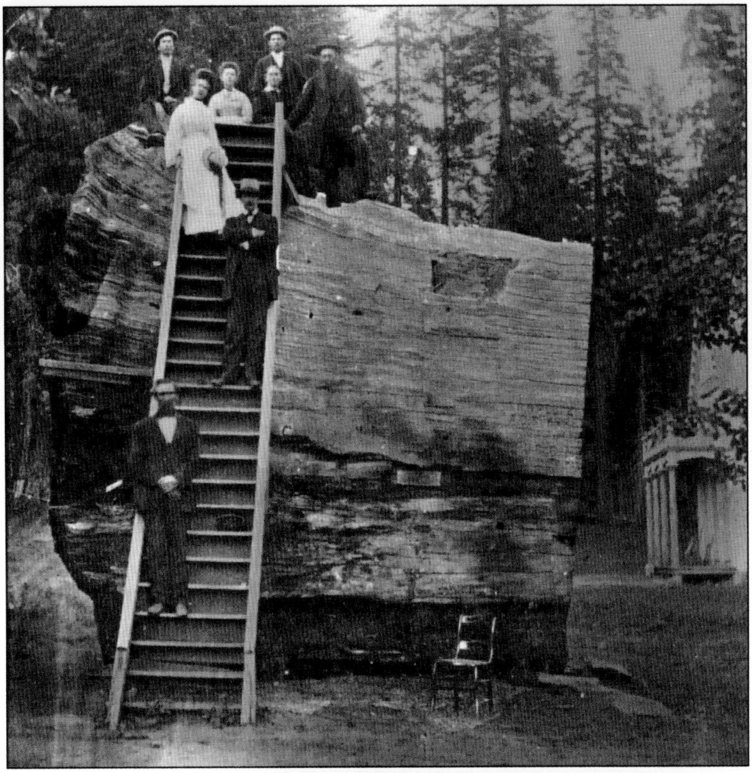

Chip of the Old Block was a popular backdrop for photographs at the Big Tree Ranch, as in these images from the early 1870s. These photographs are only a few known of the so-called "Haynes Addition," the Gothic Revival dormitory added to the grove by Dr. A. S. Haynes in 1858. The four-columned front portico can just be seen to the right. (CBTSP.)

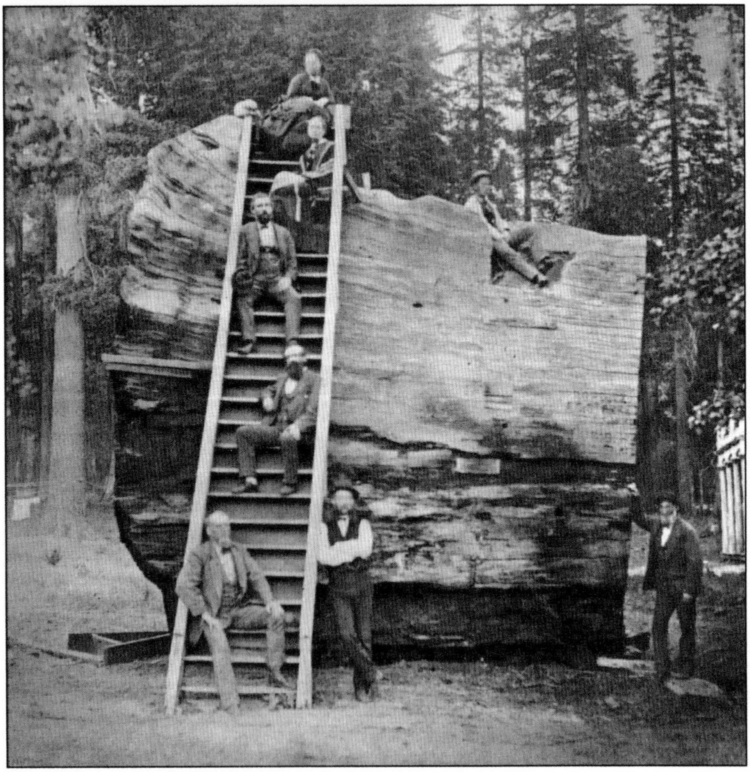

After the Discovery Tree was felled, it was partially embedded in the ground. Separated from the rest of the fallen trunk, an unknown number of men and draft animals raised Chip up using screw jacks. The cavity below was filled with dirt as Chip was rolled back and forth. Also noteworthy is that Chip is shorter in these photographs because of slices removed for exhibition. (CBTSP.)

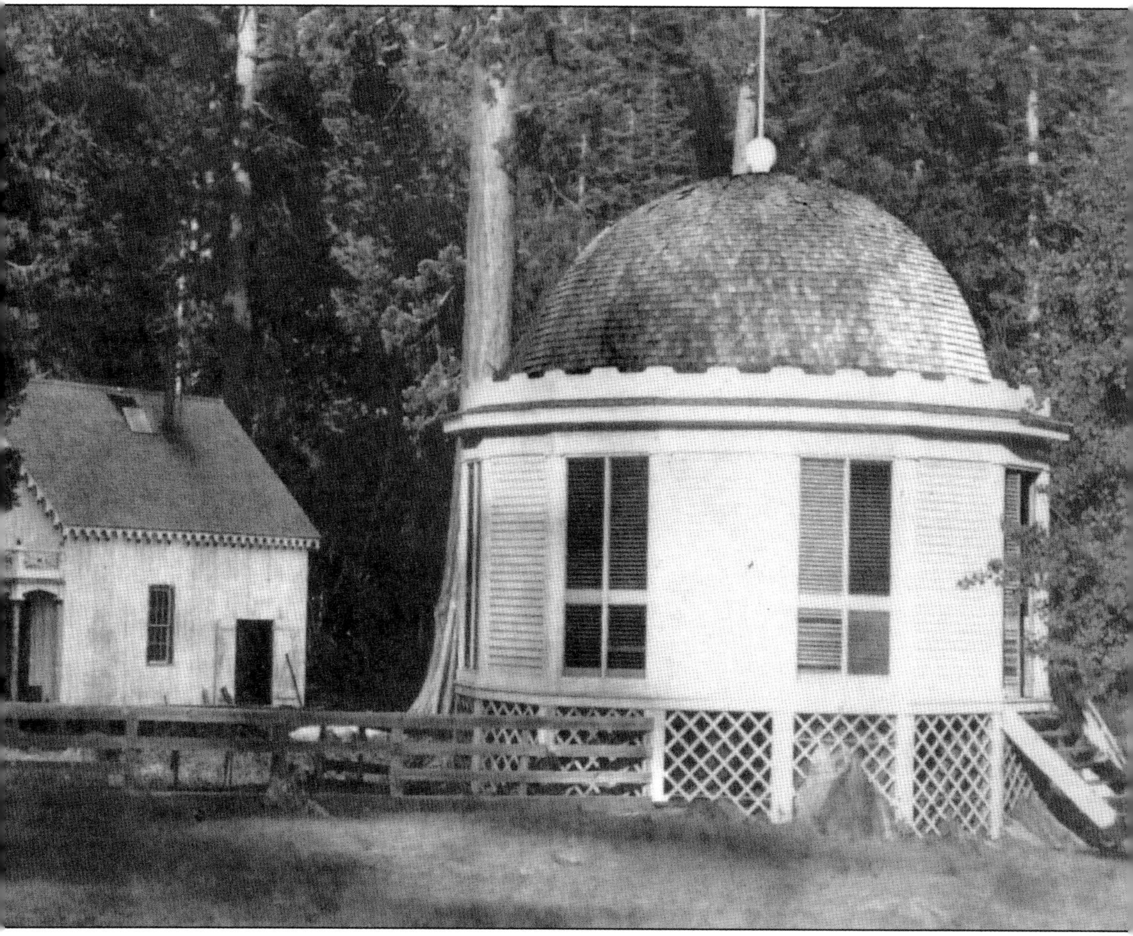

The Haynes addition can be clearly seen in this previously unknown photograph published by John P. Soule around 1870. The exact date of the structure's demise is unknown, but it is believed to be between 1880 and 1885. In 1987, an archaeological dig helped identify the building's exact location. (NYPL.)

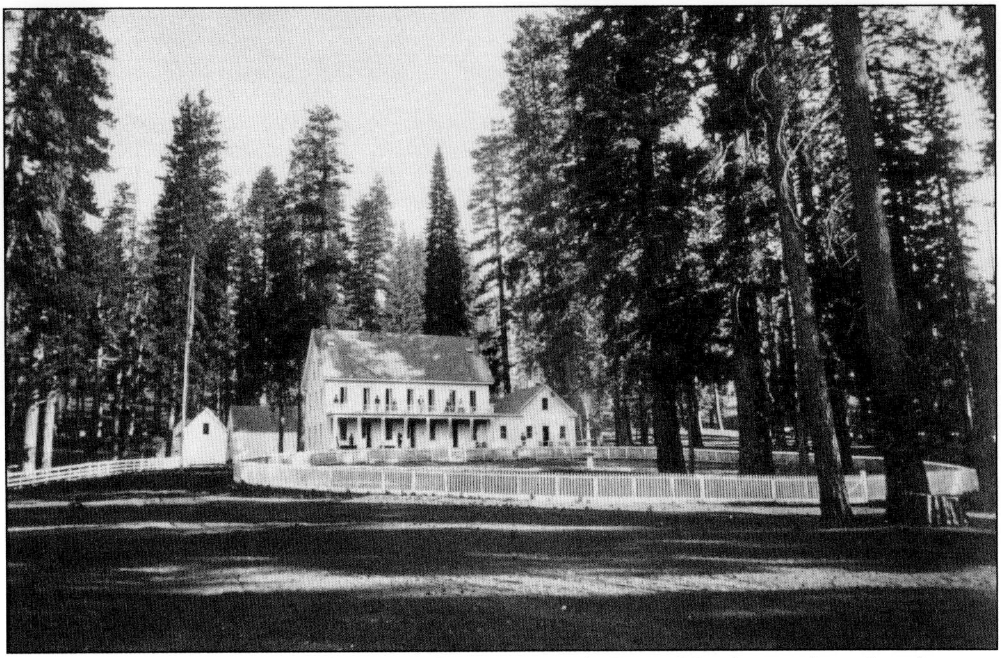

When it opened in 1861, the gleaming white Mammoth Grove Hotel was adorned with green shutters and expansive verandas along the front of the first and second floors overlooking the grove of giant sequoia. A park-like front lawn featured a spouting three-tiered fountain. The hotel boasted a parlor, barroom, dining room, a third-floor ballroom, and large bedrooms for guests. (SCP, #664.)

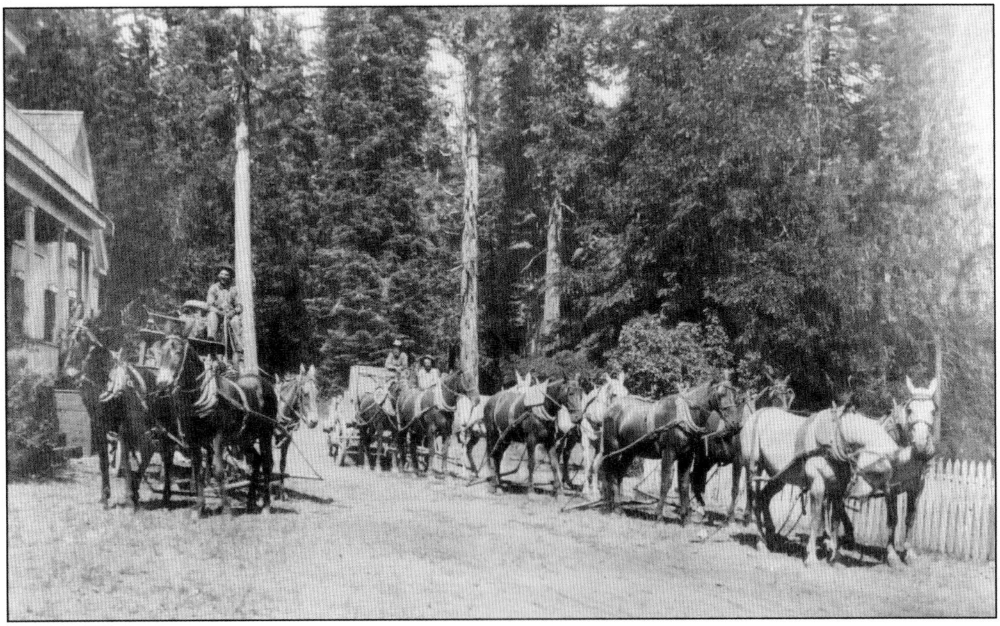

In 1862, Sperry and Perry, with eight other Murphys businessmen, formed a corporation to build and maintain the Big Tree and Carson Valley Turnpike from the grove to California's eastern border. It provided a much-needed link with Nevada. (It is not to be confused with the Big Tree Road from Murphys, which passed in front of the hotel.) (CBTSP.)

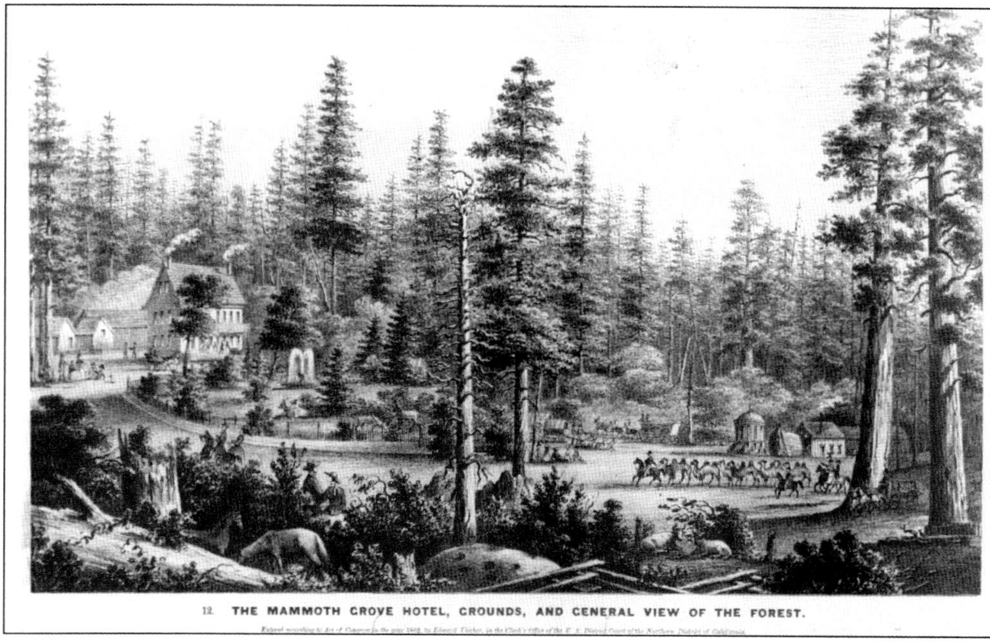

Probably the strangest travelers on this route were Bactrian (two-hump) camels. Imported from Mongolia, they were destined for Virginia City, Nevada, where they would carry burdens for silver miners, a venture that failed. Artist Edward Vischer sketched this image of the camels passing through the grove in 1861. Vischer made many sketches of the area, which were published as *Vischer's Views of California*. (CBTSP.)

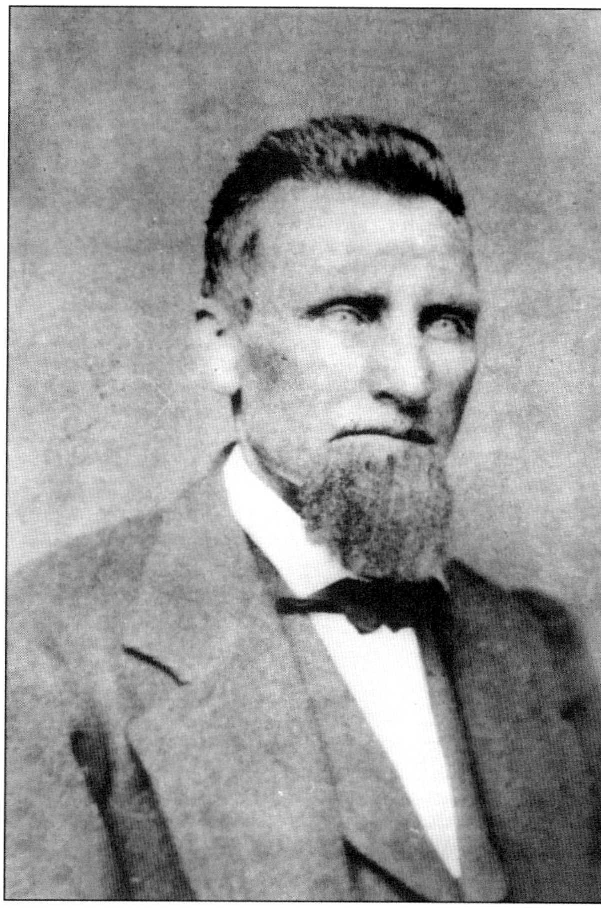

John A. "Snowshoe" Thompson was a well-known traveler on the Big Tree Road. Beginning in January 1856 and continuing for the next 20 years, Thompson carried mail over the wintry Sierra Nevada and back, using skis he constructed based on memories from his Norway youth. He carried a pack weighing between 50 and 80 pounds, making the eastward journey in three days and the return in two. (OTM.)

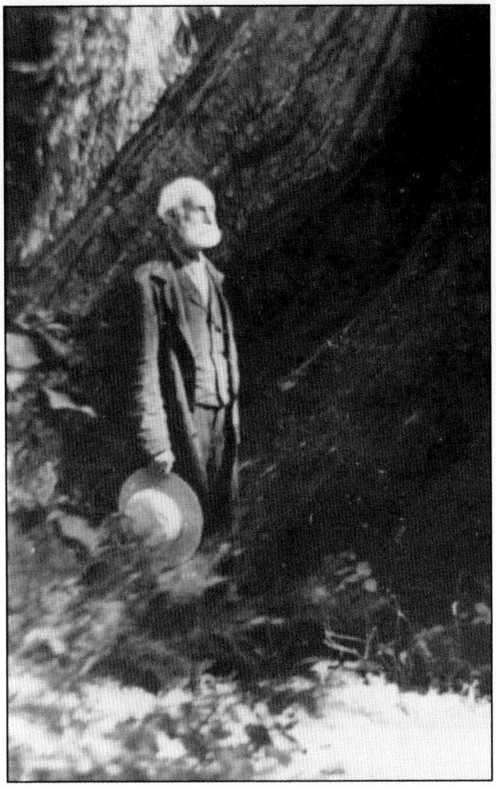

A. J. "Trapper" Smith kept an eye on things for Sperry and Perry in the South Grove from 1860 to 1862. He lived in the hollow of the second largest tree in the Beaver Creek Grove, as it was called. In 1862, Smith sheltered inside his tree home during a fierce windstorm that knocked down the grove's largest giant, Old Goliath, with a deafening crash. He thought his tree would be next, but it stood strong. (CBTSP.)

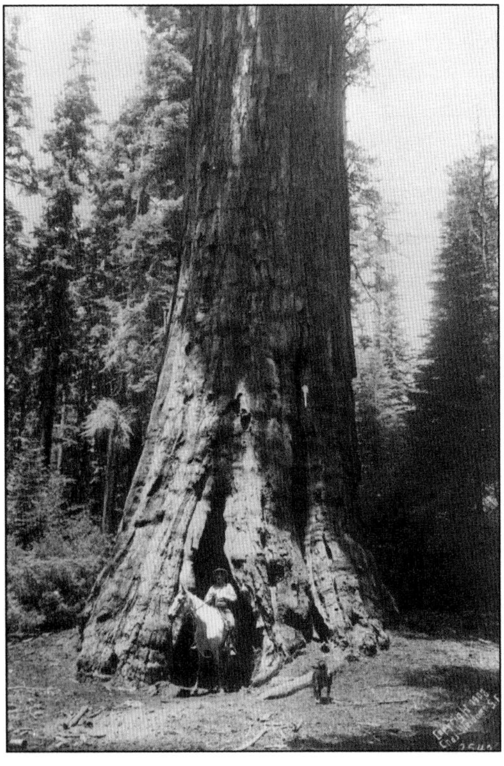

A man on horseback in 1908 poses in the entrance of "Trapper Smith's Cabin." In 1925, a U.S. Forest Service fireguard named Dan Phillipson lived inside the tree while he built a cabin nearby. (CCA.)

Many of the trees were given names, sometimes based on a tree's particular features, more often after famous people. For $50, Sperry and Perry would carve the desired name on a marble plaque that was mounted on the namesake. Although the plaques have been removed, the notch where they hung is still visible on some trees. The men in this photograph are surrounding the W. C. Bryant tree, so named by an admirer of the poet. (NYPL.)

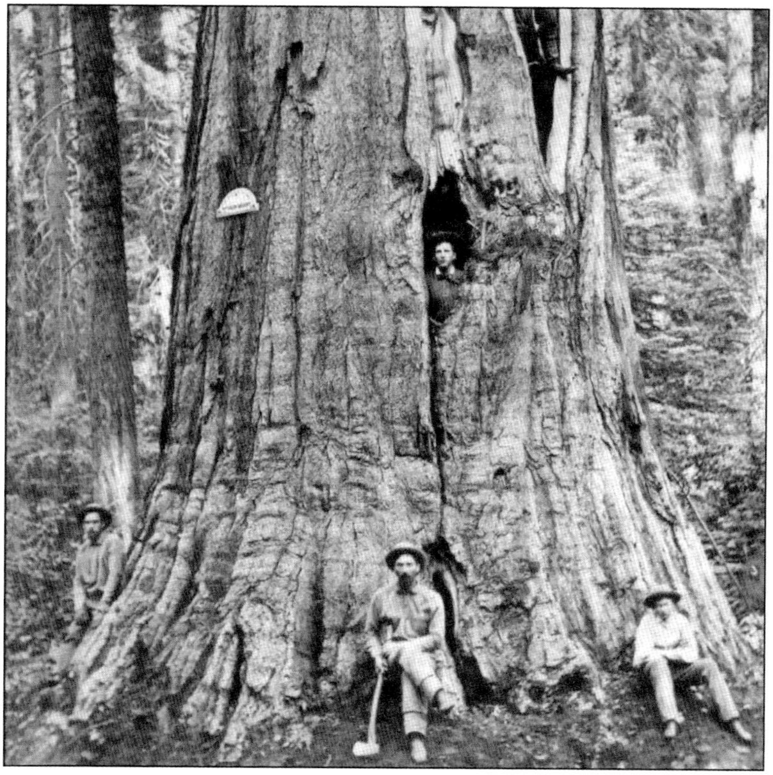

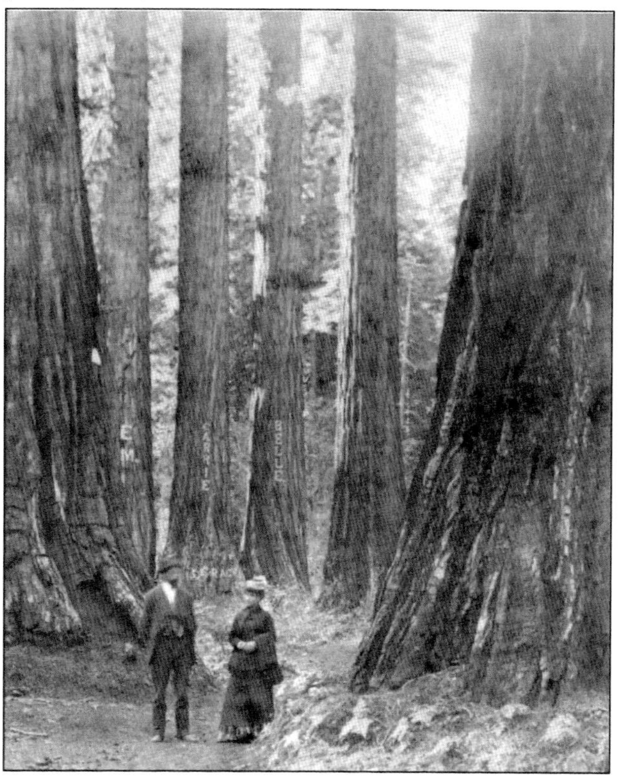

The three sequoias growing closely together in the back left of this Watkins photograph from the 1870s were dubbed the "Three Graces" by tourists. Here they are seen through the Bryant and Seward trees. Other famed trees were the "Miner's Cabin," "Salem Witch," "Hercules," "Old Bachelor," "Empire State," "Pride of the Forest," and "George Washington." (NYPL.)

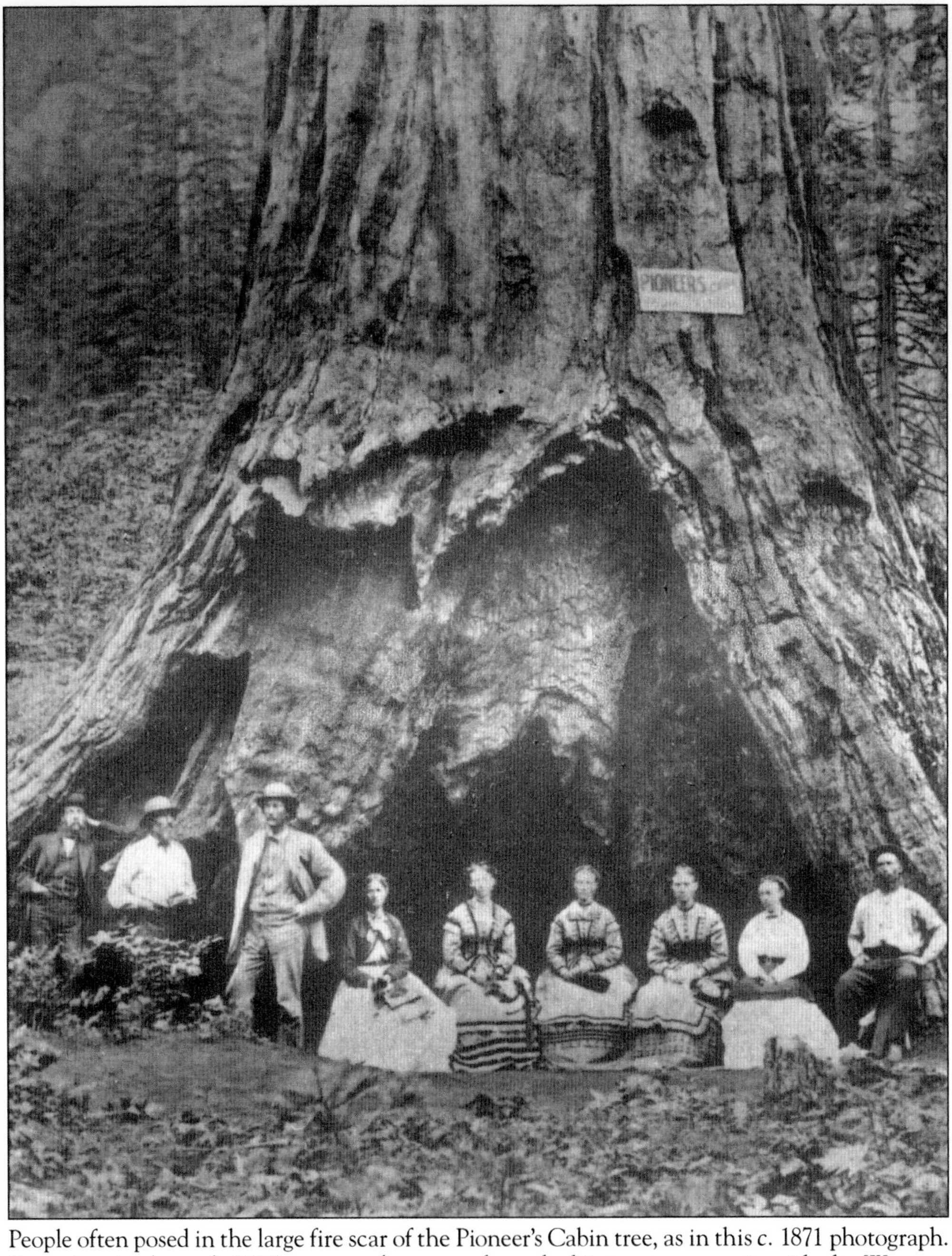

People often posed in the large fire scar of the Pioneer's Cabin tree, as in this c. 1871 photograph. Sometime in the early 1880s, a tunnel was cut through this tree to compete with the Wawona Tunnel Tree in the Mariposa Grove of Giant Sequoias near Yosemite. (OTM.)

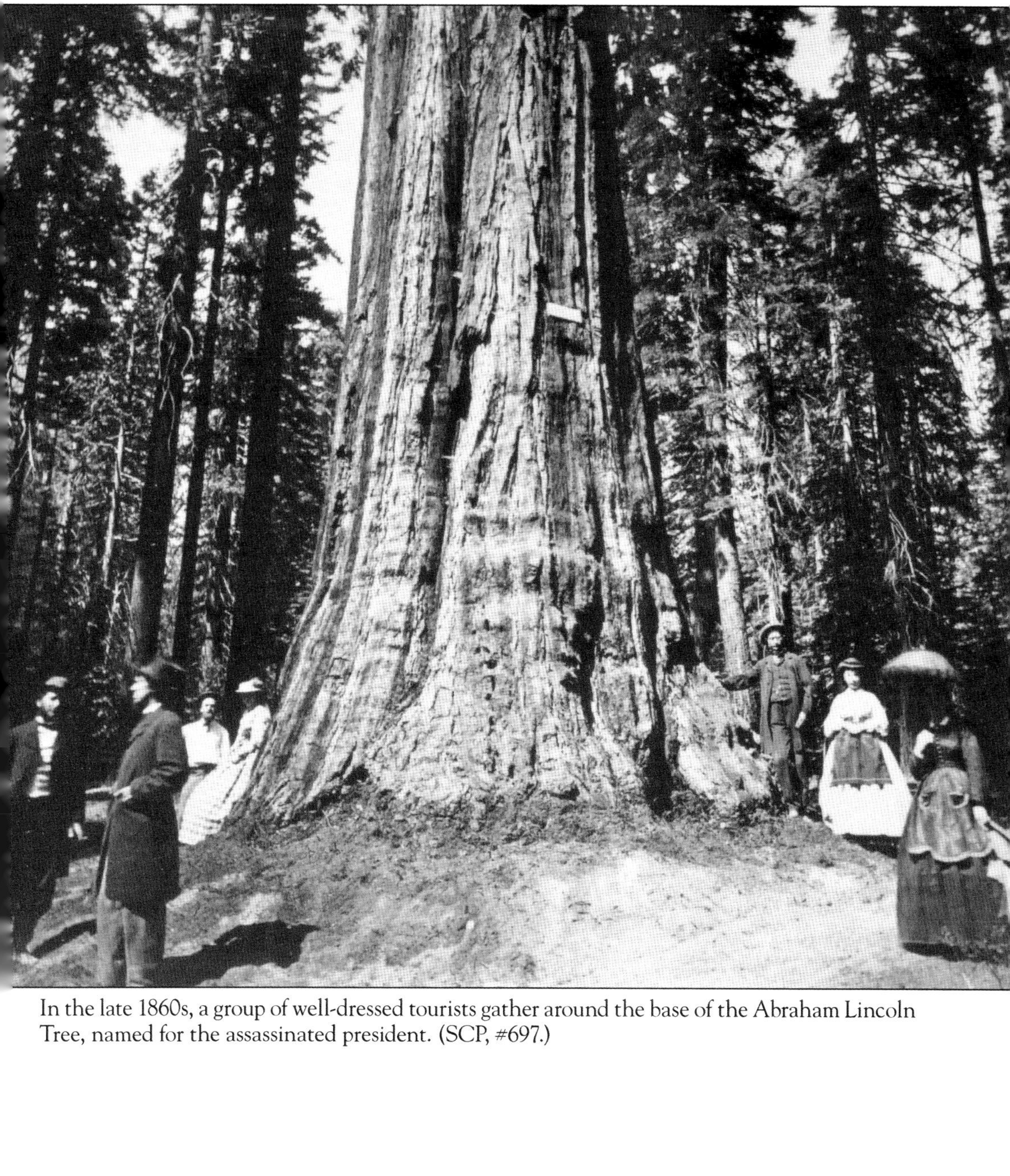

In the late 1860s, a group of well-dressed tourists gather around the base of the Abraham Lincoln Tree, named for the assassinated president. (SCP, #697.)

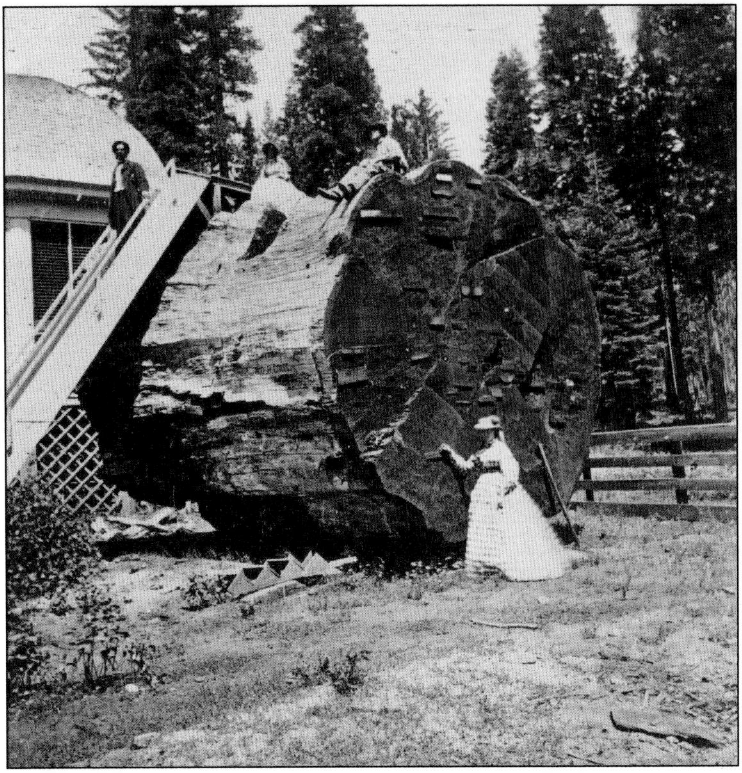

This woman shows off the latest in lady's fashion for 1866 while she poses with a few friends by Chip of the Old Block. Early travelers to the grove were usually from the upper classes of society, who had the time and money to travel. Despite the rigors of the trip, ladies of the day would bring their finest clothes and accessories. (This item is reproduced by permission of the Huntington Library, San Marino, California.)

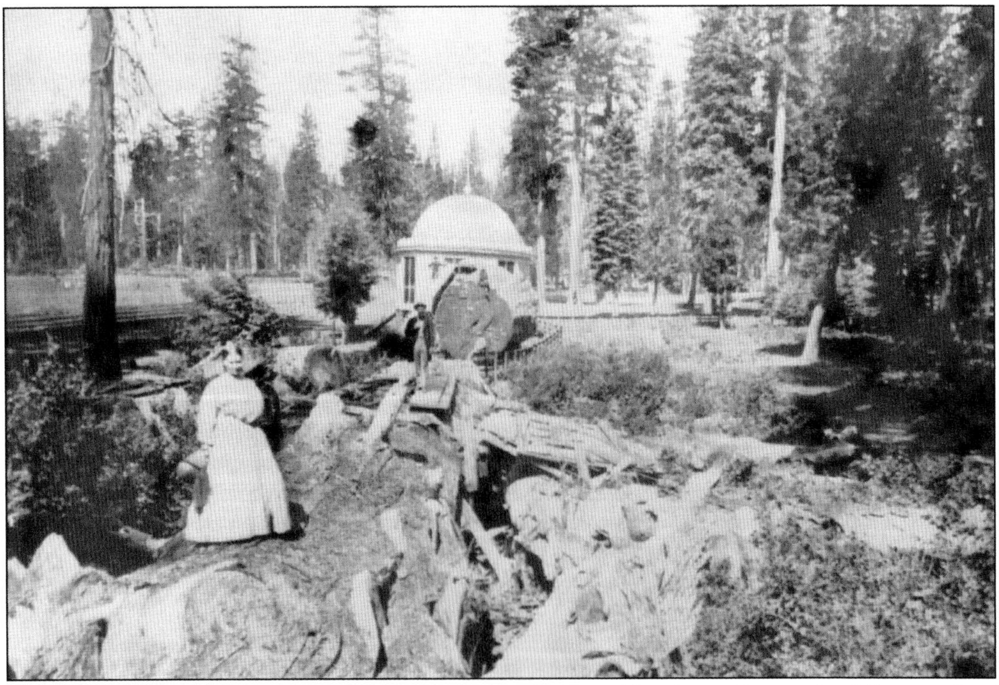

During the heavy winter snows of 1861–1862, the saloon and bowling alley on the fallen trunk of the Discovery Tree collapsed. A woman and man scramble over the wreckage in the late 1860s. (LOC, Lawrence and Houseworth Collection.)

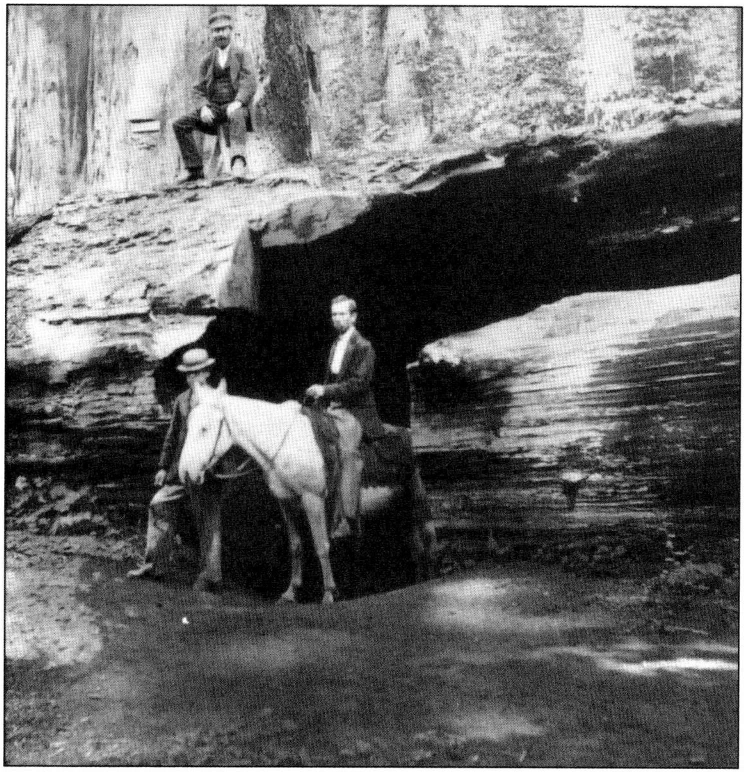

This tree, the Father of the Forest, had fallen long before the grove of mammoth trees was discovered by Dowd. Decomposition occurs very slowly in sequoias because of the tannin in their heartwood. Hollowed by fire, this was one of two trees large enough to ride through on horseback. (NYPL.)

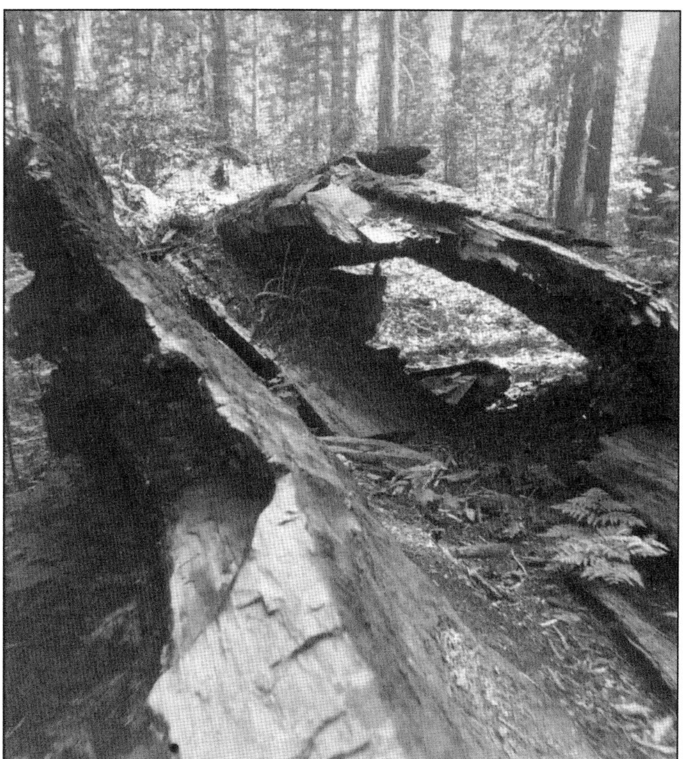

The tree originally named "Horseback Ride" collapsed, as seen here. William Brewer, a member of the first geological survey of California under state geologist Prof. Josiah D. Whitney, wrote in June 1863, "only three days before I arrived it split in pieces and caved in." (NYPL.)

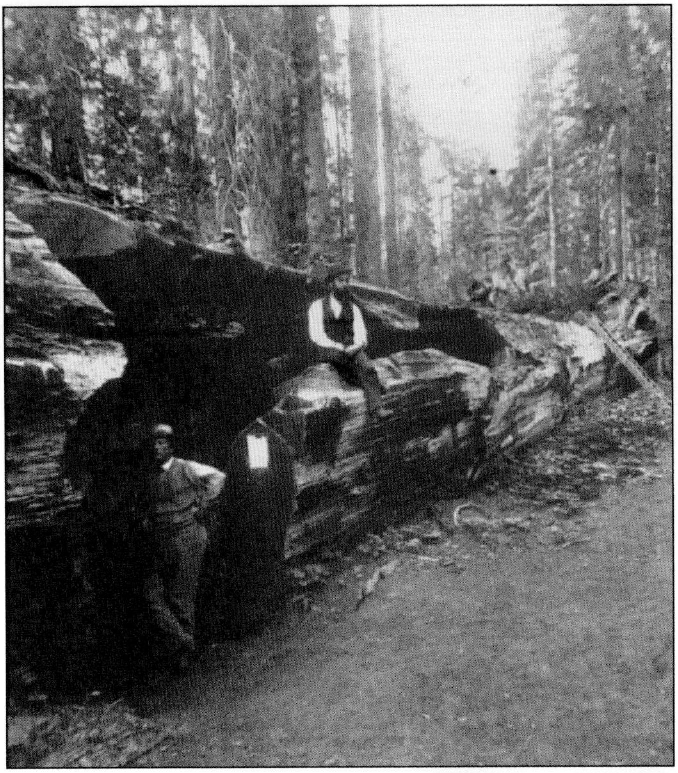

The man seated on the Father of the Forest in 1871 (left) is believed to be James Mason Hutchings, the "Father of Yosemite." He published early travel guides with extensive descriptions and illustrations of Yosemite and the "mammoth trees of Calaveras." He regularly visited the grove, and from 1900 to 1902 operated the Mammoth Grove Hotel. The gentleman standing at the entrance is likely C. L. Pond, who published stereoviews, including both images on this page. He appears in a number of grove photographs, including the one of Chip below. (Left, BOS; below OTM.)

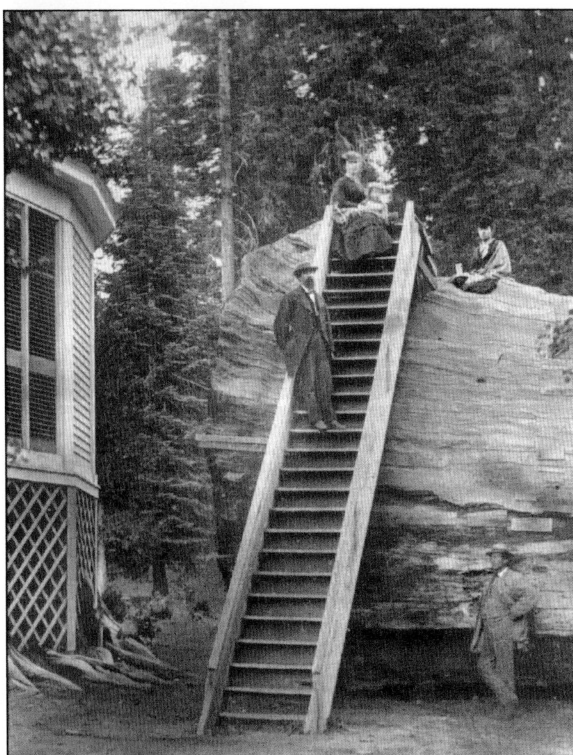

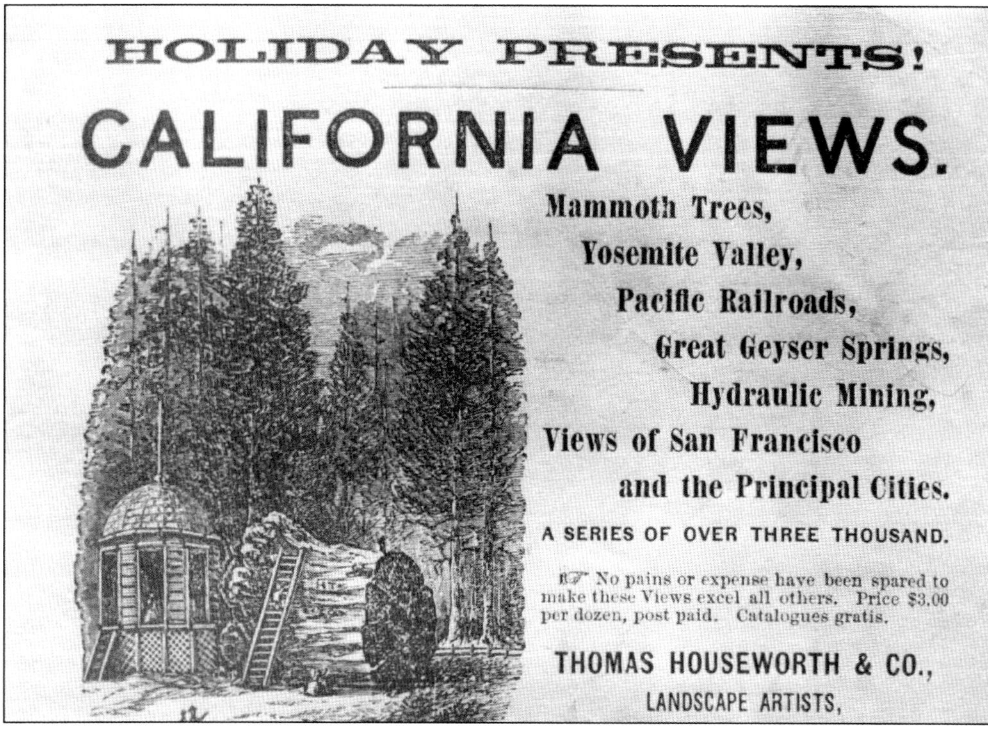

The Calaveras Big Trees were popular among photographers of the day. This *c.* 1870 advertisement is for Thomas Houseworth's *California Views*. Originally from New York, Houseworth came to California in 1849 with George Lawrence. They worked as miners in Calaveras and Trinity counties before opening an optical shop in San Francisco in 1851. In 1859, they began selling stereoviews. Their photographs are among the earliest surviving images of the big trees. (CBTSP.)

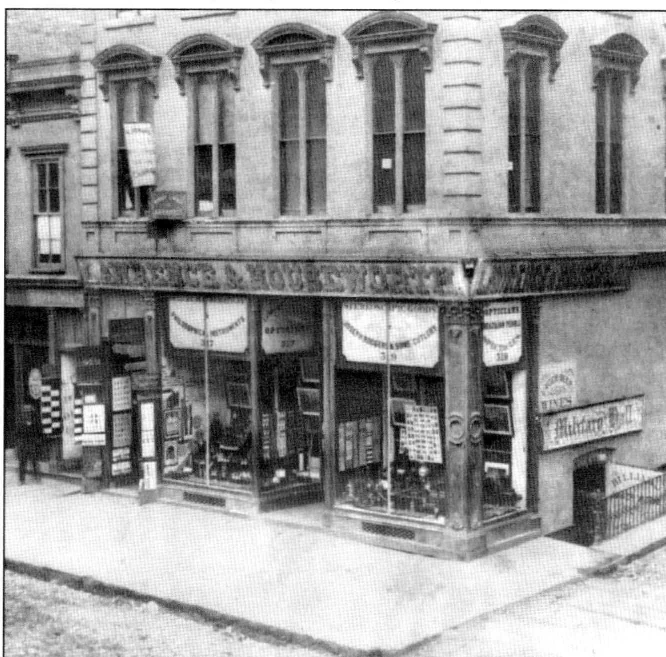

From their San Francisco studio, shown here in 1866, Lawrence and Houseworth purchased negatives from photographers and published them, usually without credit. They worked with Eadweard Muybridge, Charles L. Weed, Martin Mason Hazeltine, and George Fiske, among others. Other photographers and publishers who printed images of the big trees include Carleton Watkins, J. P. Soule, C. L. Pond, E. and H. T. Anthony, and J. C. Scripture, who spent many summers at the hotel. (LOC, Lawrence and Houseworth Collection.)

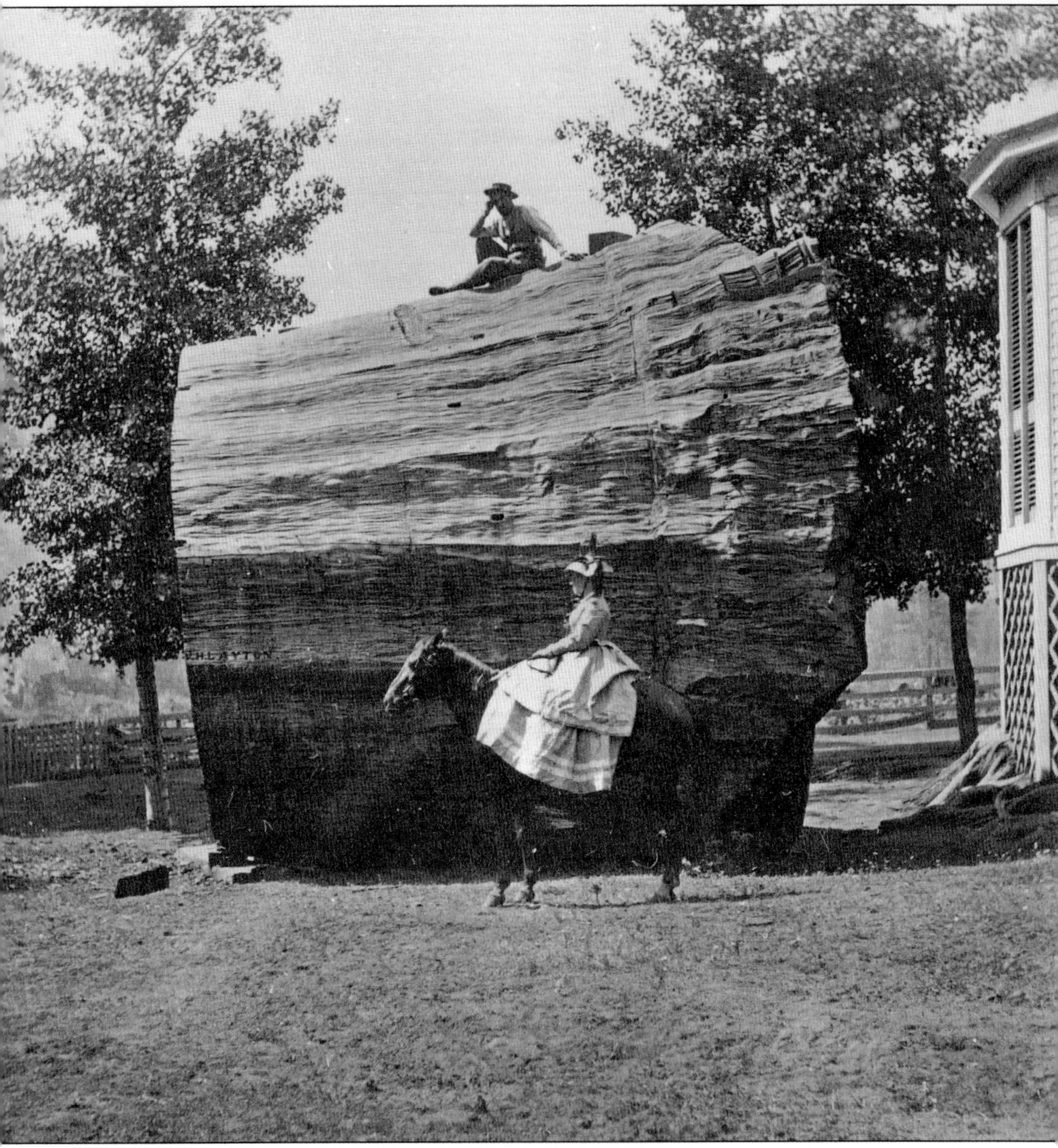

This photograph was captioned: "Section of the Original Big Tree—and celebrated horse 'Selem'." The horse was the beloved pet of James Sperry and his wife, Mehitable, whom he married in 1864. Her poetry was published in several California newspapers, including a 27-verse poem praising Selem. Well known to tourists at the Big Tree Ranch, Selem died in 1878. (This item is reproduced by permission of the Huntington Library, San Marino, California.)

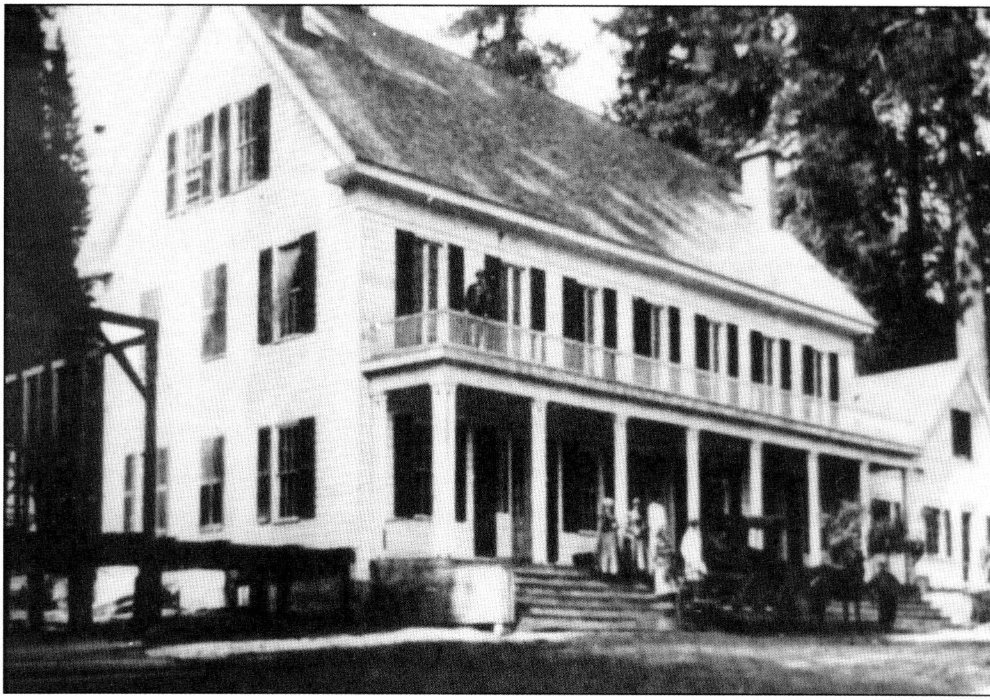

John and Eliza Perry managed the new hotel upon opening in 1861, while Sperry continued overseeing their venture in Murphys. In 1865, a two-story cottage built east of the hotel was the Perry's summer residence. Today it is the ranger station. When a U.S. post office was established at the hotel in December 1865, Perry was named postmaster. The Big Tree Ranch became so popular that a two-story wing was added to the hotel, seen under construction (above) in 1871. The unusual side view below of the hotel before the addition shows the barn and other outbuildings behind the hotel. (Above, OTM; below, CCA.)

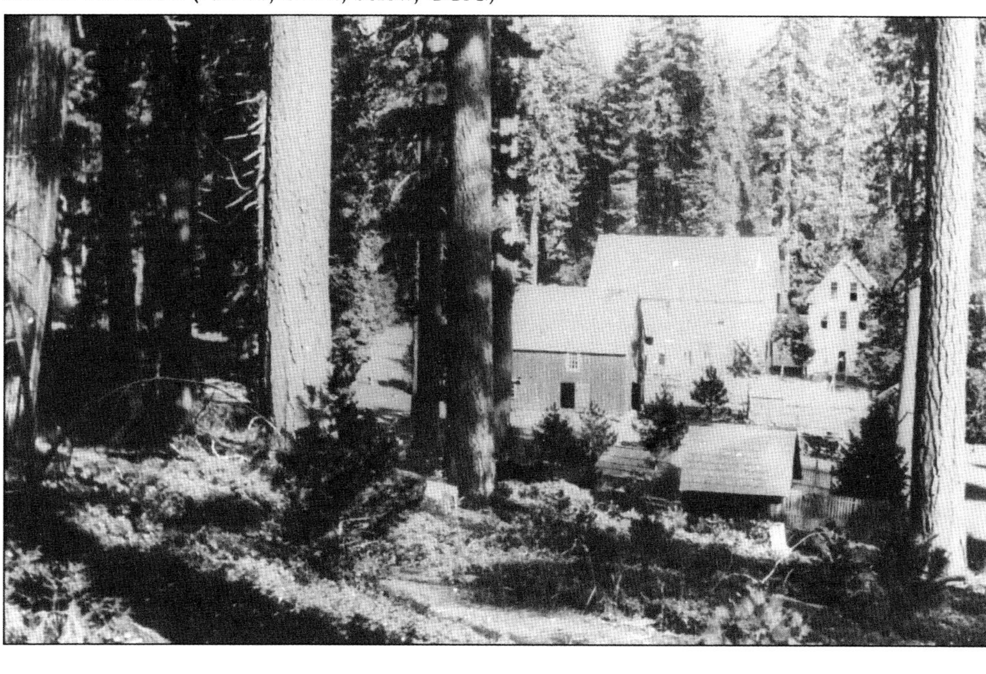

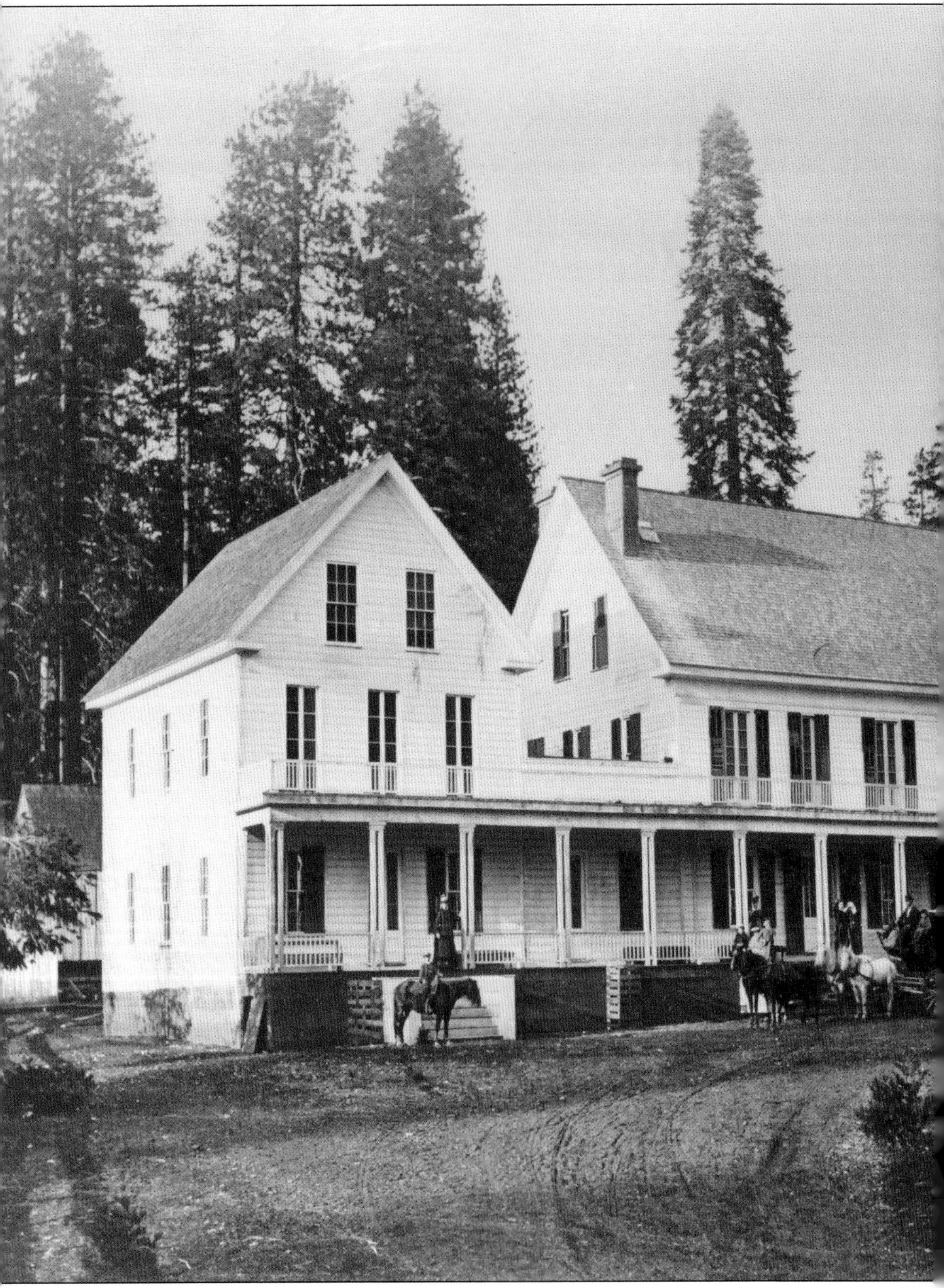

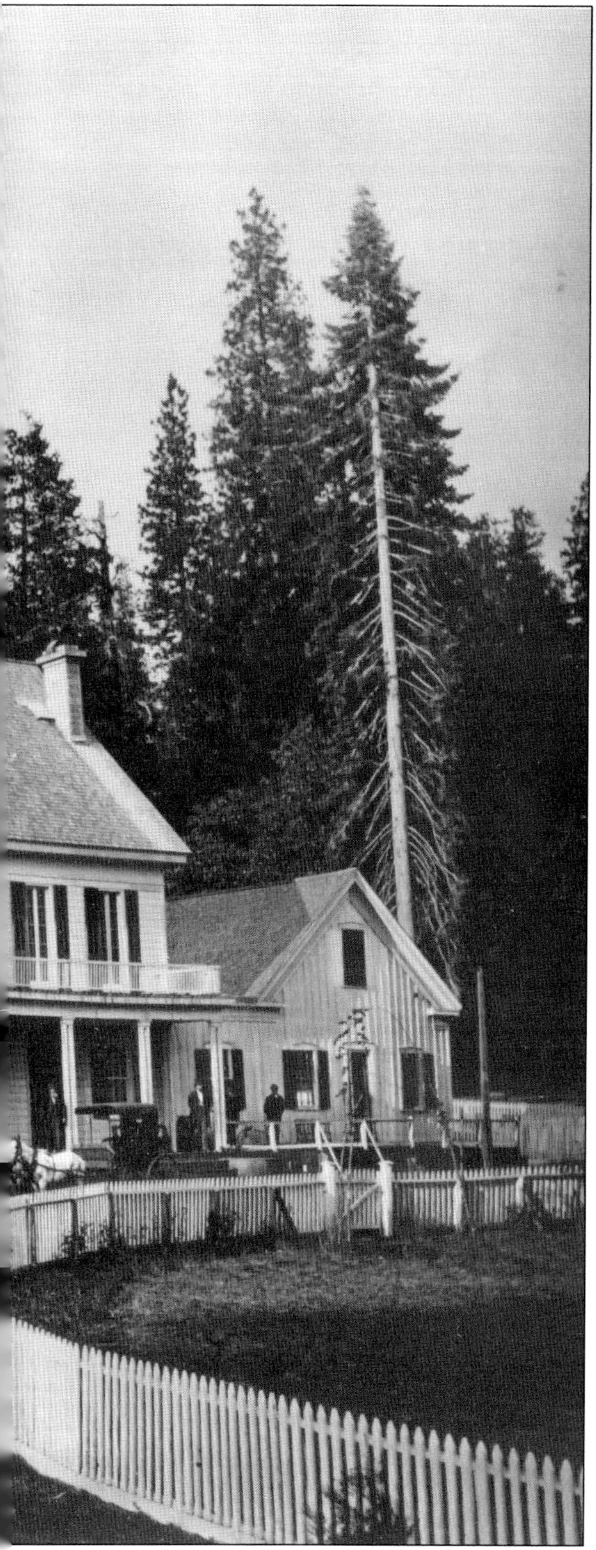

This iconic image of the Mammoth Grove Hotel was taken in 1874. The boy on the pony (left) is Sperry's eldest son, Willard. John Perry died in 1874, and Sperry bought Eliza Perry's interest for $25,000. The Marquis de Brigés, Eugene Elias Malbec de Montjoc, and his mother, the Marquise de Brigés, Maria Rosaria Barsena of France, joined Sperry as new partners. The partnership soon soured, and Sperry filed suit in October 1875 to dissolve it in court. Sperry's initial victories were challenged all the way to the U. S. Supreme Court, where he ultimately prevailed in 1877. The court ordered the property sold and the proceeds split between the parties. Sperry's ace was his brother Simon W. Sperry, the wealthy owner of Sperry Flour in Stockton, California, who submitted the highest bid at $14,500. The court confirmed the sale on April 24, 1878. On July 23, Simon resold the groves to his brother for $15,000. (CBTSP.)

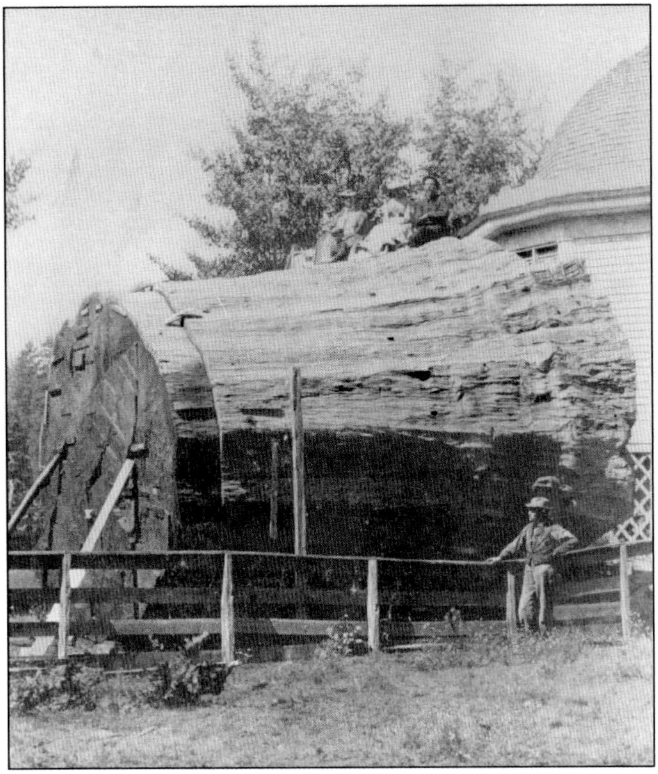

The completion of the transcontinental railroad in 1869 opened travel between the coasts and launched a new era for this country. Two entrepreneurs saw novel opportunities for a big trees exhibition. In 1870, F. S. Jellerson and A. Ricker purchased the right to remove a slice from the original Discovery Tree. The bark has been removed and the slice may be cut through in this photograph. (CBTSP.)

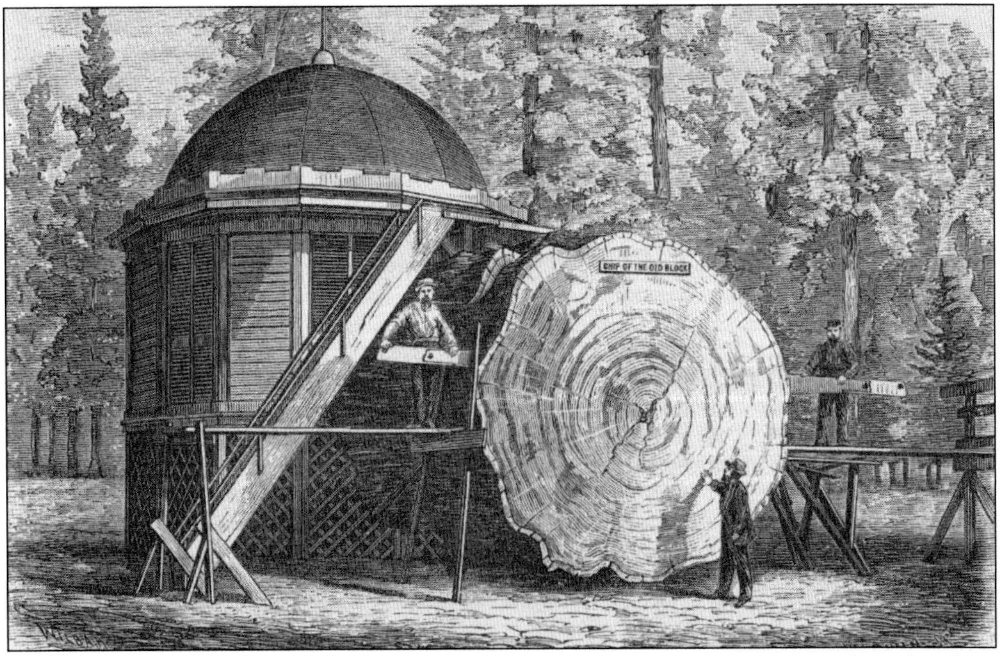

This sketch of a Kilburn brothers photograph depicts Jellerson and Ricker cutting their slice from Chip. Sperry and Perry continued the tradition of exploiting the grove, but less destructively. Wood was carved from fallen trees and bark from living trees to make souvenirs for tourists, including cribbage boards, picture frames, walking sticks, checkerboards, and pin cushions. (CBTSP.)

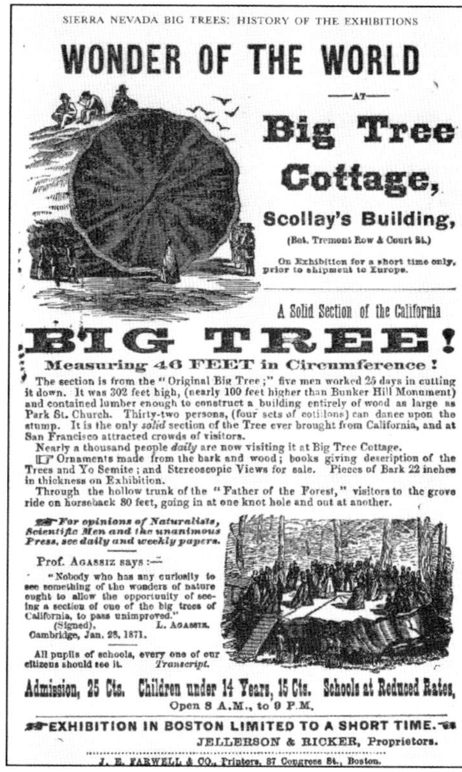

This broadside advertised Jellerson and Ricker's Big Tree exhibit in Boston. Launched at Woodward Gardens in San Francisco in November 1870, it moved to Boston in January 1871. After two and half months, the exhibit moved again to New York City in April, then on to London's Kew Gardens. (CBTSP.)

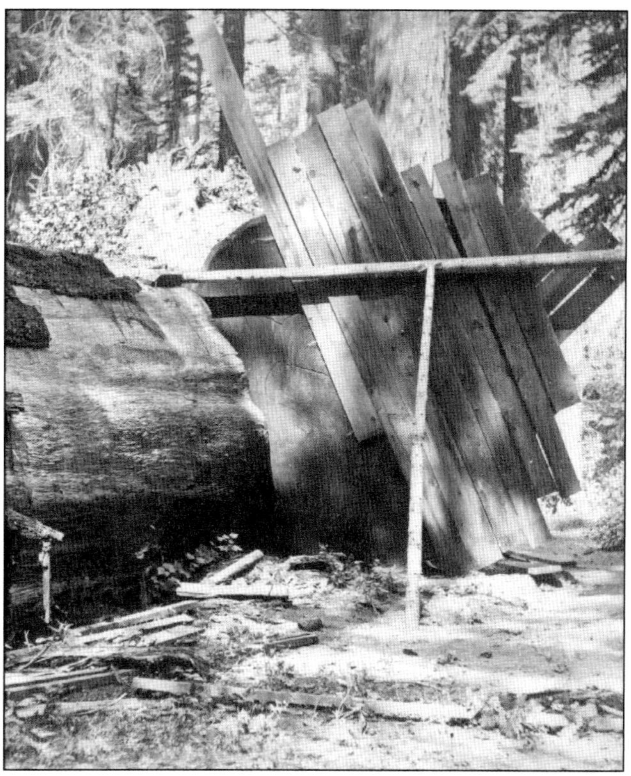

A slice was removed from the fallen Hercules tree for the Paris World Exposition of 1867, but it was never sent. Toppled by a winter storm in 1862, the tree achieved notoriety for two reasons: it was one of the biggest trees in the grove, and John Wooster had carved his name and the date June 2, 1850, into it two years before Dowd's "discovery." (NYPL.)

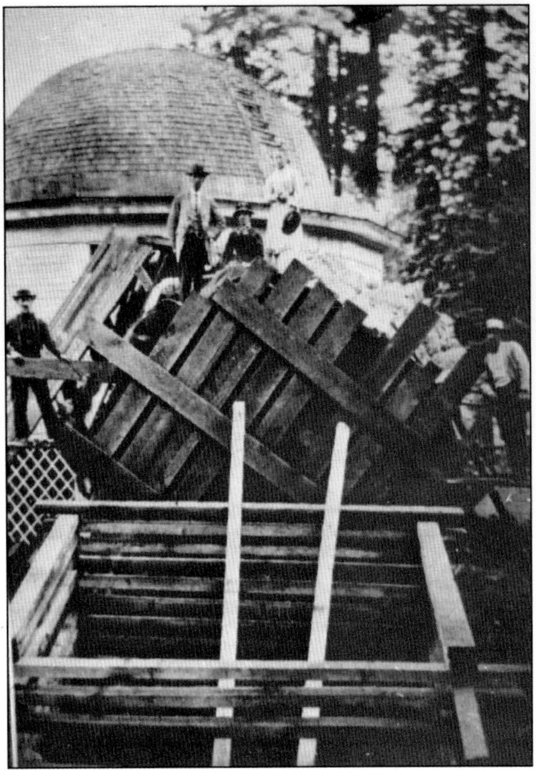

These undated photographs were likely taken in 1867 when Sperry and Perry removed a slice from Chip in the event someone inquired for one. Below, Mehitable Sperry and her friends pose on the freshly cut slab. (Left, OTM; below, CCHS.)

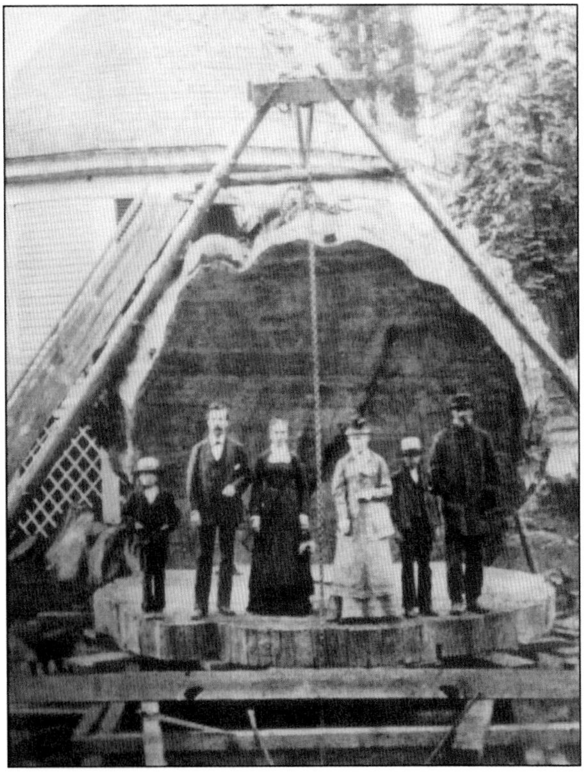

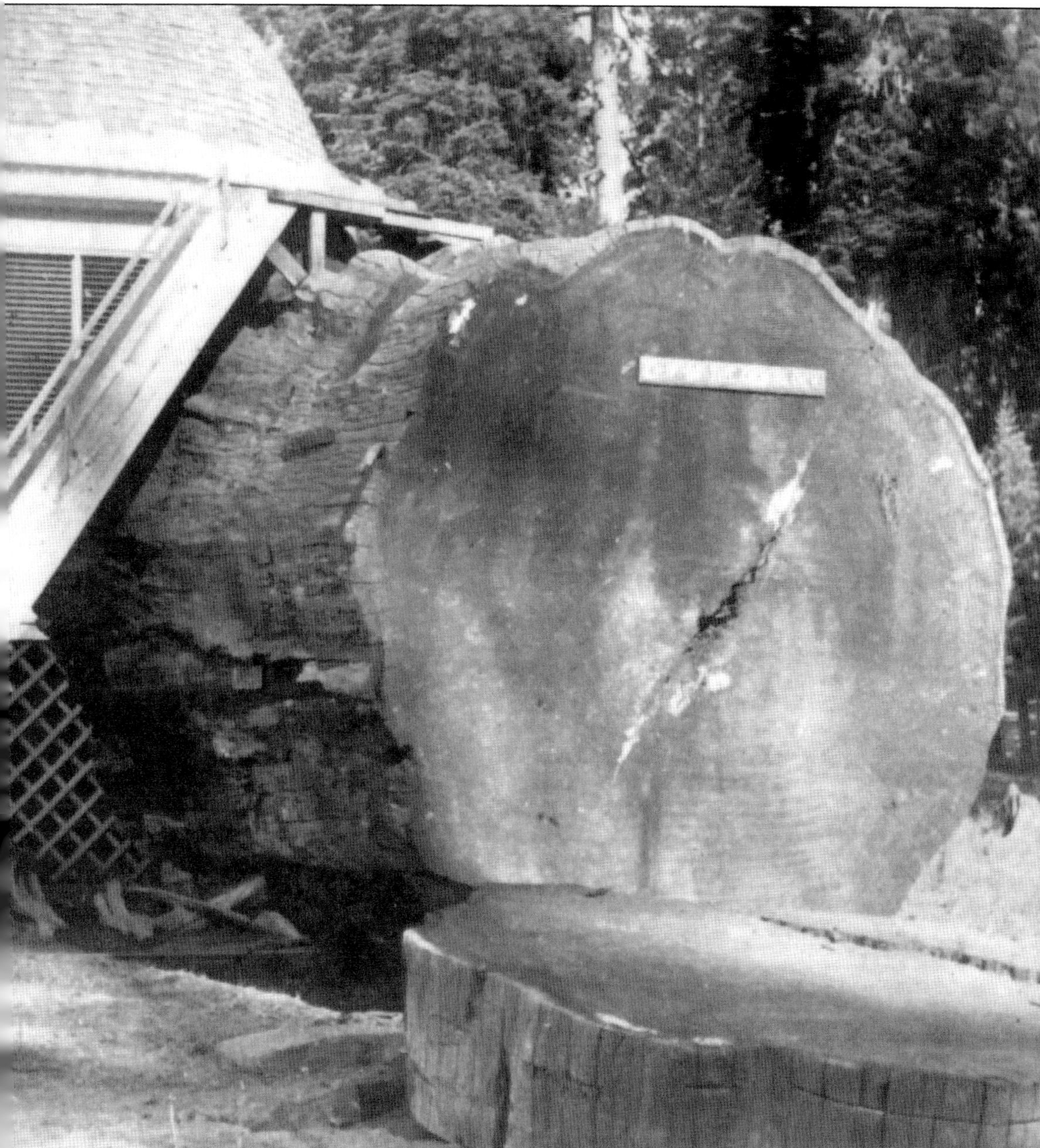

Another much larger slice was removed from Chip in this undated photograph. This may be the final cut from Chip taken for the California exhibit at the 1884–1885 Industrial and Cotton Centennial Exposition in New Orleans. An illustration of the big tree display appeared in *Harper's Weekly* on February 7, 1885. Giant sequoias were at first believed to be 3,000 to 4,000 years old. In 1863, the California Geological Survey team carefully counted the rings on Chip of the Old Block. Prof. Whitney provided the first accurate assessment of the tree's age at between 1,255 and 1,300 years when it was felled. (NYPL.)

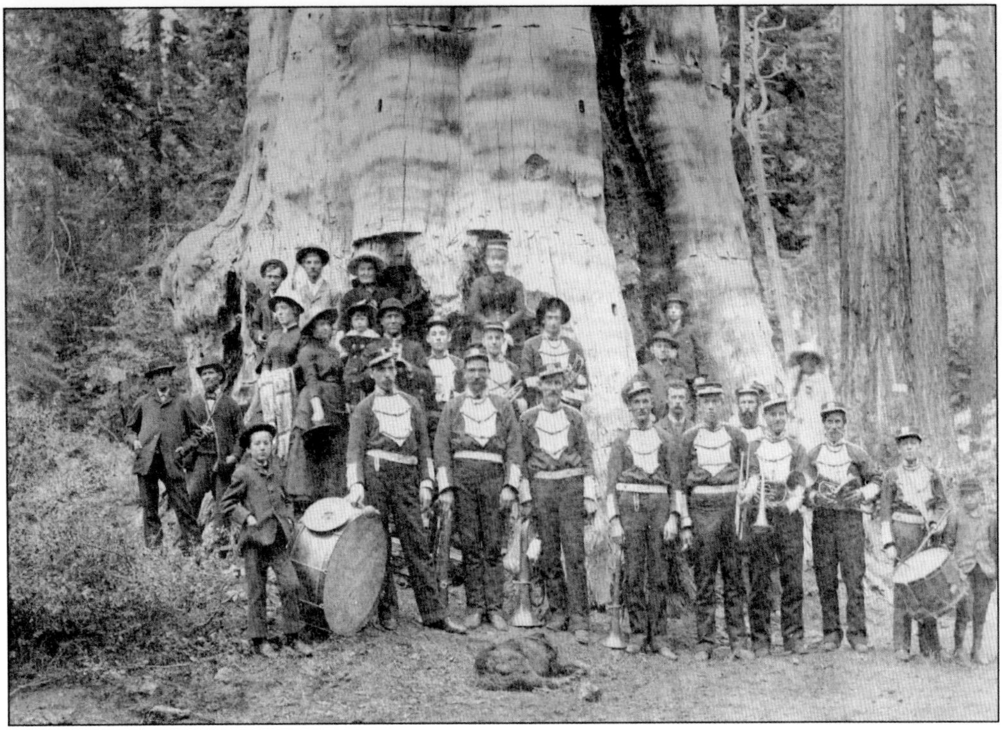

Murphys was the nearest town of any size to the big trees. As it grew, it offered the amenities found in many towns across the country, including a coronet band. Here the members of Murphys Coronet Band and some of their relatives pose in front of the disfigured Mother of the Forest (above) and the Pioneer's Cabin Tree (below). These photographs were taken after 1881, the year in which a tunnel was cut through the Wawona Tree in Yosemite. Sperry followed suit a short time later to keep up with the competition. (Both, OTM.)

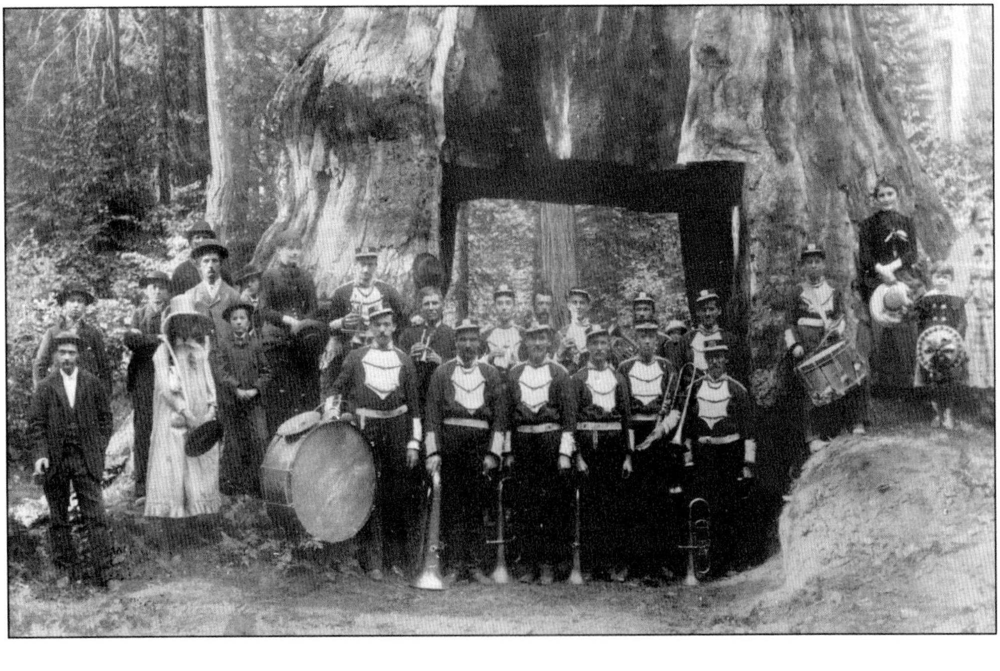

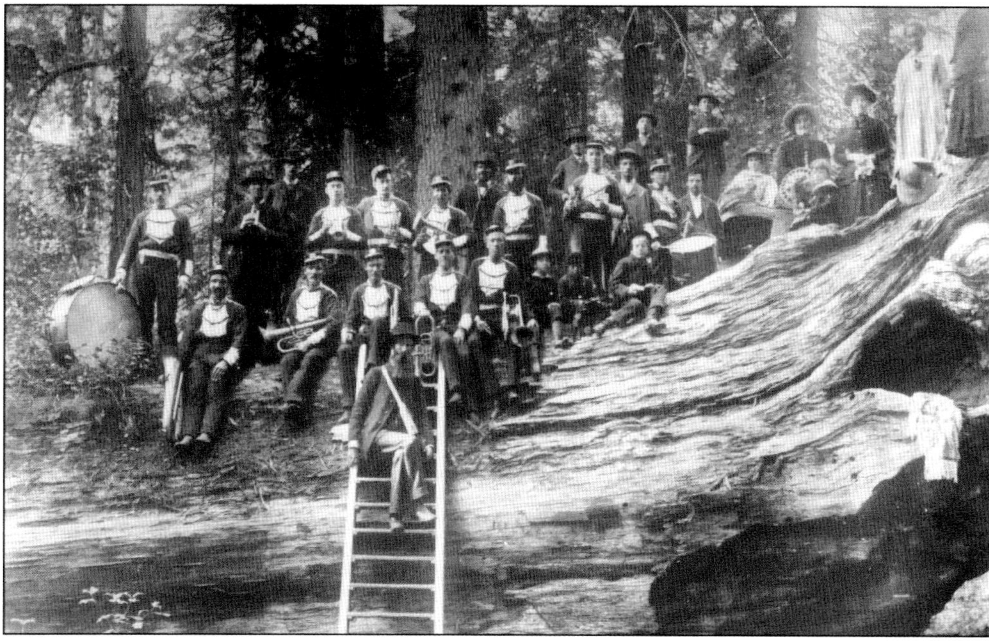

Over the years, people have speculated that the bearded gentleman in each of these photographs is famed naturalist John Muir. He visited the Calaveras Grove only twice, in 1876 and 1900. The supposed Muir is seated on the stairs with the Murphys Coronet Band (above) at the Father of the Forest. Clearly this photograph was taken at the same time as those on the previous page, after 1881, and based on period clothing, before 1890. The Pride of the Forest Tree photograph (below) with another "Muir" was likely taken in the mid-1870s. Experts have been unable to confirm that it is, in fact, Muir. (Above, OTM; below, CBTSP.)

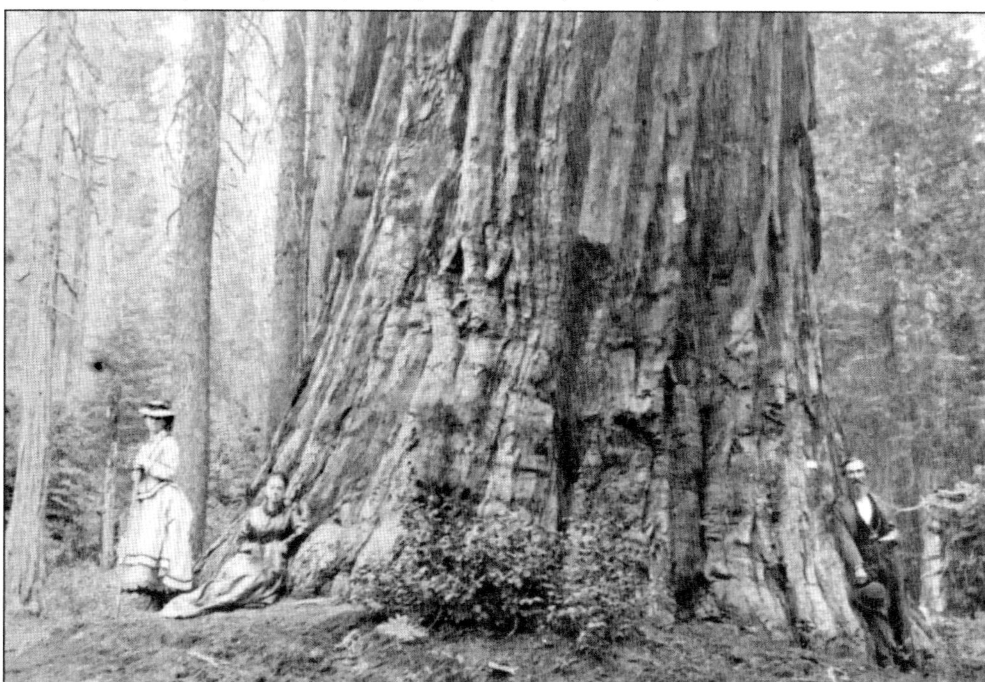

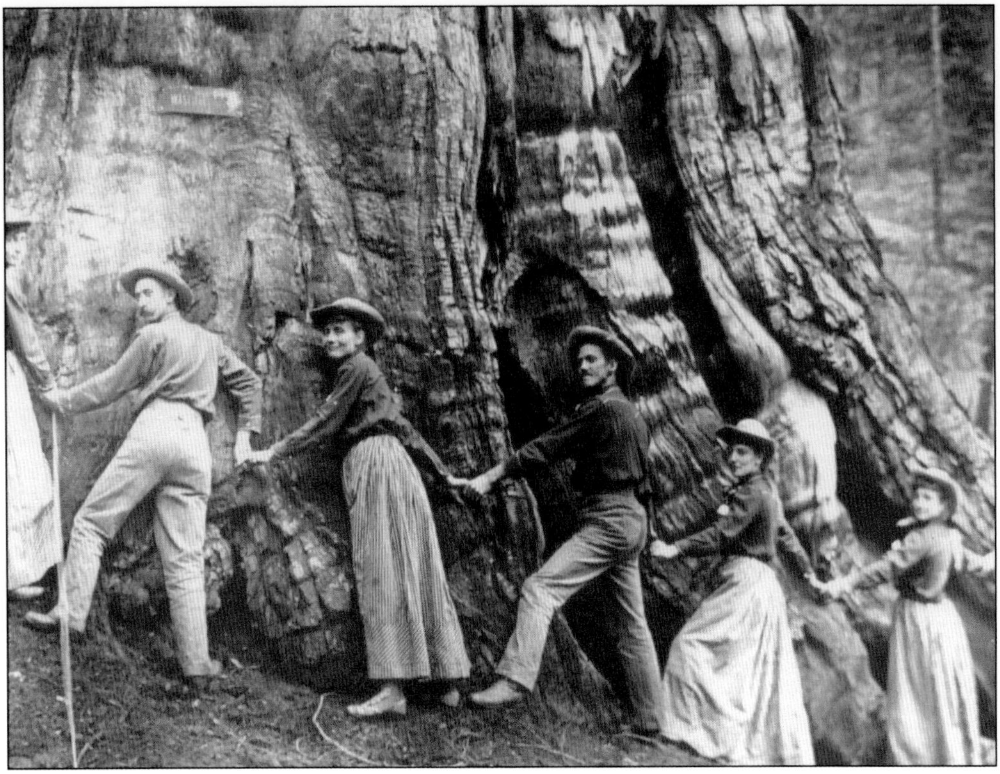

By the 1880s, travel was no longer limited to the wealthy, and new visitors were attracted to the Calaveras Grove. These men and women were part of a group that visited in two stagecoaches in the late 1880s or early 1890s. They engaged in a popular activity—seeing how many people it took to encircle the mammoth trees. (OTM.)

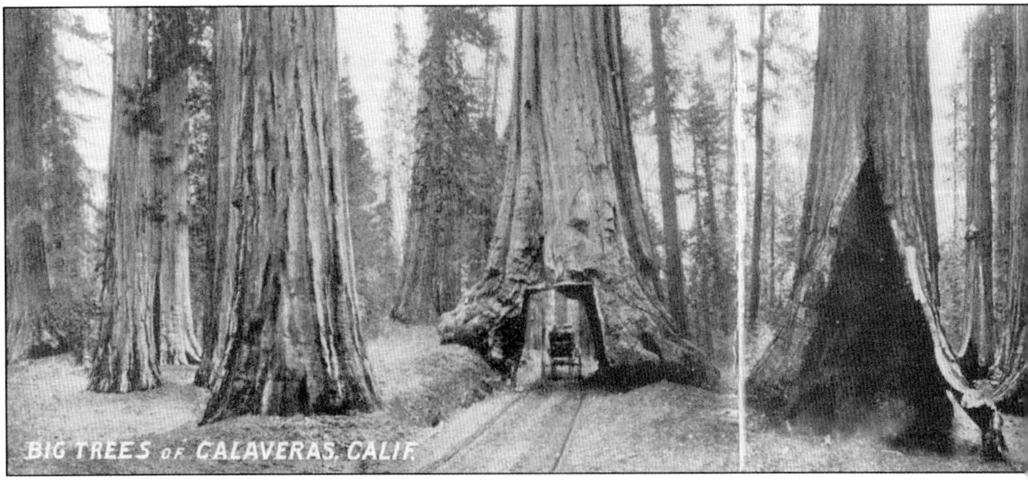

The Calaveras Big Trees Grove was brilliantly captured in this panoramic penny postcard from the 1880s. Robert Collyer, a famous Unitarian minister from New York City, told the *San Francisco Examiner* in 1887, "I have been to see the big trees in

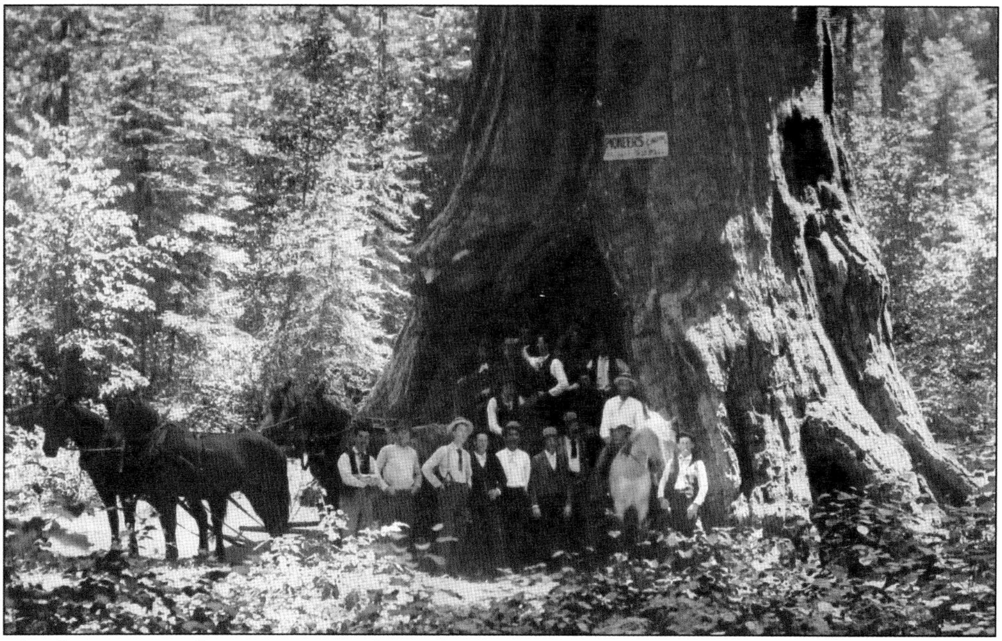

This large group of men, some in a horse-drawn wagon, pose inside and around the entrance to the Pioneer's Cabin Tree. Visitors can still walk through this tree today. The tree is no longer able to support the growth of a top because of the huge cut, yet it manages to survive, although just barely. (CBTSP.)

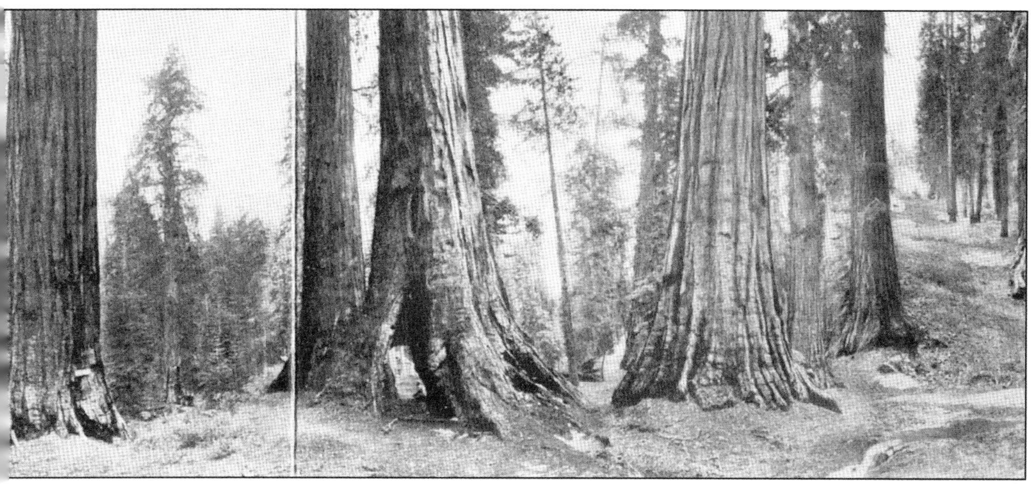

Calaveras County, and they were altogether beyond what my imagination had conceived. Photographs are merely relative and do not give you a true idea of their immense stature." (CCHS.)

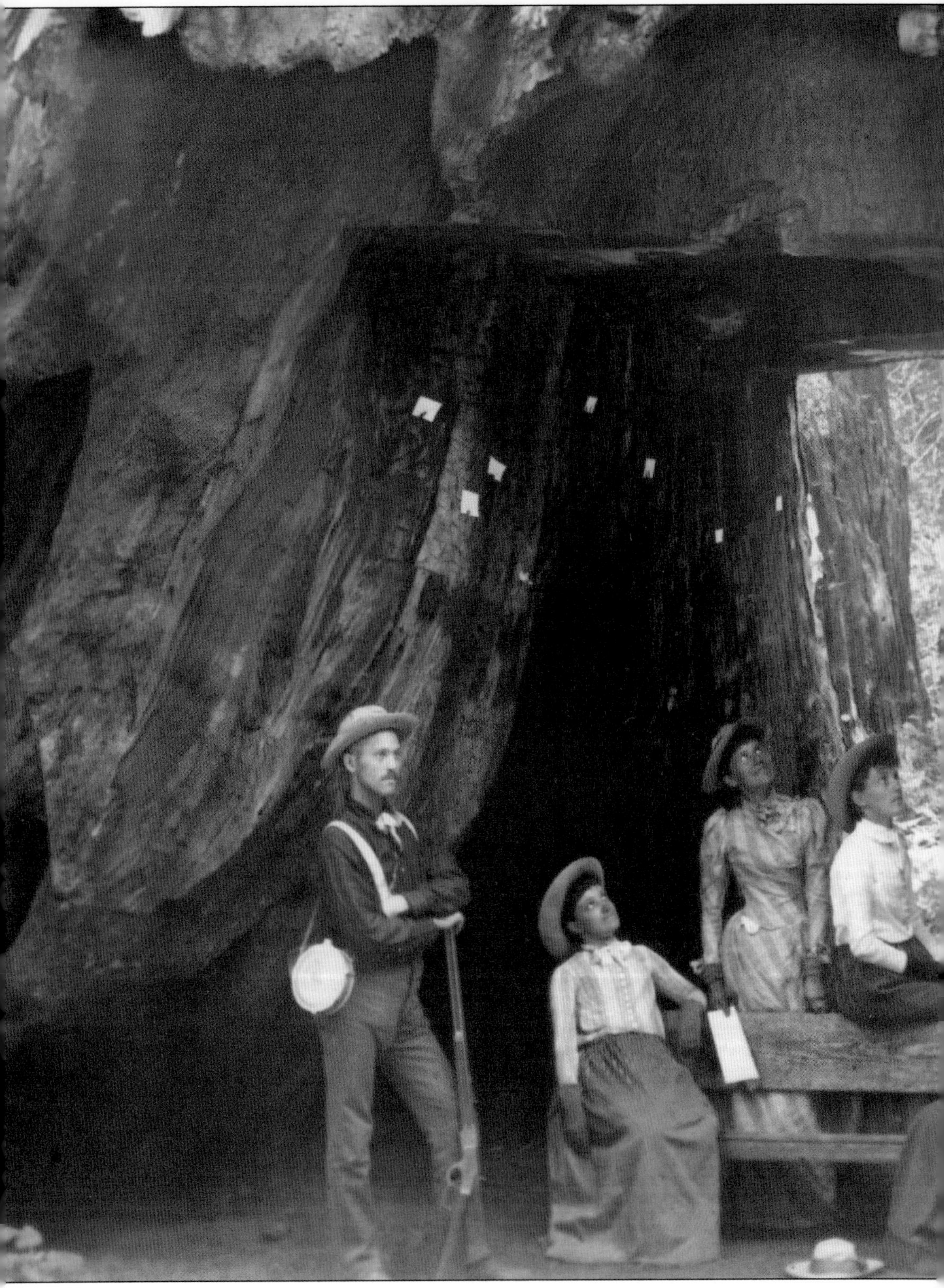

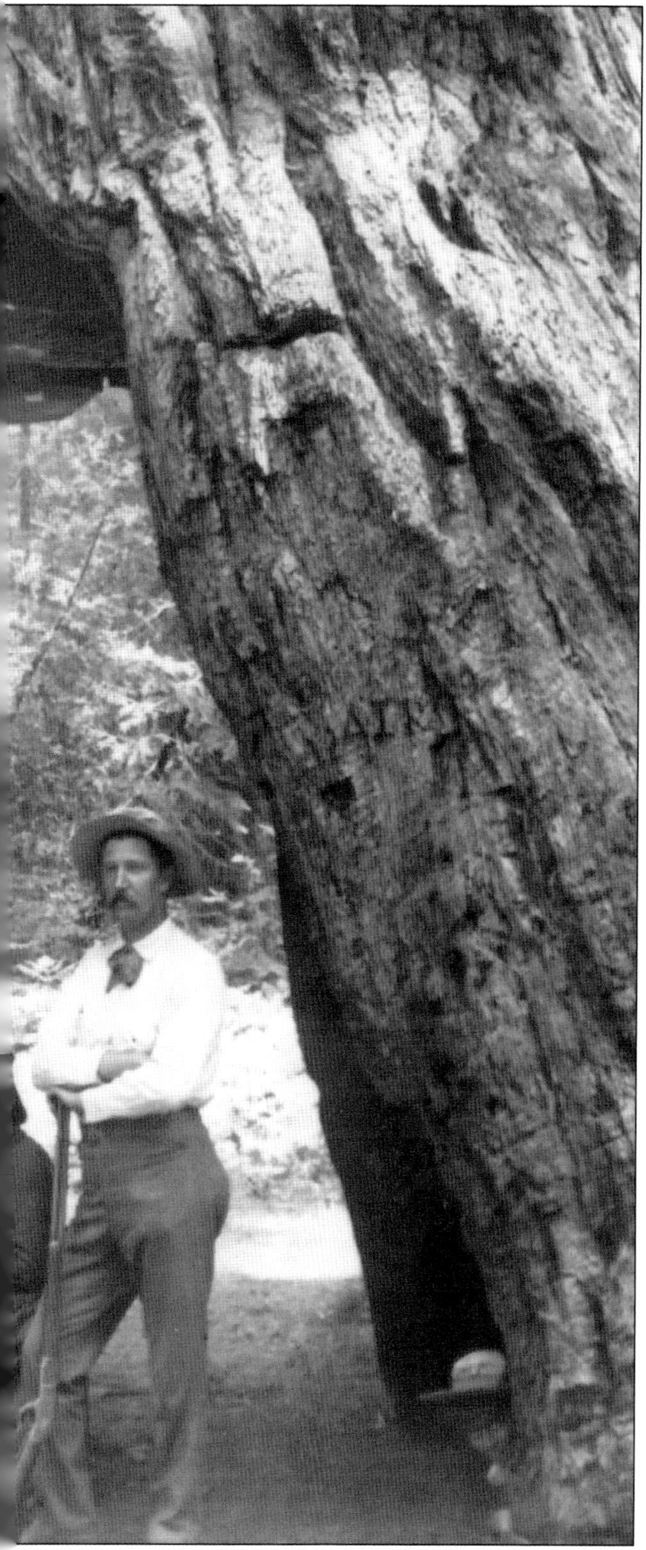

At the Pioneer's Cabin Tree in the early 1890s, some visitors strike a serious pose while others engage in a bit of whimsy. Follow the upward gaze of the three young women to see a man hiding above them. His hat has fallen at their feet. Another person peeks out at the lower right. The white squares inside the opening (left) are pieces of tin that have been punched with the names of visitors and nailed to the tree, sometimes with a spent cartridge. People also carved their names, initials, and dates into trees, a practice outlawed in the 1930s. (CBTSP.)

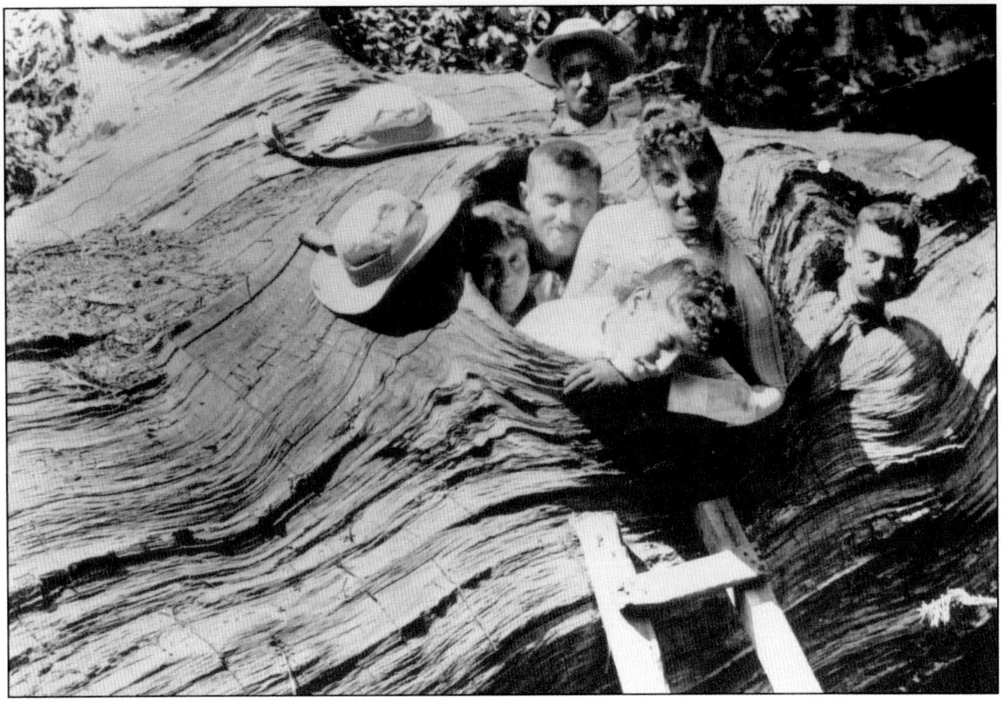

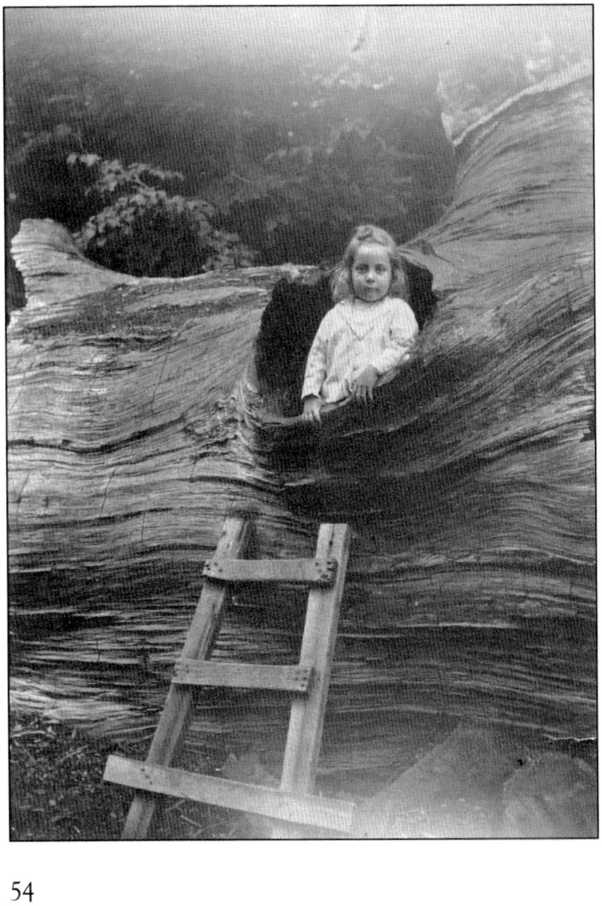

The knotholes of fallen trees have been a popular spot for photographs in the grove for more than 100 years. The men and women above poking out of the Father of the Forest appear to be the same fun-loving group of visitors from the previous page. In the photograph of the Father of the Forest at left, a young child peers out of a knothole in the 1890s. (Above, OTM; left, CBTSP.)

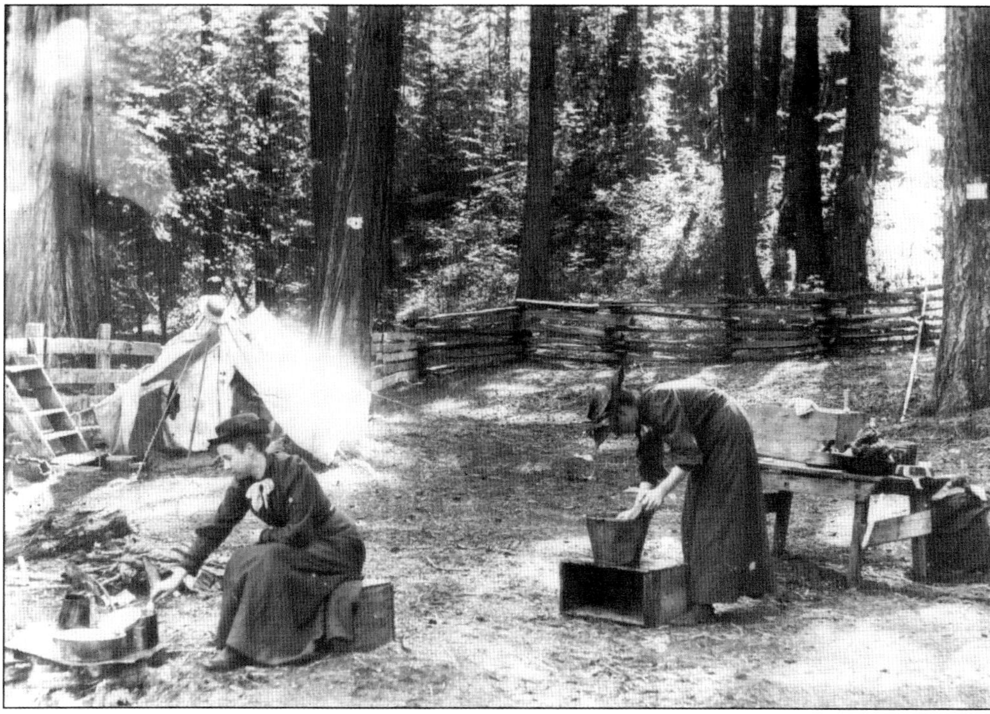

Camping has always been a popular activity at the Calaveras Big Trees Ranch. These women in 1893 appear to be preparing a meal in their rustic campsite. (CBTSP.)

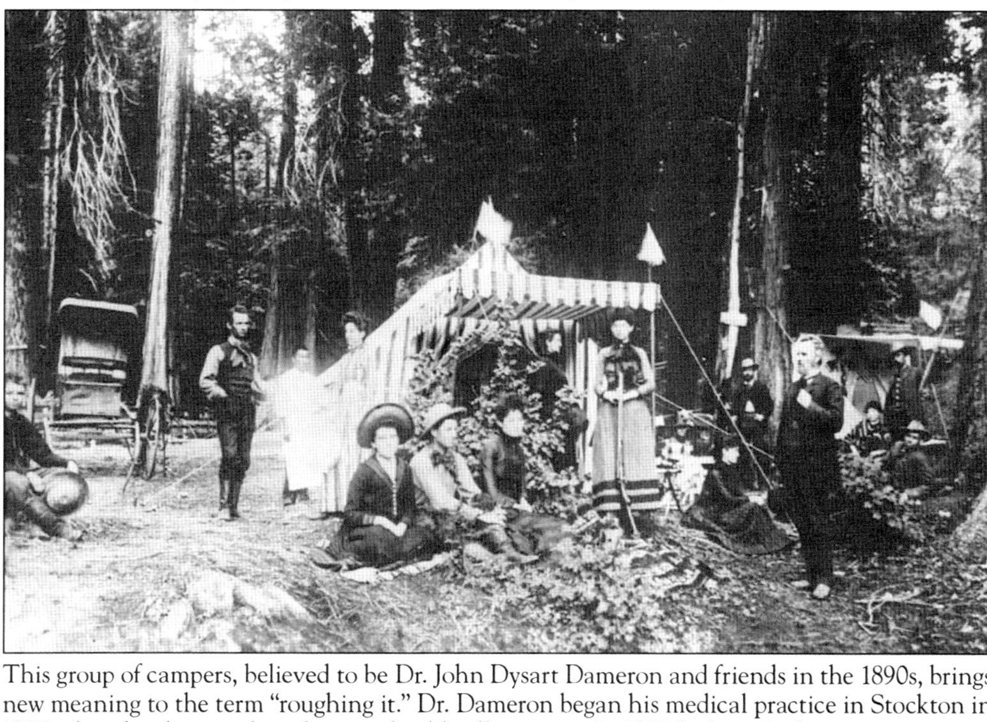

This group of campers, believed to be Dr. John Dysart Dameron and friends in the 1890s, brings new meaning to the term "roughing it." Dr. Dameron began his medical practice in Stockton in 1895, where he also was elected county health officer twice. In 1901, he launched a training program for nurses and, in 1912, founded a hospital in Stockton that still bears his name. (BOS.)

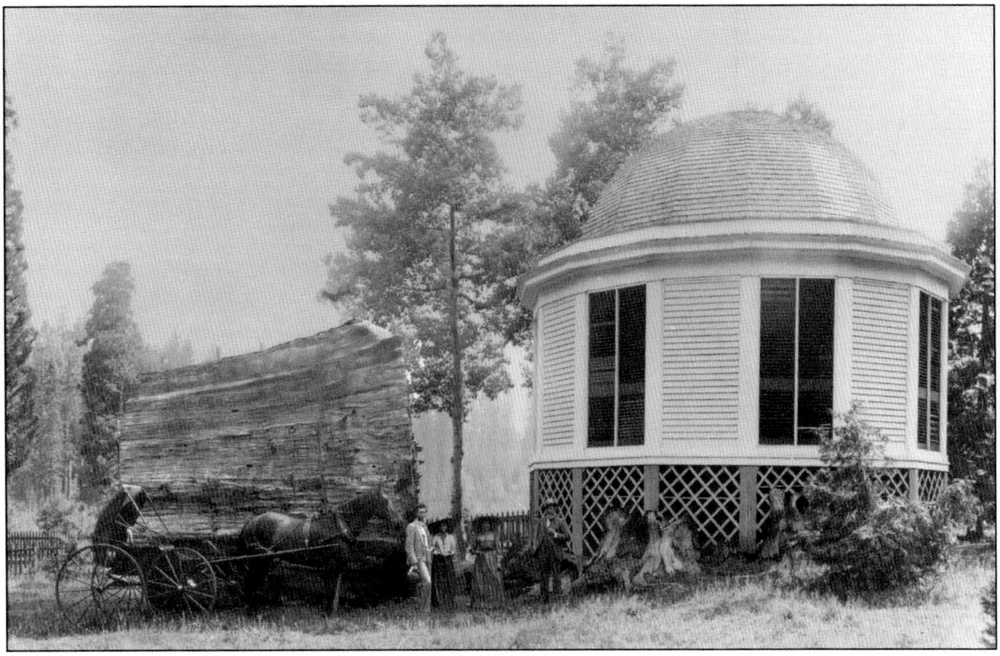

Both photographs on this page were taken in 1890 by Désiré Fricot, the son of wealthy mining magnate Jules Nicolas Fricot, originally from France. The Fricot family owned and operated mines in Calaveras and Nevada Counties. Désiré was one of the leaders of the movement to preserve the big trees through the creation of a state park. (CBTSP.)

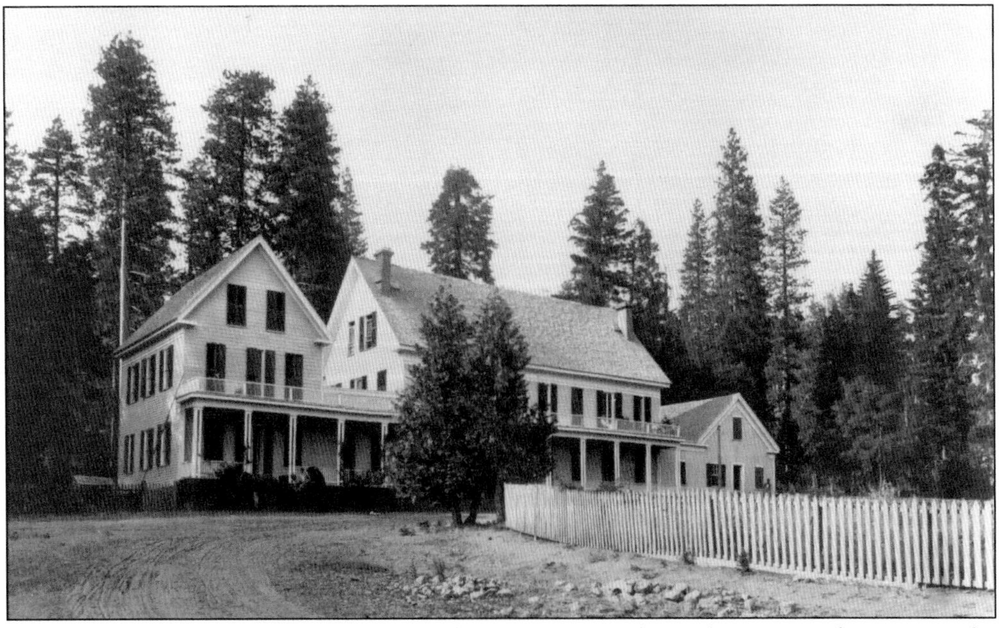

The Sperrys spent summer tourist seasons between 1878 and 1891 living at and managing the Mammoth Grove Hotel, which had changed little in 15 years. In April 1890, James Sperry transferred ownership of both groves to the newly formed Calaveras Big Trees Company. The corporation was headquartered in San Francisco, and he was a director. (CBTSP.)

James and Mehitable Sperry are seen here on the porch of their residence in Murphys, one of the oldest homes in town today. They had four children, Willard, Evelyn, Marion, and James C. After her parents retired to Berkeley, Marion remained at the grove, apparently running the hotel and serving as postmistress. James C. was active in the preservation movement to convert the grove into a state park in the 1920s, as was his cousin Ethel Sperry Crocker. (CCHS.)

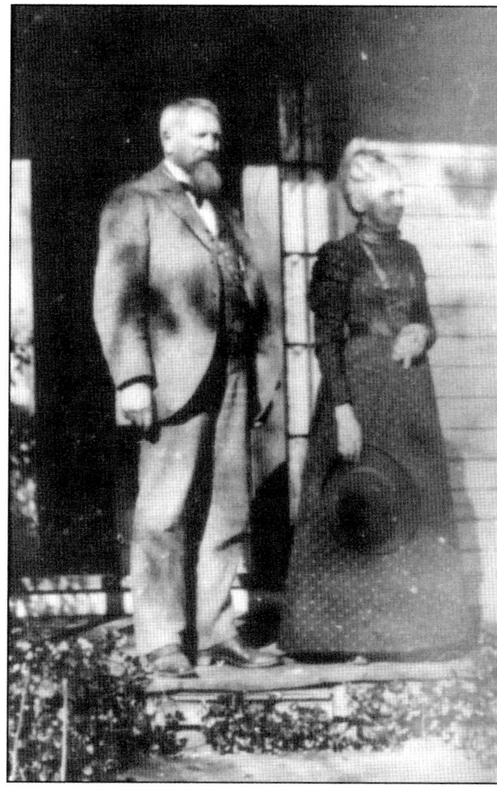

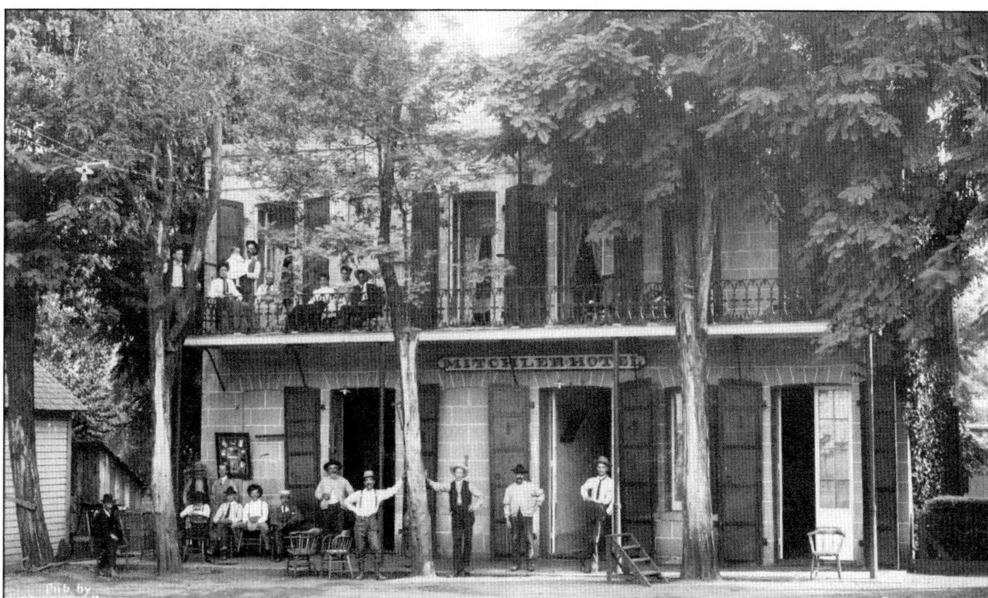

Sperry had long ago sold the hotel in Murphys to Eliza Perry for $1,000 after her husband's death. She eventually sold to Harvey Blood, former operator of the Big Trees and Carson Valley Turnpike, the toll road from the North Grove to California's eastern border. By the time this photograph was taken in the 1890s, C. P. Mitchler owned the hotel. It remained in his family until 1945. (CCA.)

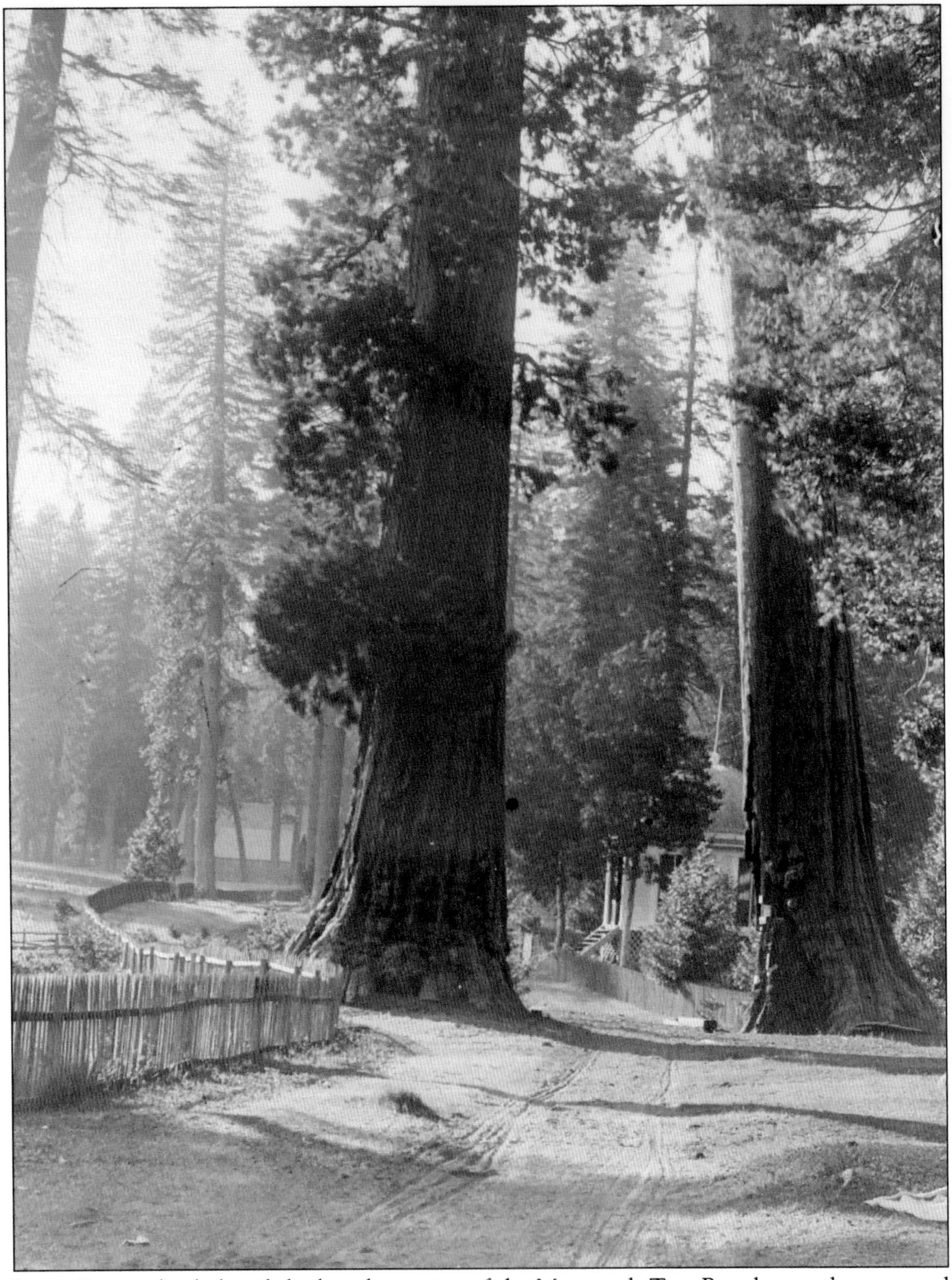

James Sperry clearly loved the bucolic setting of the Mammoth Tree Ranch, seen here around 1890. However, by then the Calaveras Big Trees were less popular than the increasingly fashionable destination of Yosemite and its nearby sequoia groves. Throughout the decade, large tracts of publicly owned land in the western states were preserved in national forests and parks, including the Sequoia and General Grant National Parks. Sperry had similar ideas for his beloved big trees. He hoped the government would purchase his property to establish a state or national park, but no offer was forthcoming, despite his offer to sell at a steep discount. (CBTSP.)

Four

THE WHITESIDE YEARS

Finding no government interest in purchasing the famous Big Trees, James L. Sperry began actively shopping for a buyer in 1899. The unlikely purchaser came in the form of Robert B. Whiteside, a lumberman from Duluth, Minnesota, who had been buying timberland throughout Calaveras County. On December 29, 1899, Whiteside paid $1,000 to the Calaveras Big Trees Company for a 90-day option to purchase the North and South Groves for $100,000. In less than a week, news of the proposed sale leaked out. The San Joaquin Valley Commercial Association was the first group to act. On January 6, 1900, it passed a resolution asking Congress to create Calaveras Big Trees National Park. Newspaper articles appeared in San Francisco on January 12 and soon spread across the country. Many groups and individuals, such as the Sierra Club, Pioneer Club, and Stanford University president David Starr Jordan, rallied to save the groves from the lumberman's ax.

Prominent among these were the women of San Francisco's California Club. Mrs. Lovell White spearheaded the movement to initiate federal legislation with assistance from Mrs. Alexander Sharon in Washington, D.C. In rapid succession, and without a dissenting vote, a resolution passed the House on March 3 and the Senate on March 7. Mrs. Sharon was present when President McKinley signed the bill on March 8. Unfortunately the legislation only authorized negotiation to purchase the North and South Groves. No funds had been allocated to do so. For his part, Whiteside was perturbed by his portrayal in the press as a "bogey man." His actions and statements only inflamed the issue. He reportedly told the secretary of the interior he would not sell for less than $1 million. "That Calaveras Grove subject is getting a little worn with me . . . I will say that it is a business proposition with me and I shall make money out of it," he told a reporter from the *San Francisco Call* on March 6, 1900. Despite the outrage and efforts, the grove passed into Whiteside's hands on April 1, 1900. Yet he and Sperry had apparently reached a gentleman's agreement that he would not cut the mammoth trees for so much board feet of lumber.

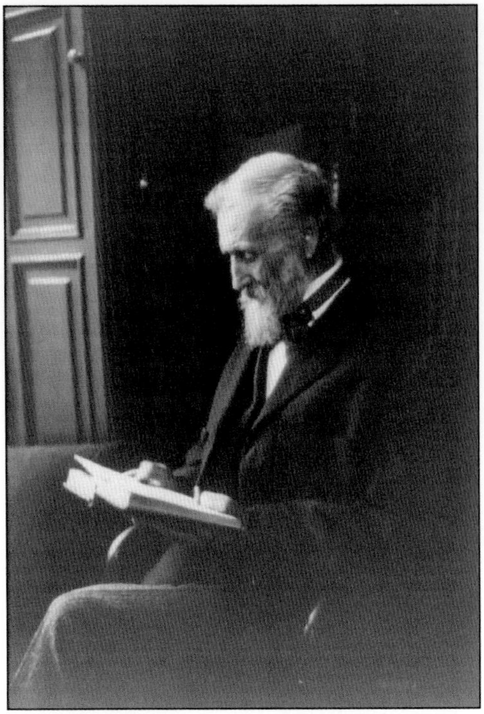

John Muir, cofounder of the Sierra Club in 1892, lobbied to save the Calaveras Grove, although he was surprised at the public outcry. He pointed out that "more than three times as many sequoias had been cut into lumber every year for the last 26 years . . . with scarce a word of protest on the part of the public." He attributed the change of heart to the fact that the grove had been the first discovered and was the best known. (LOC.)

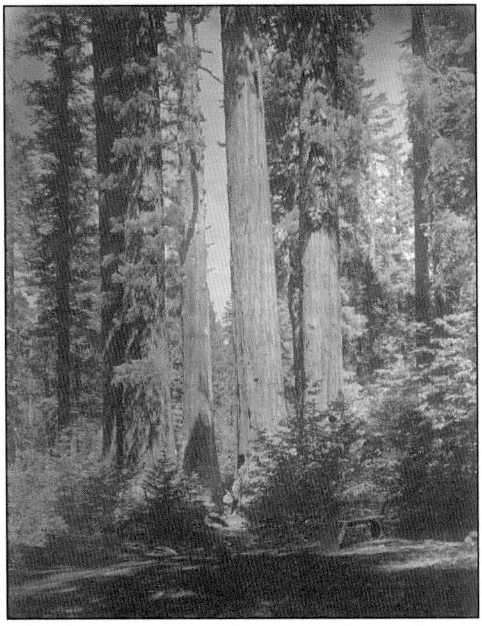

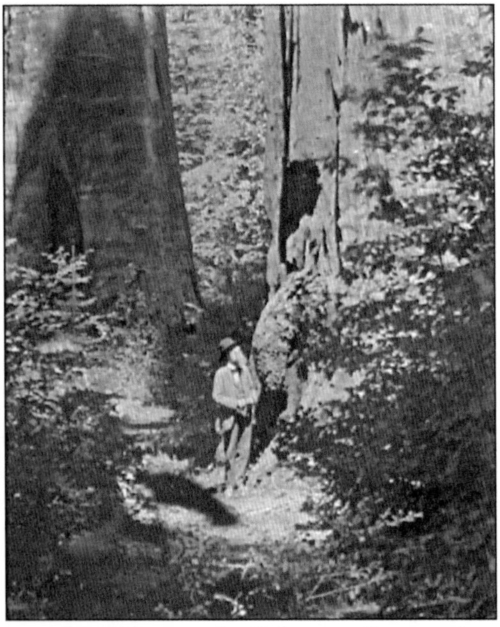

The photograph at left is the only verified photograph of Muir in the Calaveras Grove, taken near the Mother of the Forest in August 1900 by scientist C. Hart Merriman. Muir was on an extended trip through the Sierra Nevada and spent two nights at the Big Trees Hotel in the company of Marion Sperry and James and Emily Hutchings, Muir's one-time employer and the new lessee of the hotel under Whiteside's ownership. At right, a close-up from the photograph more clearly shows Muir. (Both, F24-1333 John Muir Papers, Holt-Atherton Special Collections, University of the Pacific Library. Copyright 1984 Muir-Hanna Trust.)

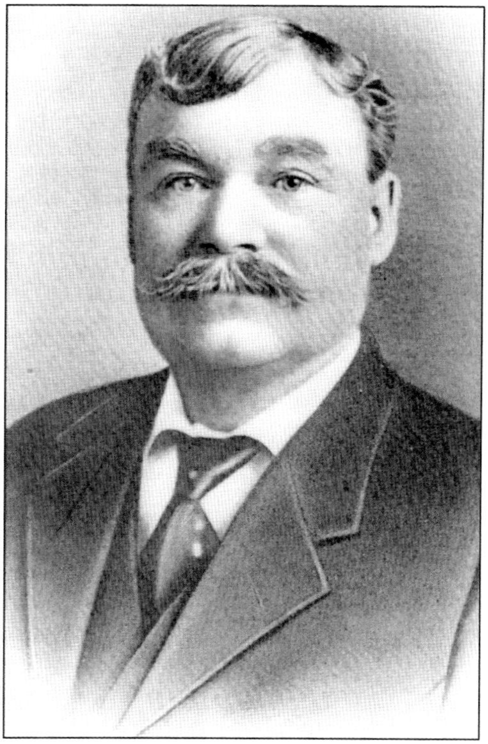

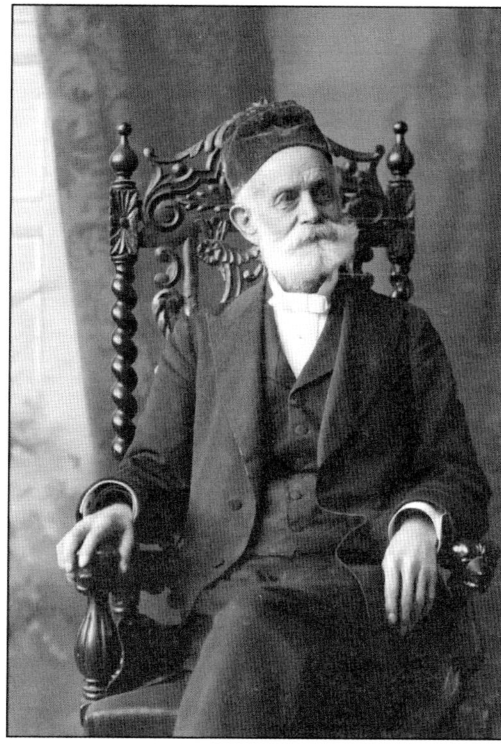

Wealthy Minnesotan Robert B. Whiteside (left) purchased the North and South Groves of big trees, including the hotel, from Sperry in 1900. He came to the U.S. from Canada in 1881 at age 25 with $3,500. After initial failure, the hardworking and shrewd Whiteside had become one of Minnesota's wealthiest men. James Mason Hutchings (right), pictured in 1890, leased the Mammoth Grove Hotel from Whiteside from 1900 to 1902. Known as the "Father of Yosemite," Hutchings came to California shortly after emigrating from England in 1848. He gained a fortune during the Gold Rush and lost it before achieving success again in publishing and other interests. (Left, Ely-Winton Historical Society; right, California History Room, California State Library, Sacramento, California.)

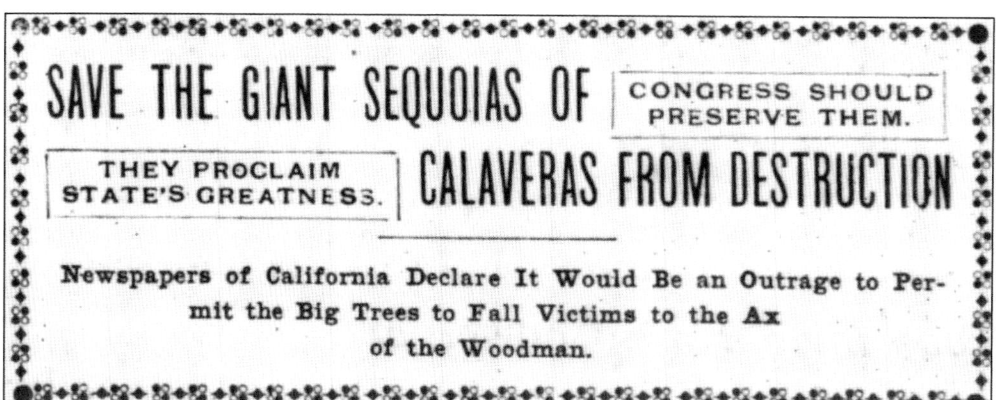

SAVE THE GIANT SEQUOIAS OF CALAVERAS FROM DESTRUCTION

CONGRESS SHOULD PRESERVE THEM.

THEY PROCLAIM STATE'S GREATNESS.

Newspapers of California Declare It Would Be an Outrage to Permit the Big Trees to Fall Victims to the Ax of the Woodman.

This headline from the *San Francisco Call* on March 3, 1900, sums up the sentiments of Californians throughout the state about the pending sale. Less than two years later, in February 1902, James Sperry died unexpectedly in Oakland from kidney disease at age 71. (California Digital Newspaper Collection.)

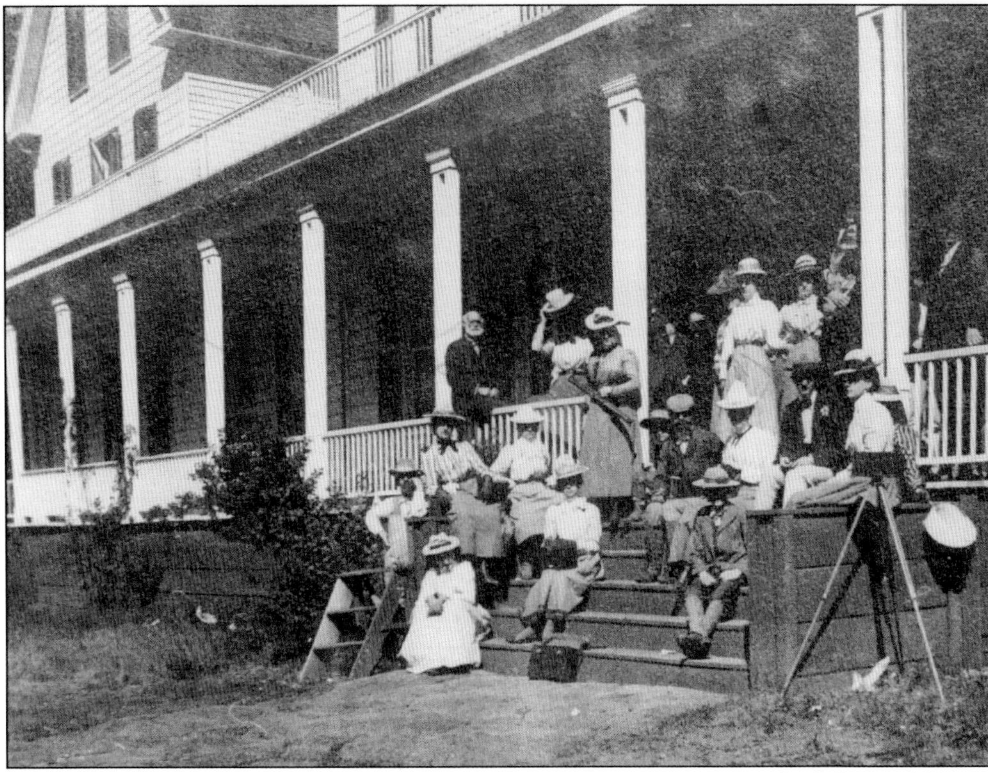

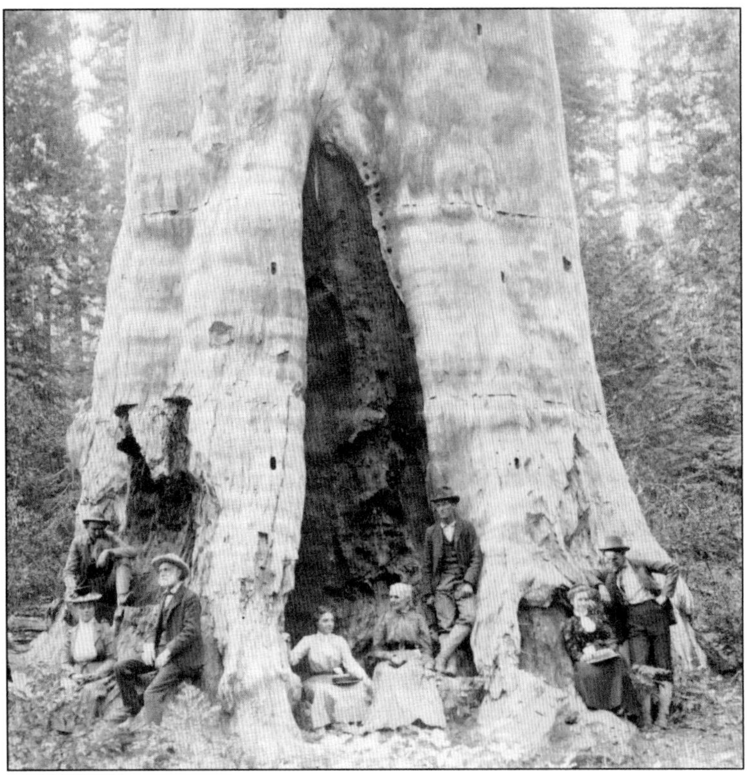

On July 11, 1900, members of the Sierra Camera Club visited the grove. They pose on the steps of the hotel above with innkeeper Hutchings, seated on the railing. The scarred Mother of the Forest (left) is the setting for another group of visitors in 1902 with Hutchings (the bearded man). After losing his fortune, Hutchings again achieved success as writer and publisher of the *Miner's Ten Commandments*, which sold 97,000 copies. (Above, OTM; left, LOC.)

Hutchings sits astride the horse in both photographs published by Underwood and Underwood in 1902. In 1855, he led the first tourist party into Yosemite Valley and became one of its earliest settlers. He also built the first Yosemite hotel. A prodigious promoter, his *Hutchings' Illustrated California Magazine*, published from 1856 to 1861, detailed the wonders of Yosemite and California. An early and regular visitor to the Calaveras Grove, Hutchings described its features in his magazine and books. (Right, LOC; below, OTM.)

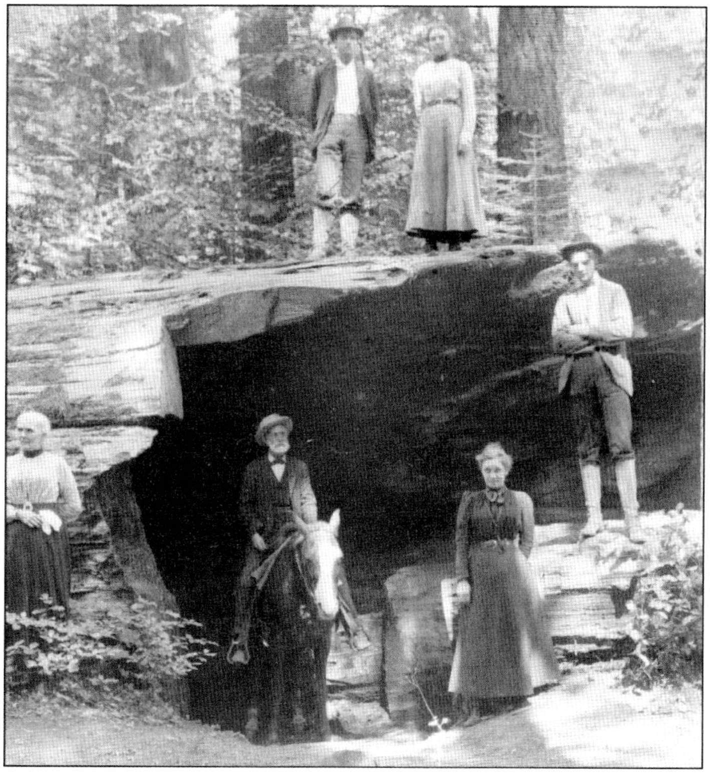

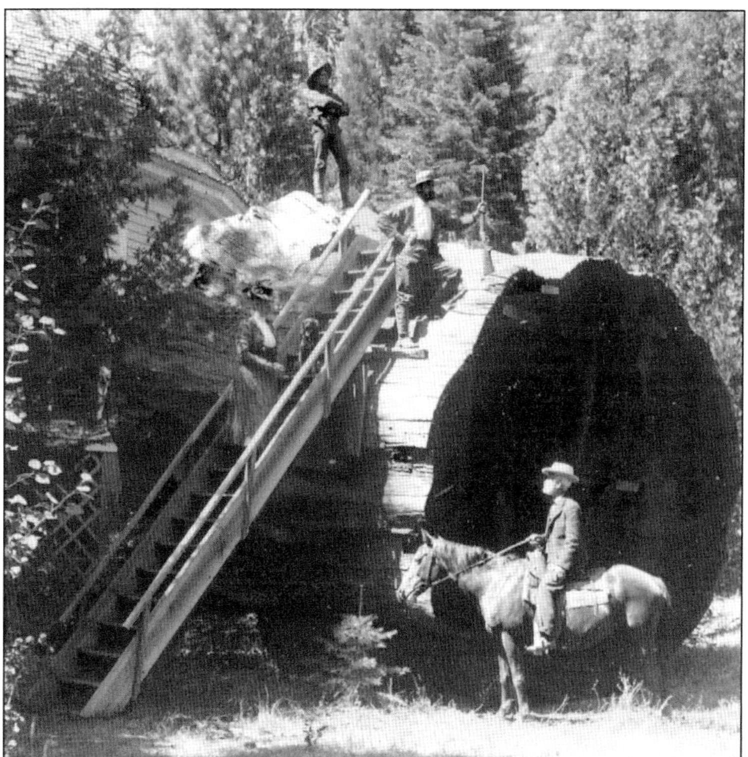

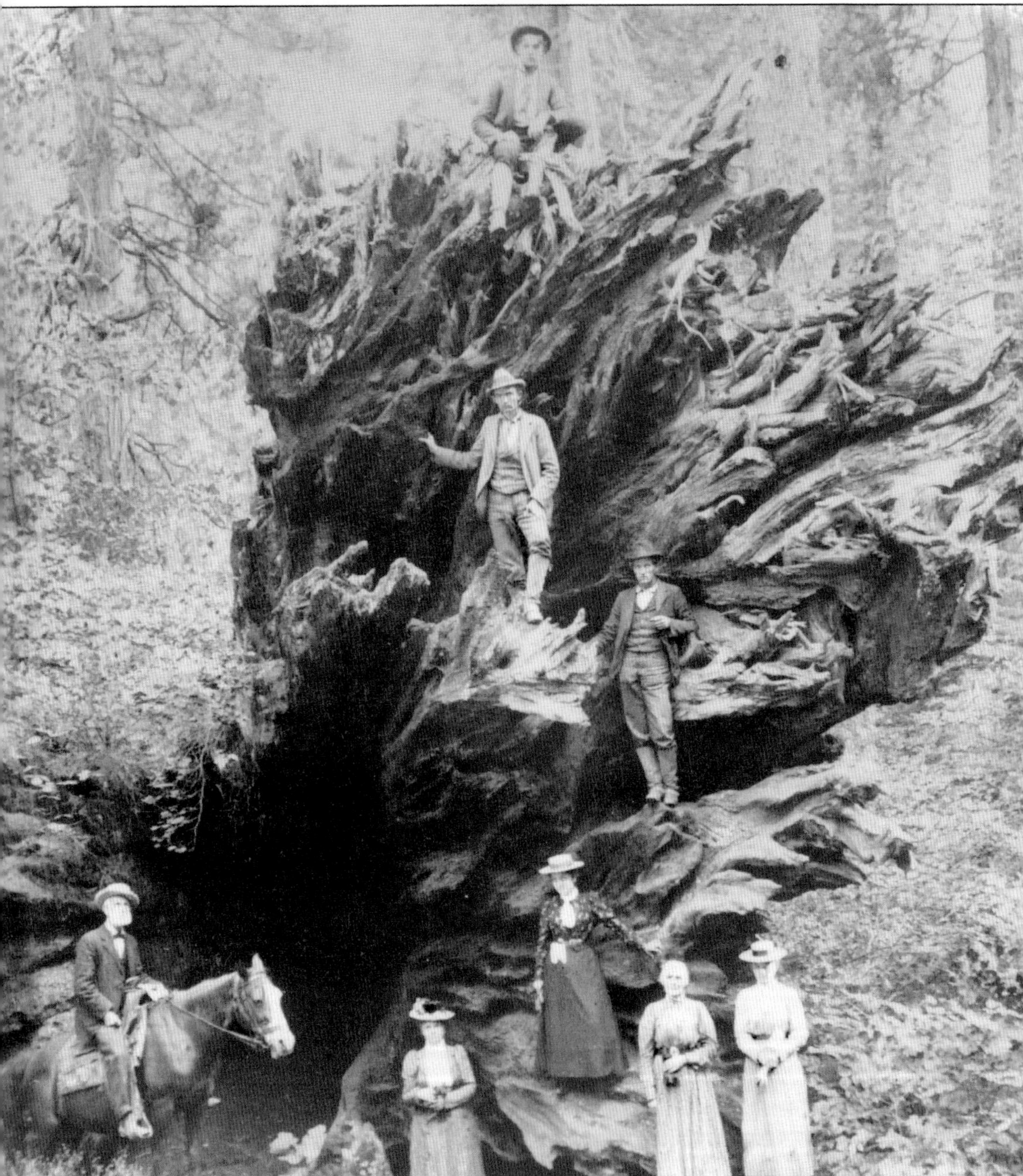

Hutchings and his group pose with Eagle's Wing, the roots of a fallen giant sequoia. At the end of the 1902 season, Hutchings retired. The 82-year-old and his wife, Emily, headed to Yosemite for a camping trip before returning to San Francisco. On the steep trail into Yosemite Valley on October 31, 1902, the horses pulling their carriage spooked. Both were violently thrown to the ground, and Hutchings died moments later. He is buried in the Pioneer Cemetery in his much-loved Yosemite Valley. (LOC.)

Daily operations of the grove and hotel were handled by other lessees until 1905, when Job and Elizabeth Whiteside (right and left) took over operations at the grove for older brother Robert. Elizabeth, a widow with a young son, Edgar, worked for the Sperrys and must have met Job when he traveled to Murphys on Whiteside business. Stocked streams provided ample fishing opportunities. The fisherman could be another of Whiteside's brothers. (CCA.)

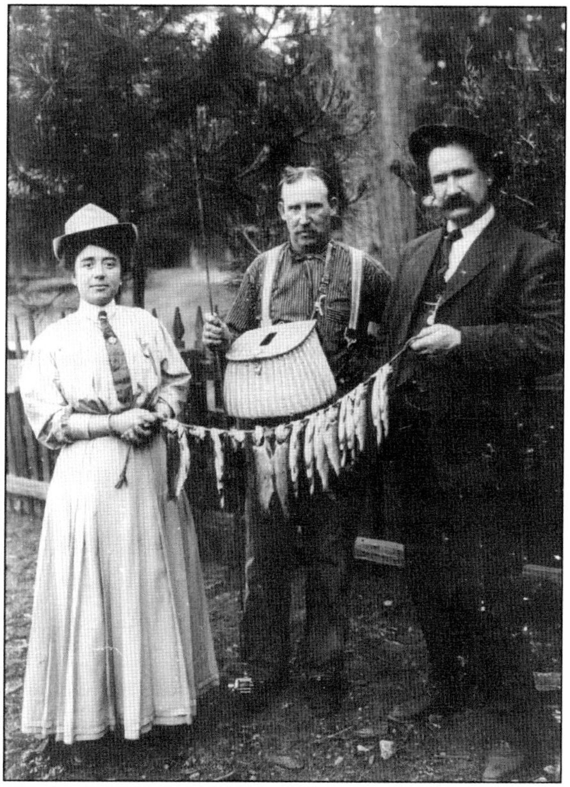

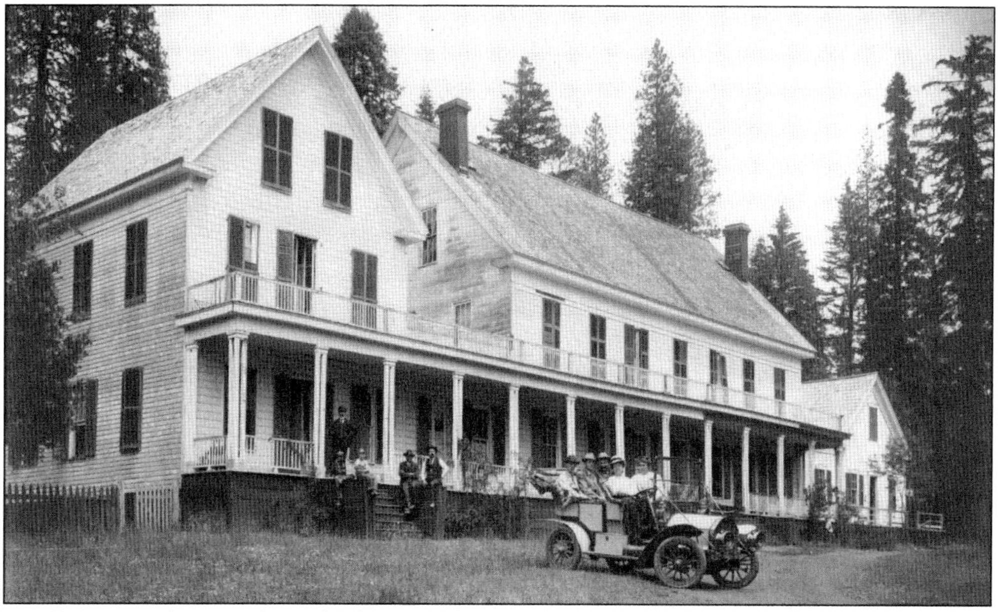

San Francisco photographer Charles Weidner photographed the Big Trees Ranch and gracious old hotel in 1908. Instead of stagecoaches, that new wonder, the automobile, is parked out front with Elizabeth Whiteside at the wheel. The grove's new owner, Robert Whiteside, appears to be in the backseat (right) and that may be his wife, Sophia, next to Elizabeth. (CCA.)

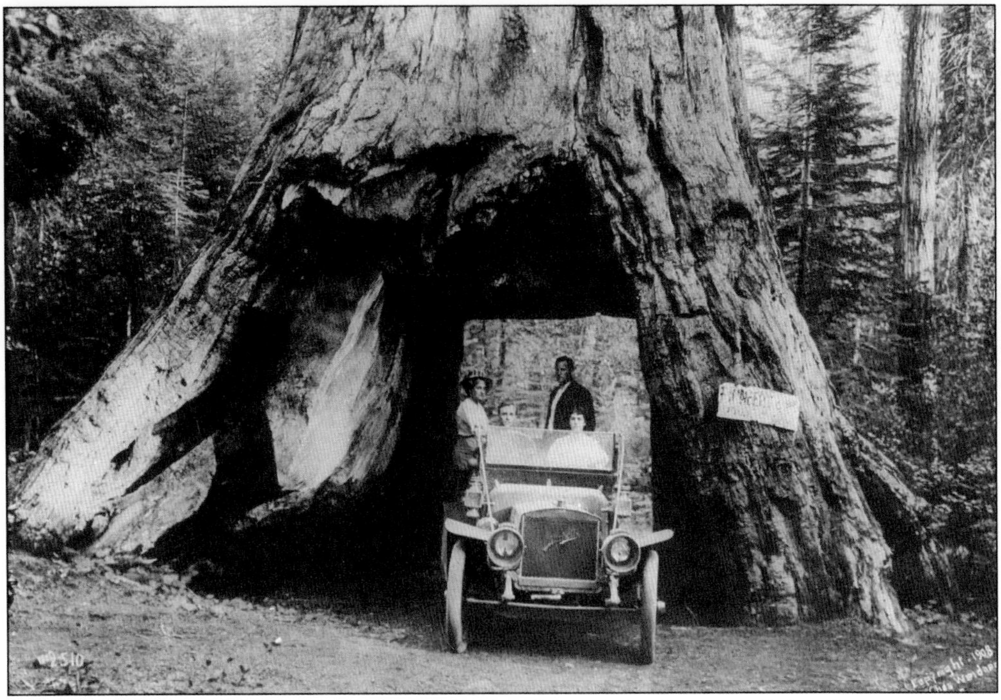

Exploring the grove in an automobile and driving through the Pioneer's Cabin Tree is a novelty in the early 20th century for this group of visitors in 1908 (above). Many other visitors continued to arrive in horse-drawn buggies or wagons. (Above, CCA; below CBTSP.)

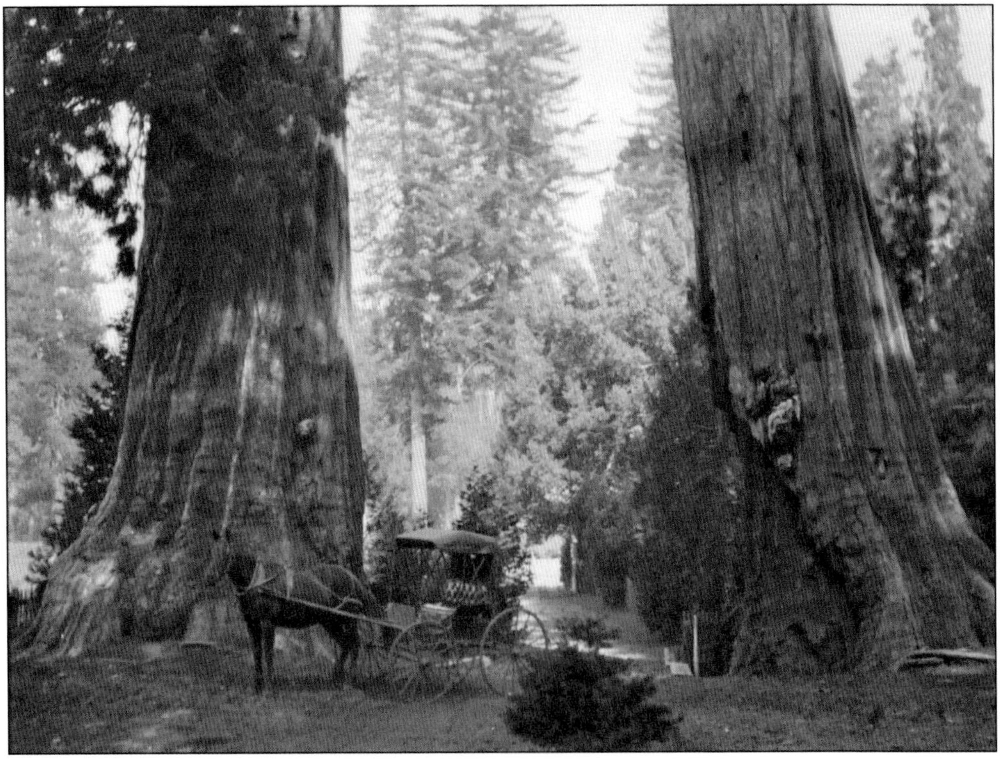

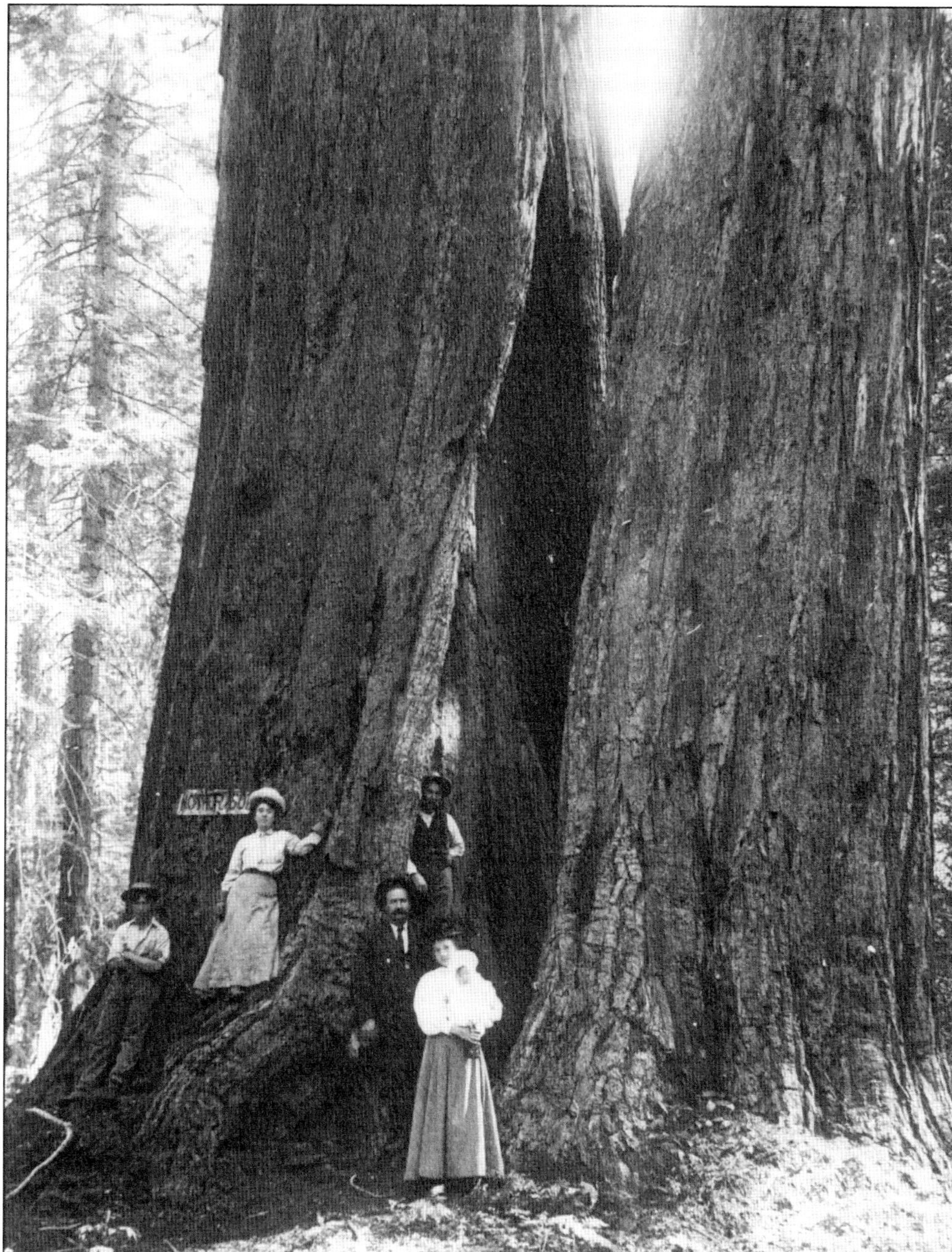

Job and Elizabeth (Lizzie), with grove visitors, gather round the Mother and Son trees. Job and his brothers Richard, John, and James all followed Robert to Duluth in the 1880s, as did two of their sisters with their husbands. Together they secured nearly 10,000 acres of prime Minnesota timberland through homestead claims in the area now known as the Vermillion Iron Range. Unbeknownst to them, the land was also rich in iron ore. Around 1887, Robert opened the Pioneer Hotel in Ely, Minnesota. It was the town's first boardinghouse and restaurant, and Job managed it. In 1898, Robert and Richard, with their wives, recorded a plat of land to create the village of Fall Lake, which was later renamed Winton. (CCA.)

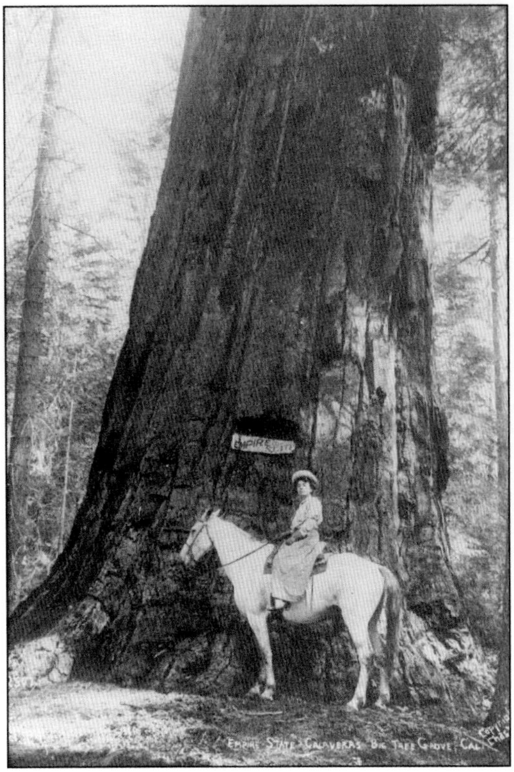

Lizzie Whiteside sits astride a horse by the Empire State Tree (left), which is the largest tree in the North Grove today. In September 1908, a spark from a steam-powered winch at Manuel's Sawmill started a fire that moved into the grove. Without her bark, the Mother of the Forest (below) easily caught fire. The *New York Times* reported on September 3, "All the forest rangers in the district, with settlers, many visitors living in camps around the grove, and the employees of the Big Tree Hotel, are fighting the flames." Mother burned for two weeks before being doused by a rainstorm. Damage to the rest of the grove was minimal. (Both, CCA.)

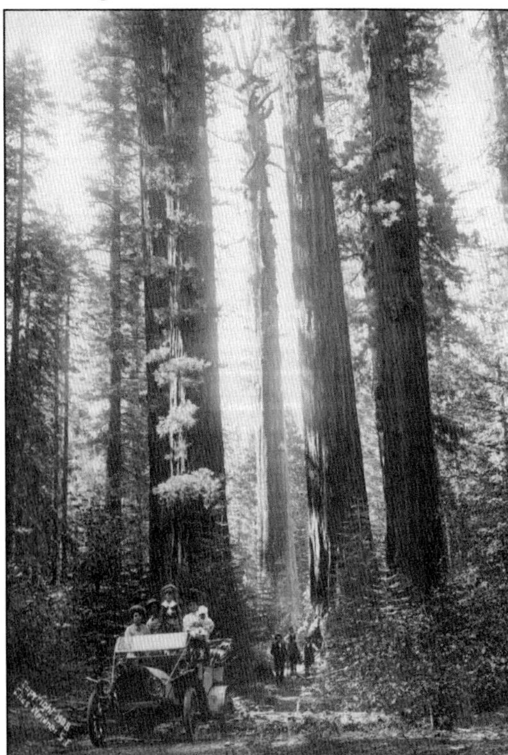

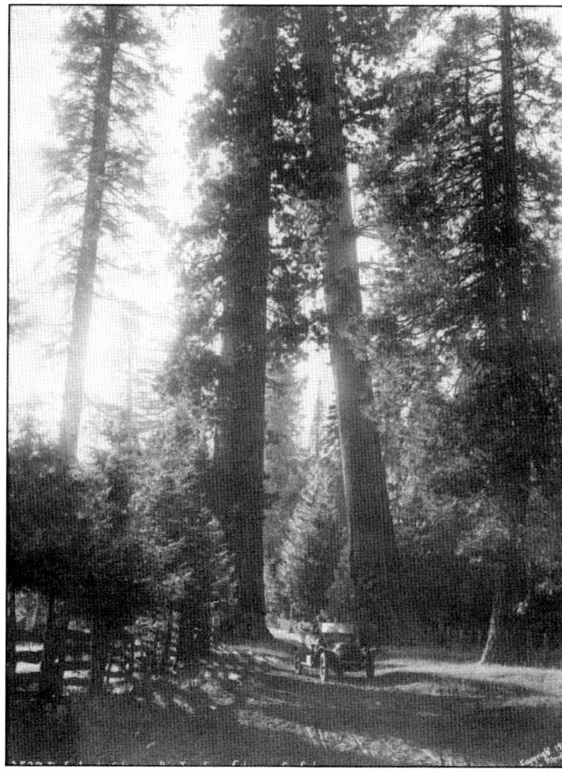

These two images of the Sentinels at the entrance to the Calaveras Grove in 1908 show how severely one of the giants is leaning. The traditional view when entering the grove between the two trees (right) shows the tree on the right leaning. The reverse view (below) provides an even better perspective. Between 7 and 8 a. m. on Thanksgiving Day, November 27, 1919, the giant toppled during a windstorm. Lizzie and her son, Sydney, were in the hotel and reported that some windows broke from the concussion. At 200 feet in height, the fallen tree blocked the road and extended into the meadow. It still lies there today, with the road rerouted around it. (Both, CCA.)

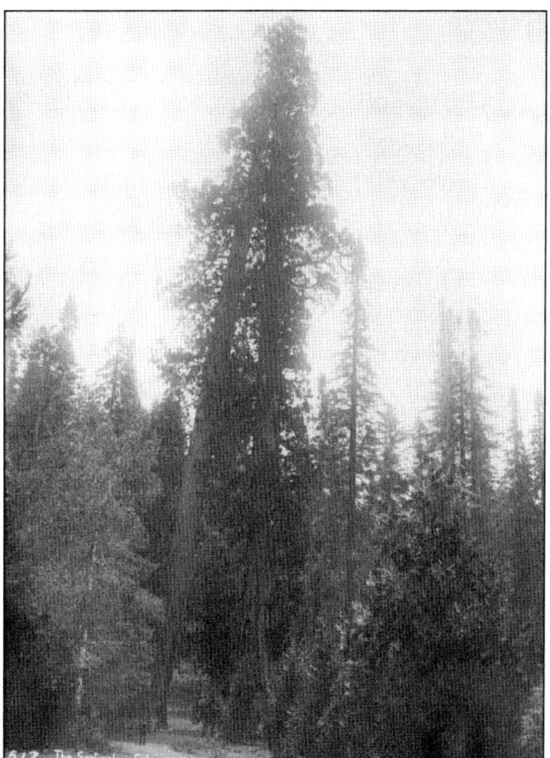

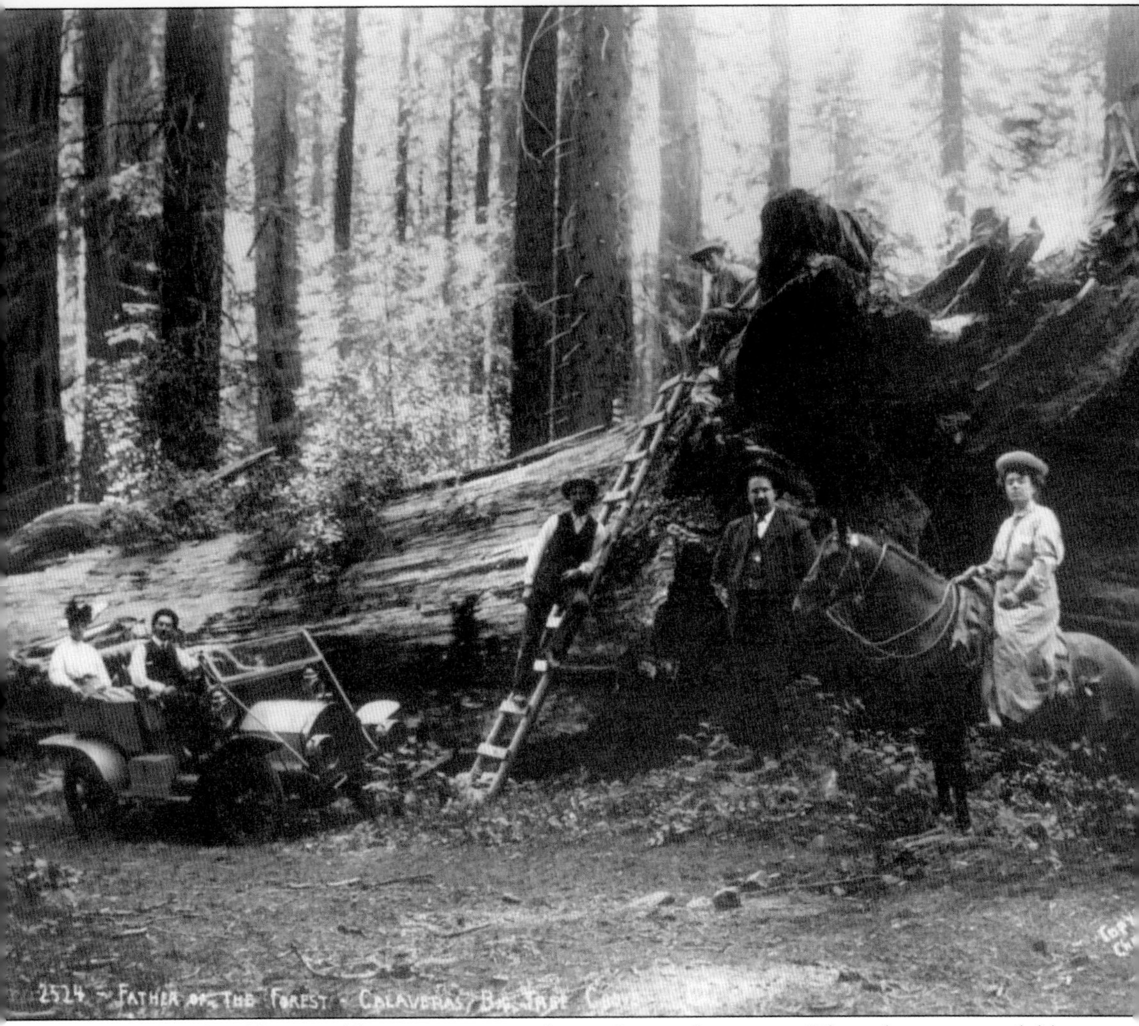

The hotel stable rented horses to tourists for exploring the groves. They also were available to hunters pursuing deer or other game. Lizzie (on horseback) and Job nearby gather with guests at the Father of the Forest. (CCA.)

Robert Whiteside is believed to be the man on the white horse crossing the Stanislaus River to explore the South Grove in 1908. Sperry and Perry opened a bridal trail to the South Grove, a two-hour ride from the hotel, in 1873. Cattlemen later built a bridge to move their stock across the river. The present-day bridge is a half-mile above where this bridge was located. (CCA.)

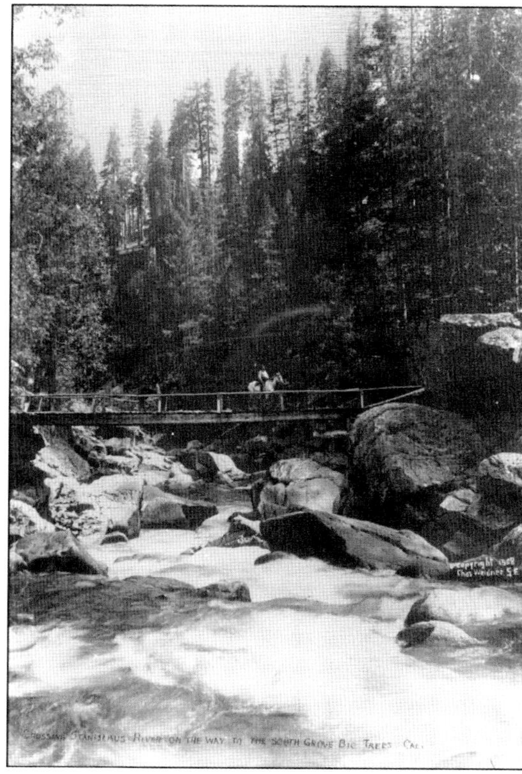

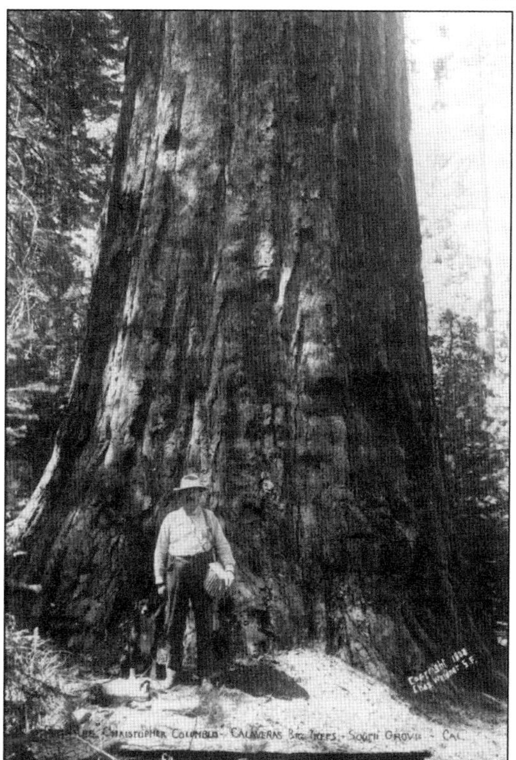

A four-legged companion accompanies Robert Whiteside to the Christopher Columbus Tree in the South Grove. He was lambasted in 1900 for purchasing the groves. Yet when his youngest child was born in August that same year, she was named Marion Calaveras Whiteside. In 1903, he was quoted in the *New York Times* as saying, "I possess nothing that I would rather hand down to my children than the Calaveras grove." (CCA.)

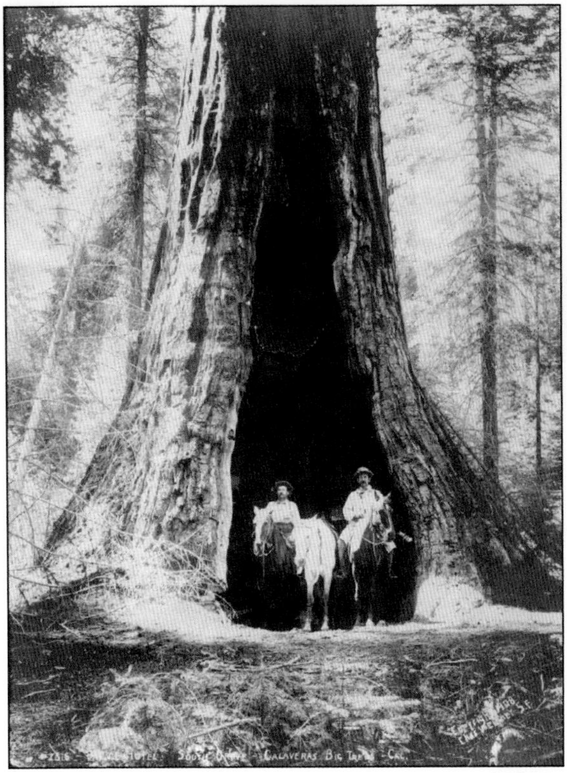

Members of the Whiteside party pose with two famous trees of the South Grove. The Palace Hotel (left) was named in the 1870s after the hotel of the same name in San Francisco because the tree's large opening reminded visitors of its central courtyard entrance. Trapper Smith's Cabin (below) provided a home to A. J. Smith in the early 1860s. (Left, CBTSP; below, CCA.)

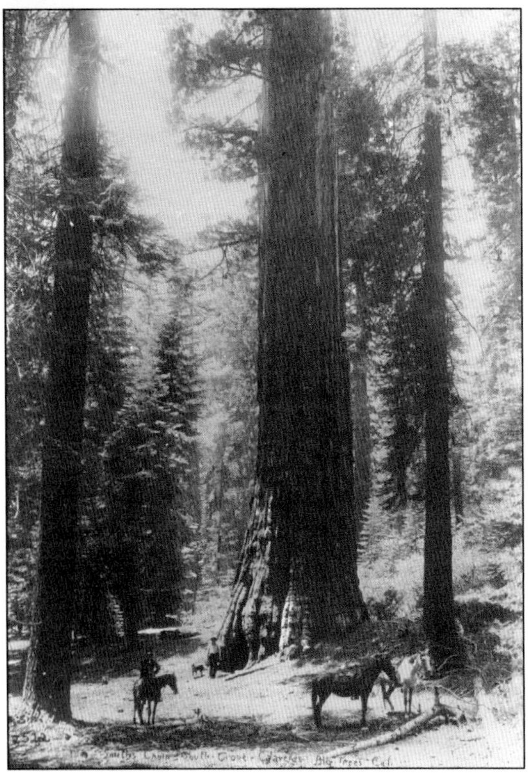

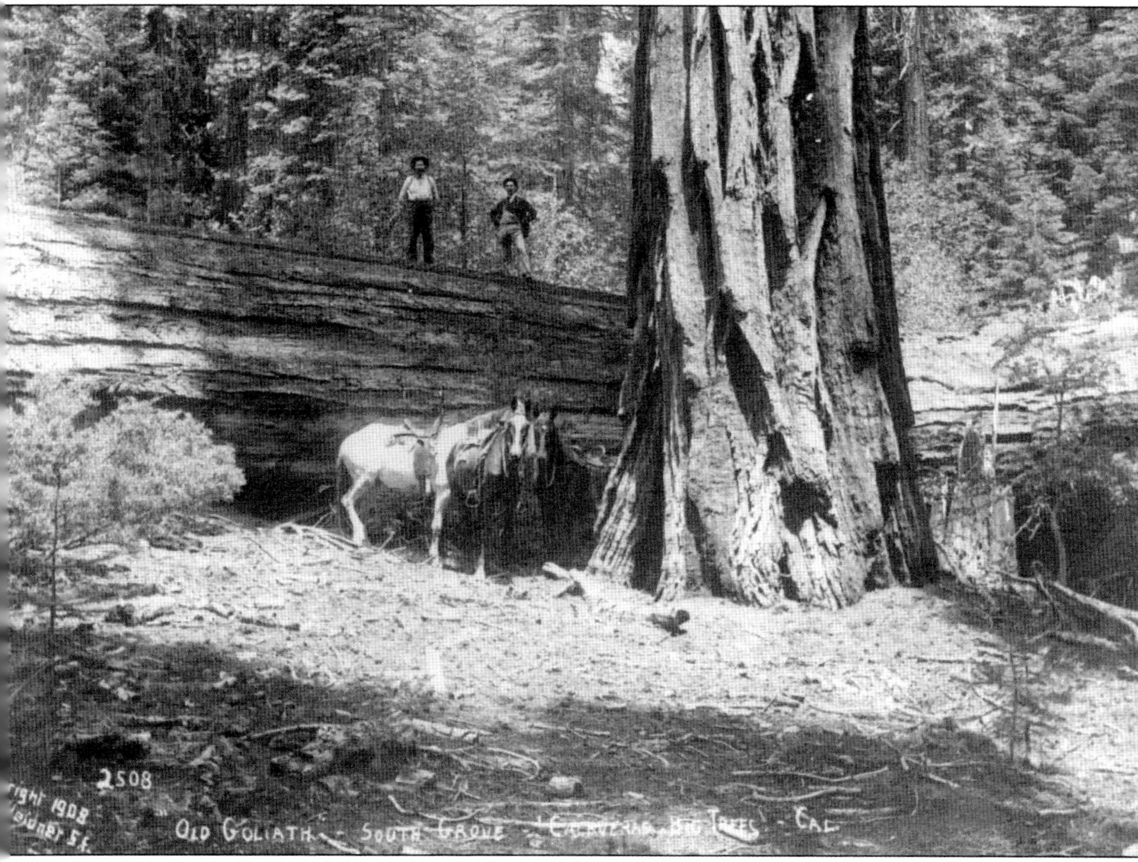

Robert Whiteside (left) and an unidentified man, likely a hotel employee and guide, stand on the fallen Old Goliath in the South Grove. Even though the South Grove had been open to visitors since the 1870s, these are the first known photographs. Toppled in 1861, Old Goliath was 300 feet high. The largest sequoias found in Big Trees State Park are in the South Grove. (CCA.)

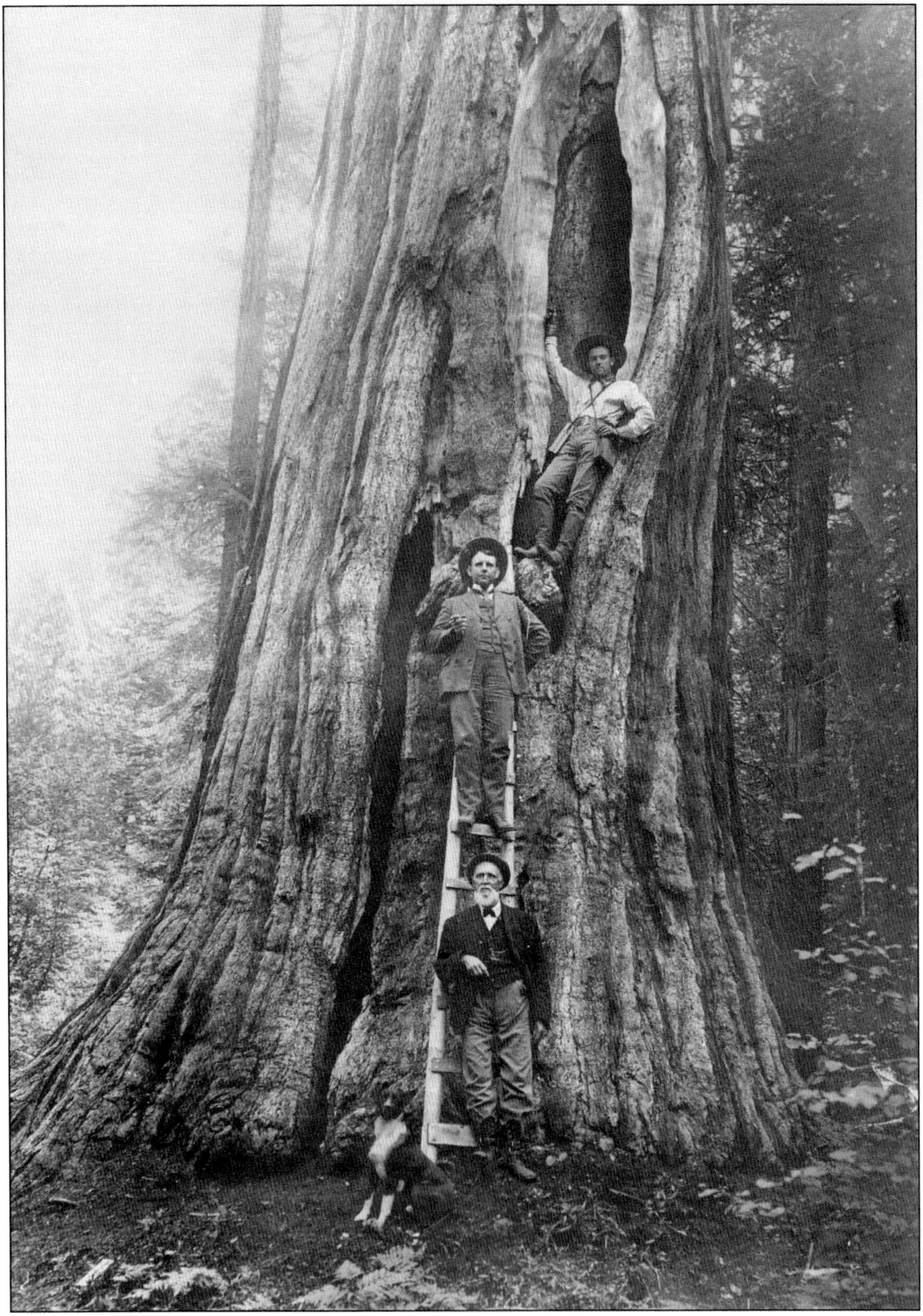

Take note of the black and white dog at the bottom of the ladder with this group of grove visitors. He appears in several photographs from this time period. This photograph, and most of those from 1908, are from the Whiteside family album, which was donated to the Calaveras County Archives. (CCA.)

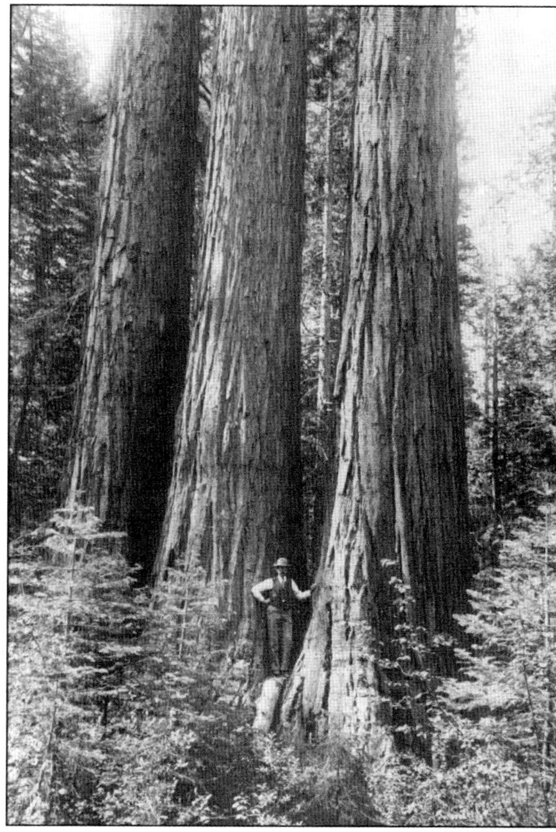

Two iconic images of the Calaveras Grove, the Three Graces and Chip of the Old Block, provide the backdrop in these 1908 photographs of local businessman Désiré Fricot. The years have taken their toll on the pavilion erected over the Discovery Stump in 1861. (Both, CCA.)

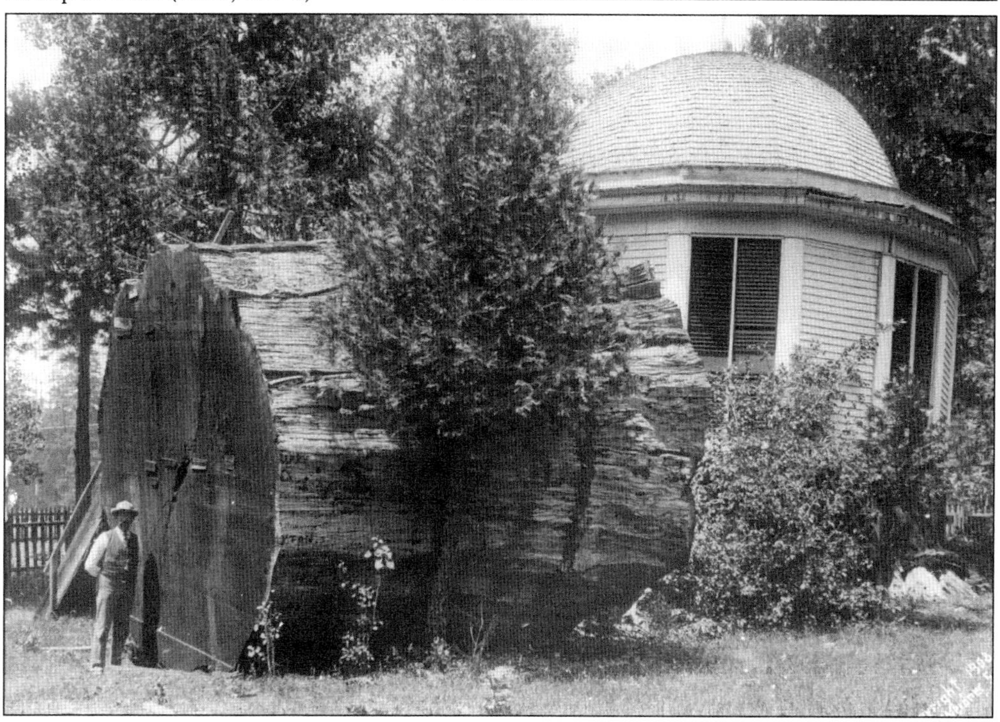

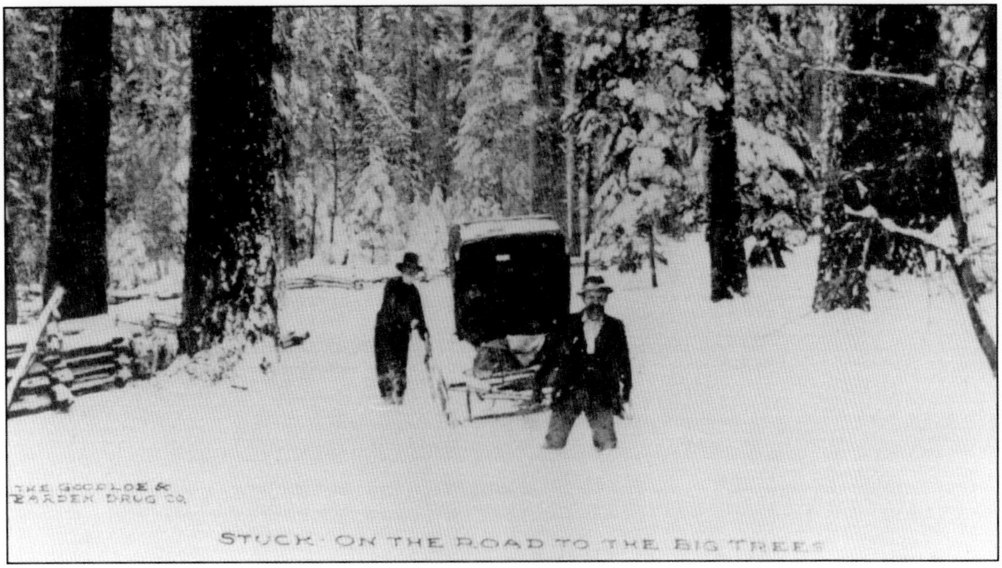

These postcards from 1906, sold by Goodloe and Barden Drug Company in Angels Camp, illustrate why the Big Tree Ranch was a summer resort. At an elevation of 4,700 feet, snowfall was often quite heavy during the winter. These hardy adventurers (above) were "stuck on the road to the big trees" according to the notation on the card. The photographer must be on the horse, because it appears the men are pulling and pushing their buggy by hand. Their reward upon arrival was a unique pose with Chip in the snow (below). Job and Lizzie Whiteside lived at the ranch during the summer season and maintained a home in Angels Camp in winter months. (Above, OTM; below, CBTSP.)

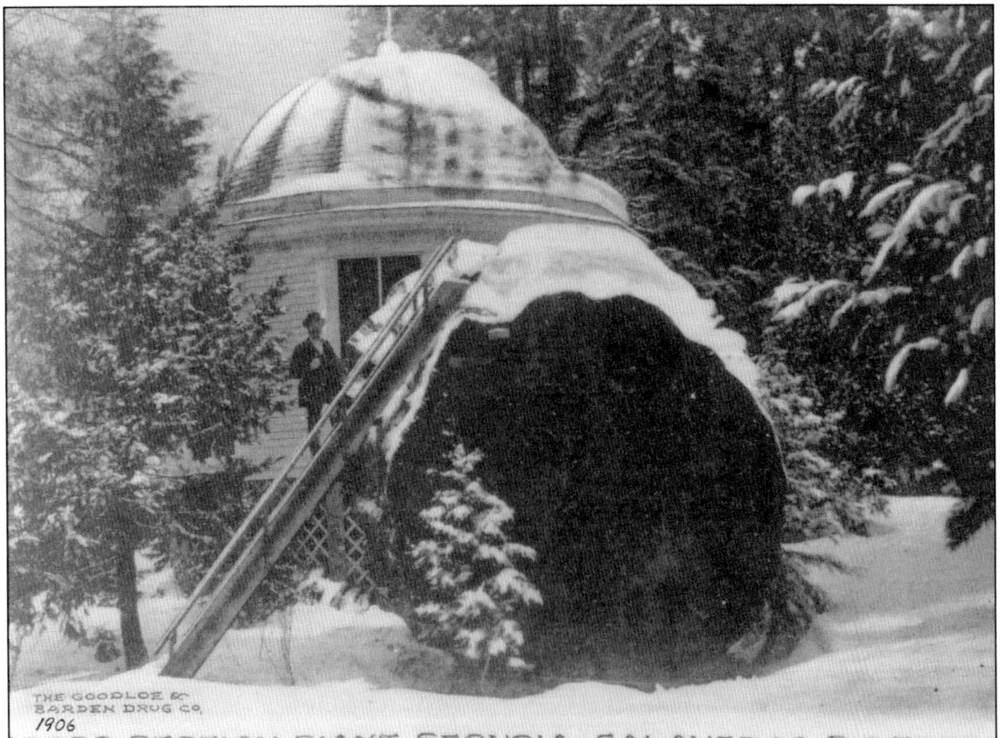

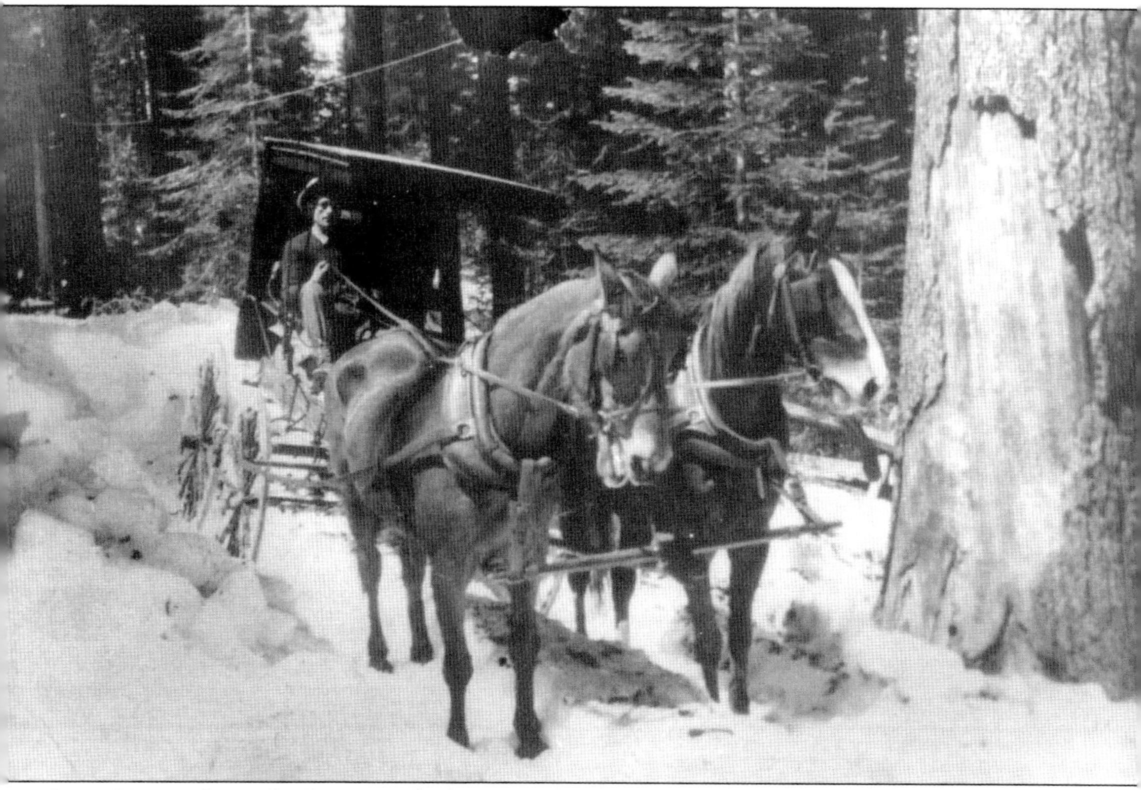

Amon Tanner drove the first rig to the big trees after winter on April 23, 1911. In the tradition of Snowshoe Thompson, Tanner was known to sometimes deliver mail on skis. As soon as possible in the spring, Tanner would break a road into the Calaveras grove of big trees with horses and rig. On this trip, it was noted he "narrowly escaped upsetting [the rig] at one point." (OTM.)

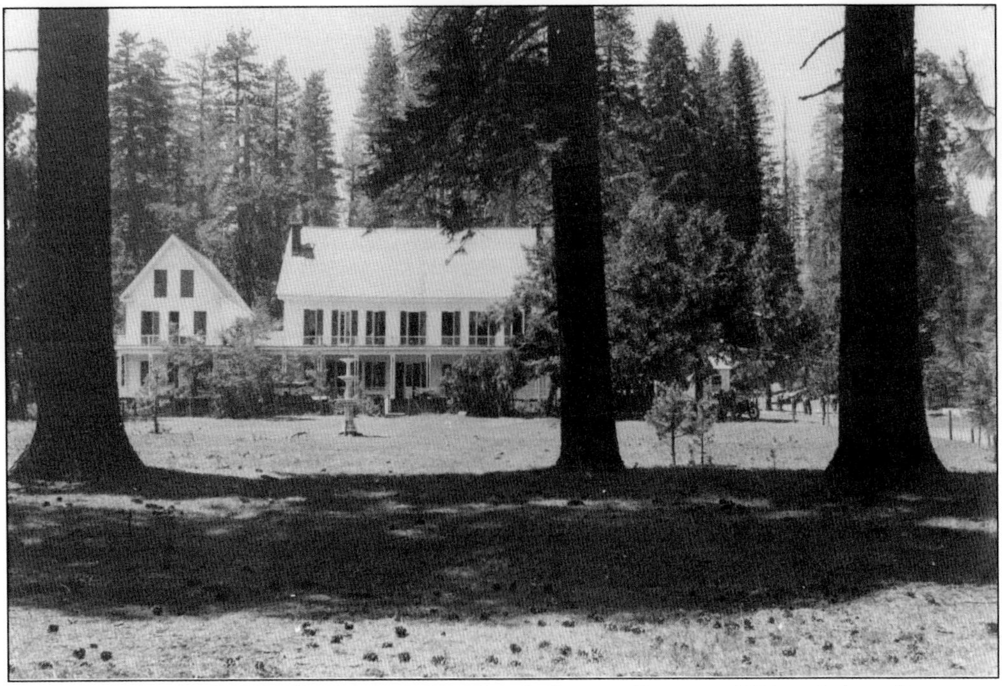

Photographer Charles Weidner returned to the Calaveras Grove in 1914 and shot this image of the hotel, with its well-known fountain. By now, the pipes had clogged and the fountain no longer worked. (CCA.)

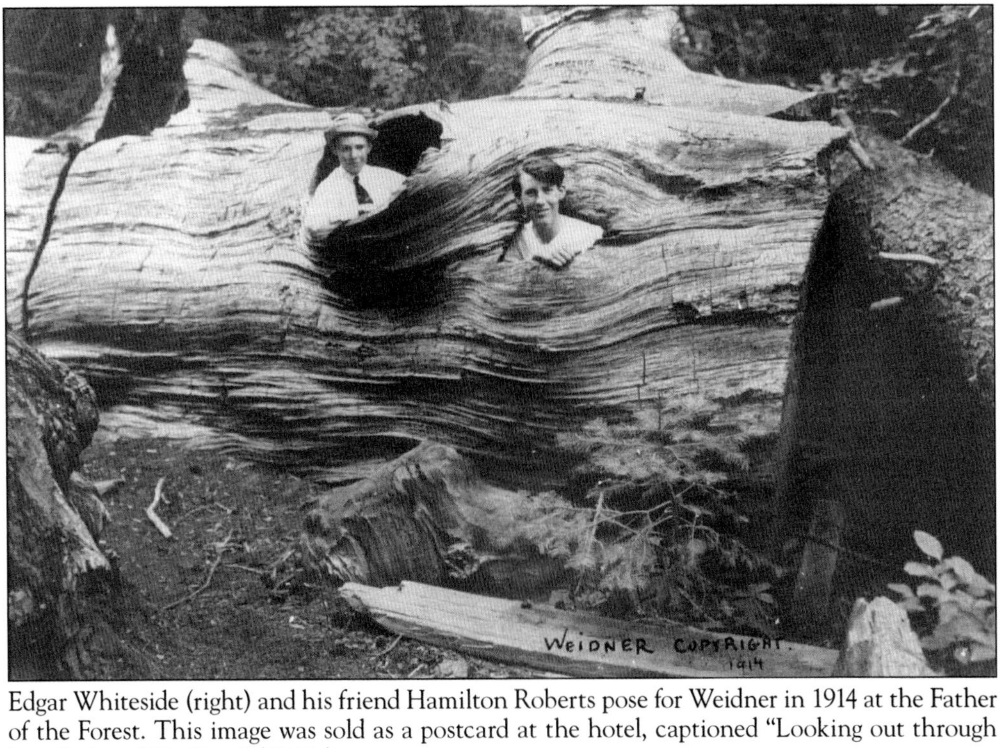

Edgar Whiteside (right) and his friend Hamilton Roberts pose for Weidner in 1914 at the Father of the Forest. This image was sold as a postcard at the hotel, captioned "Looking out through knot holes of Big Tree." (CCA.)

Job and Lizzie's son, Sydney, born in 1904, is seen in this undated photograph on the veranda of the hotel. (CBTSP.)

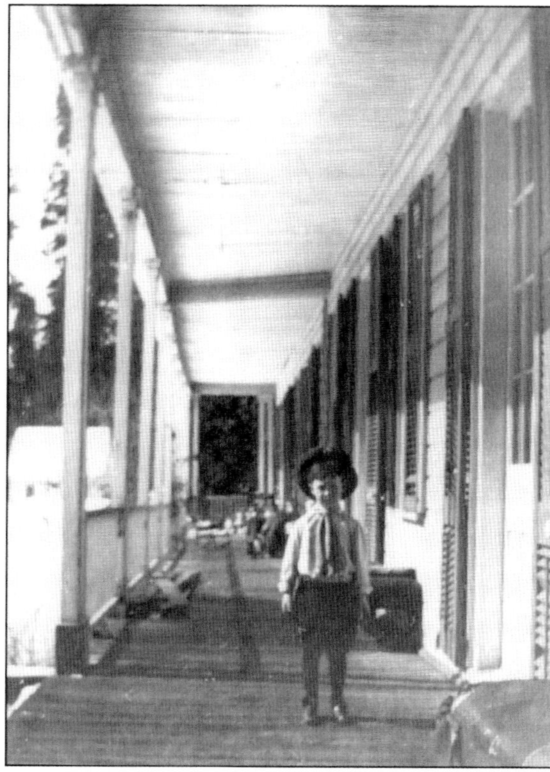

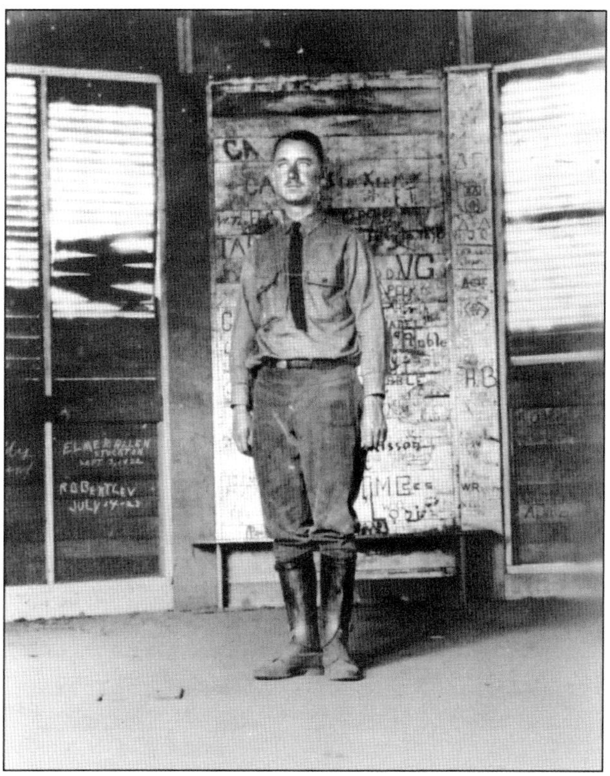

This photograph taken after 1923 shows the sad state of the pavilion's interior, now covered with graffiti. The structure finally collapsed under heavy snow in the winter of 1934. (CBTSP.)

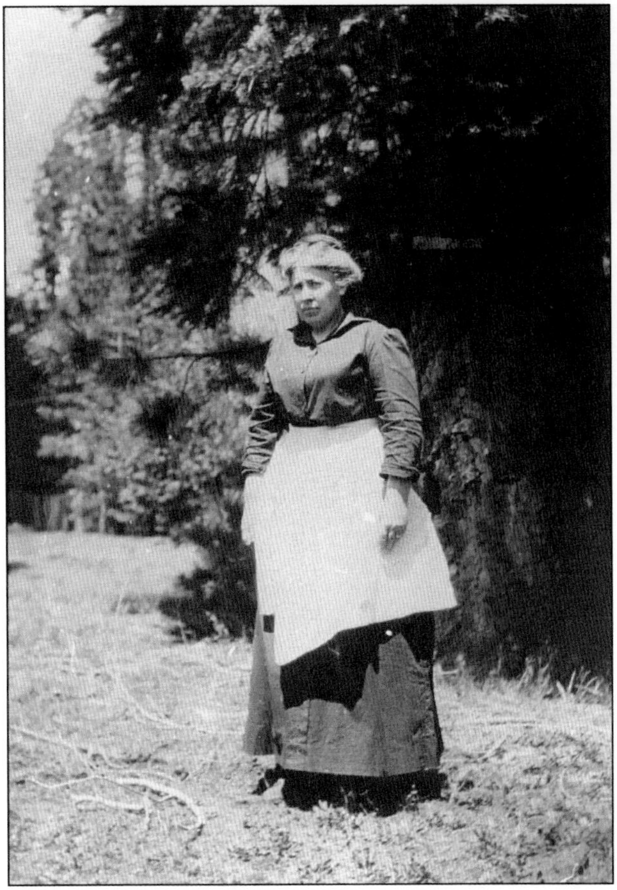

After he became paralyzed in 1914, Job Whiteside was confined to a Stockton sanatorium until his death on January 24, 1916. With help from her sons and loyal employees, Lizzie, seen in this undated photograph probably from the 1920s, managed the property until her brother-in-law sold it to the state in 1931. Lizzie Whiteside died December 20, 1940, at age 75, while visiting Sydney in Stockton. (CCA.)

Sometime around 1920, the pavilion on the Discovery Stump was re-roofed with a conical-shaped top, although other parts remained neglected. (OTM.)

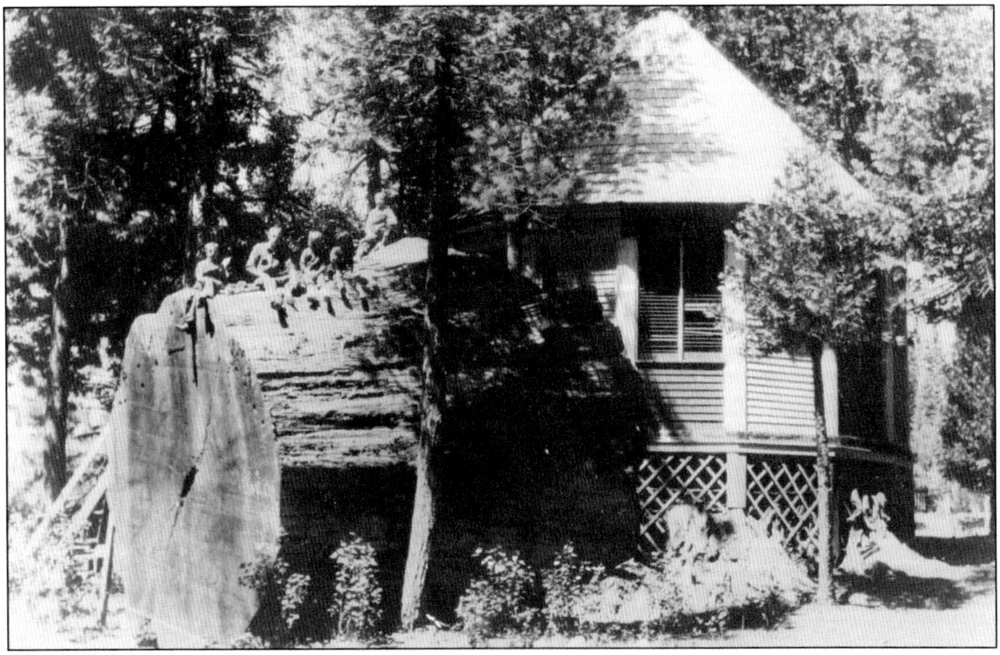

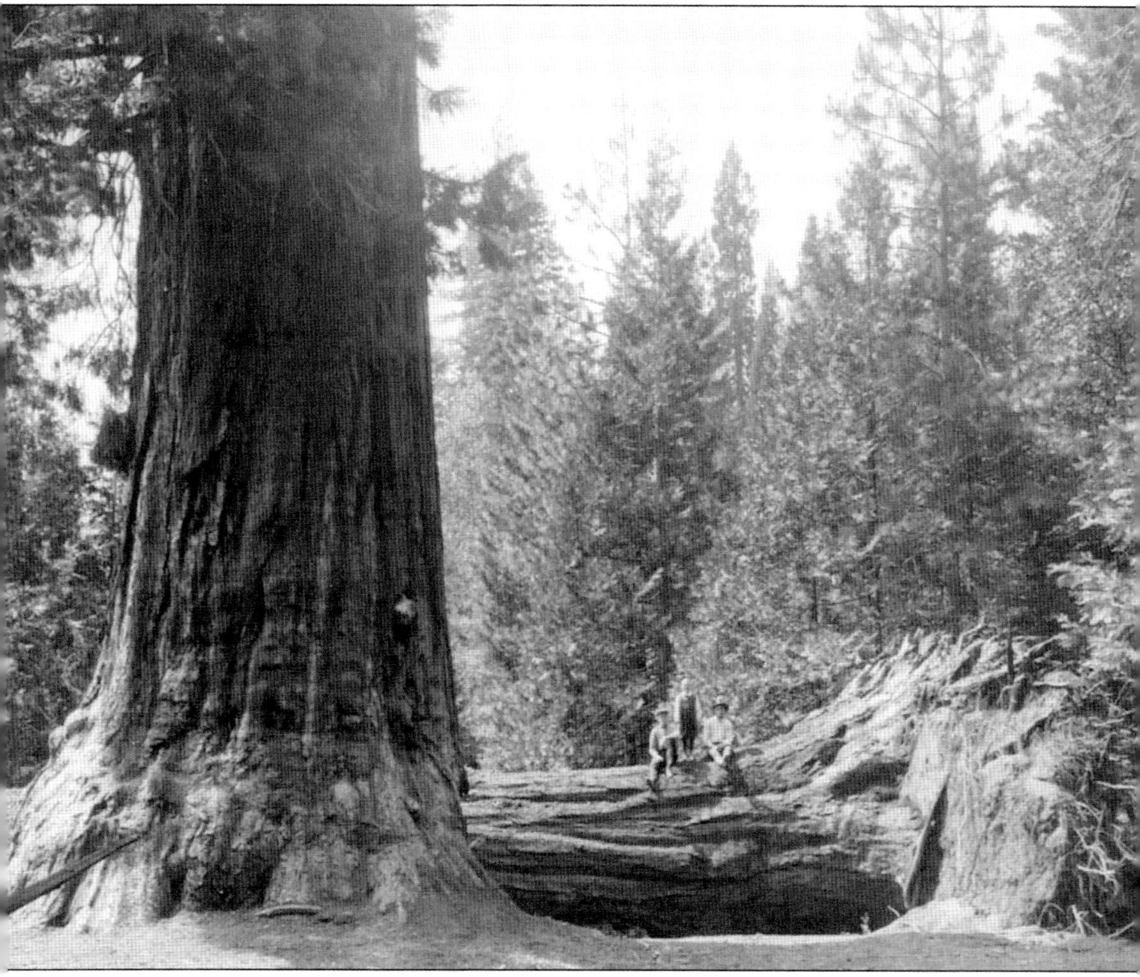

Grove preservation efforts continued after its sale in 1900. President Roosevelt signed legislation creating Calaveras Big Trees National Park in 1909 by exchanging national forest land for the Calaveras grove. The *New York Times* crowed, "Big Trees Will Be Saved." Whiteside was uninterested and the exchange never materialized. Another legislative effort failed in 1912, effectively killing the idea. By 1925, when this picture of youngsters on the fallen Sentinel was taken, Whiteside's era was winding down. (BOS.)

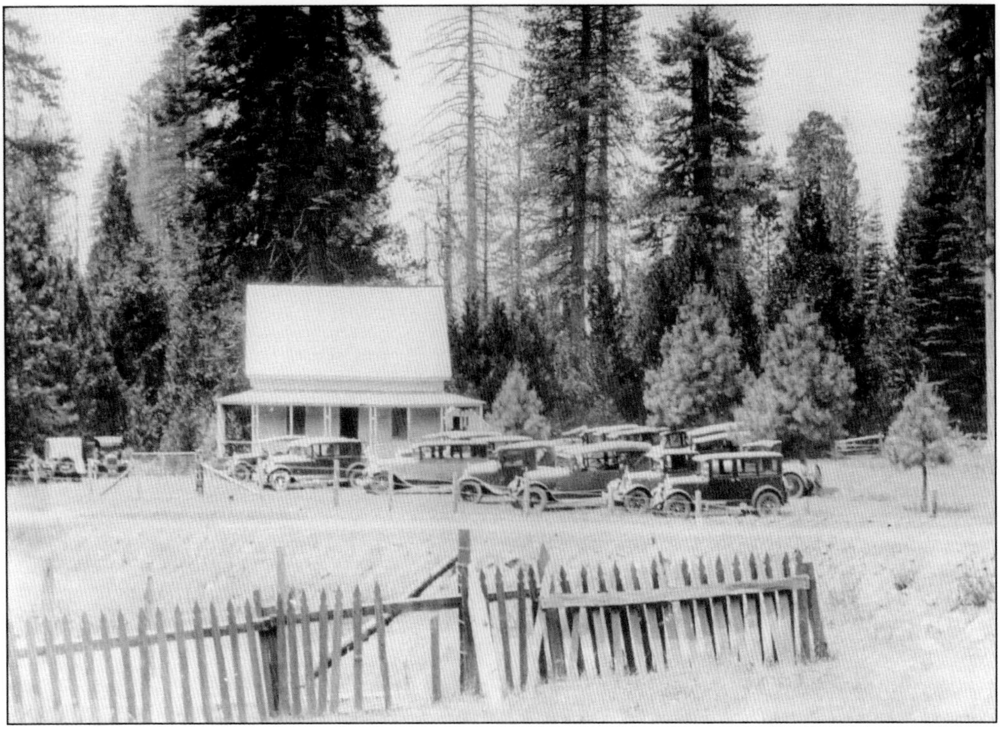

The "annex," originally built as the Perry's summer home in 1865, housed the Whiteside boys, Edgar and Sydney, when the hotel was full in the 1920s. If the cottage filled with guests, too, the boys slept under the trees. After state acquisition, early park rangers and their families lived in the cottage. Today the "White House" survives as the Ranger Station. (CCA.)

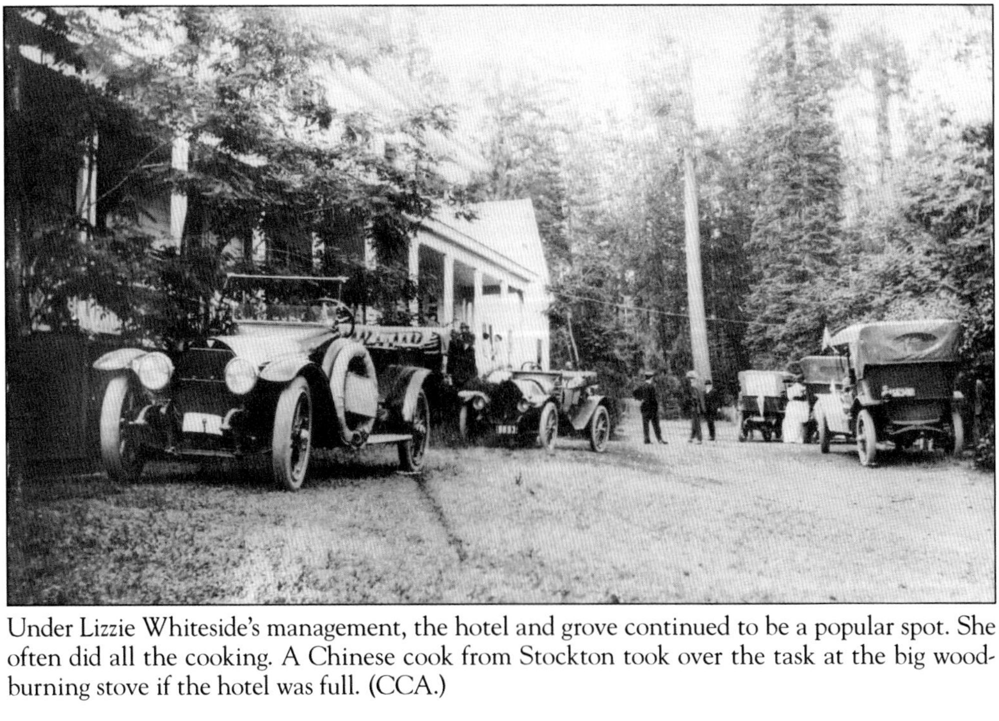

Under Lizzie Whiteside's management, the hotel and grove continued to be a popular spot. She often did all the cooking. A Chinese cook from Stockton took over the task at the big wood-burning stove if the hotel was full. (CCA.)

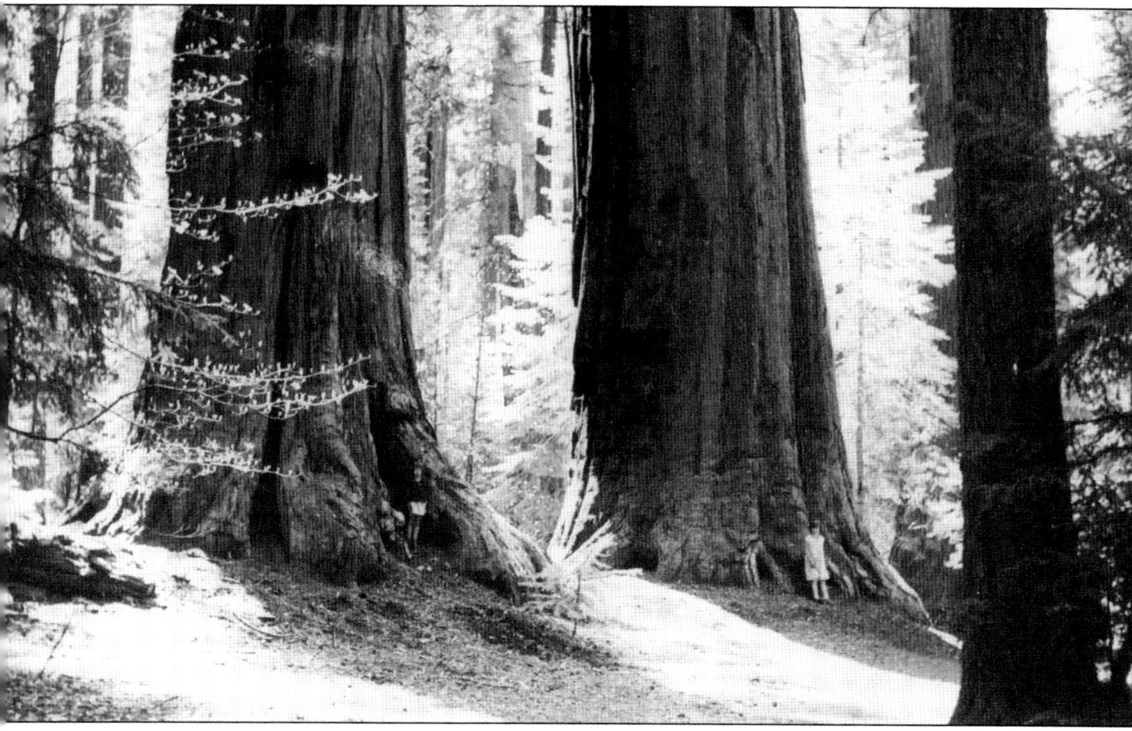

Children playing among the giant sequoias look no bigger than ants in this delightful photograph probably from the 1920s. (CBTSP.)

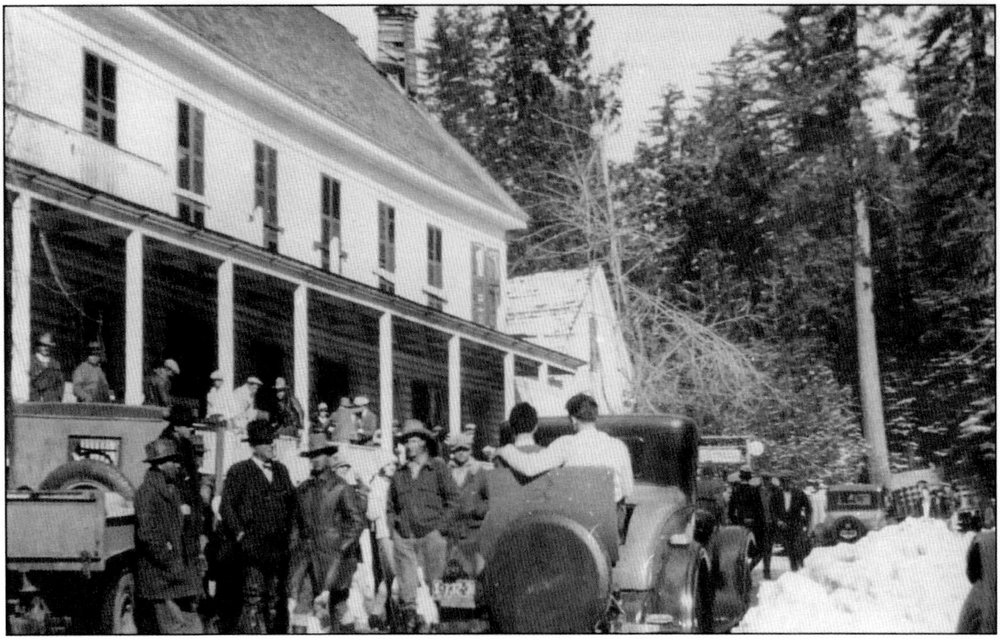

Sometime in the late 1920s, the grove season extended into winter. Snow picnics or "snow frolics" were organized by local business organizations and social clubs. Crowds gather for the festivities in front of the hotel. The run-down condition of the hotel is evident by this time. Part of the railing along the second-floor veranda is missing, shutters are broken, and the chimney appears damaged. (CCA.)

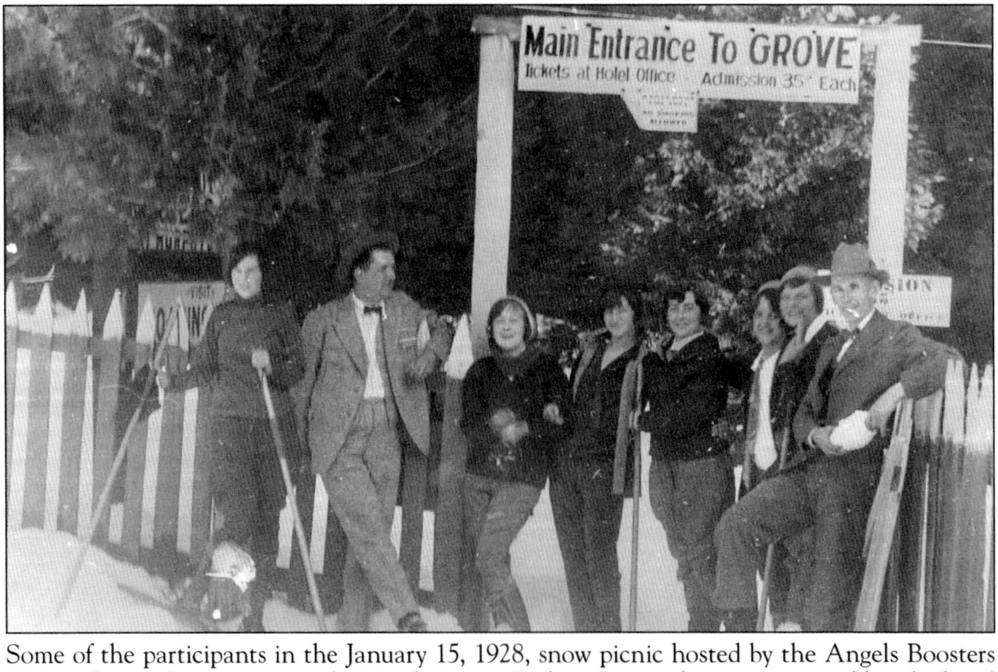

Some of the participants in the January 15, 1928, snow picnic hosted by the Angels Boosters Club gather at the entrance to the North Grove. Tickets to tour the grove were sold at the hotel for 35¢ a person. Although not a concern this time of year, the sign warns of the fire danger and says, "No Smoking Allowed." (CCA.)

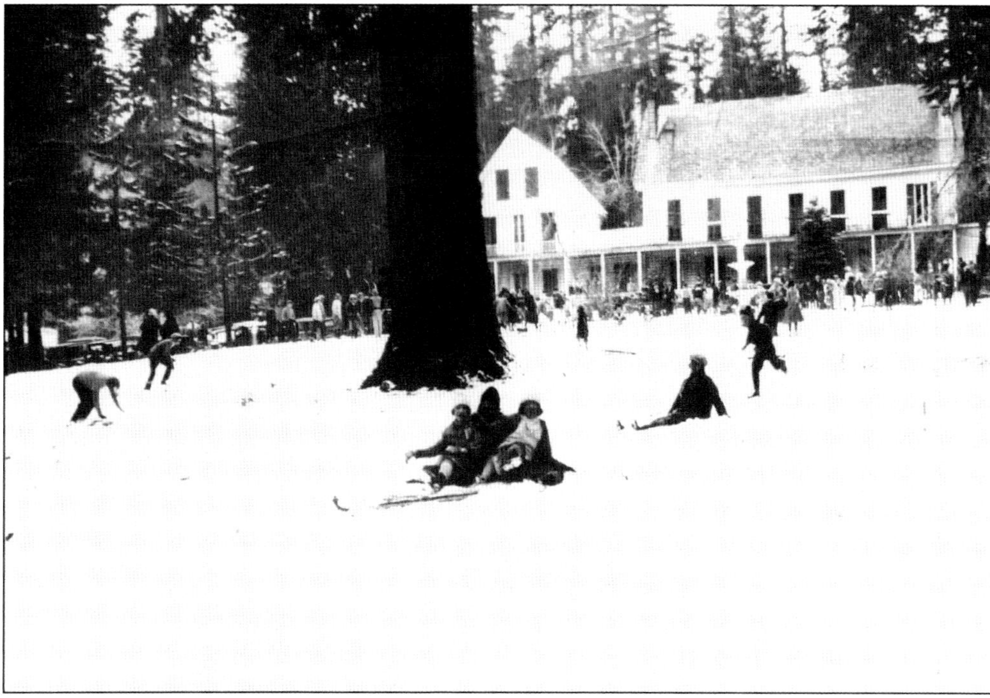

The slope in front of the hotel was perfect for sledding, snowball fights, and socializing. The hotel provided a place to warm up and purchase food and drink. Hundreds of people would come to frolic in the heavy snow. Even in Murphys, snow did not accumulate because of its lower elevation. (Both, CCA.)

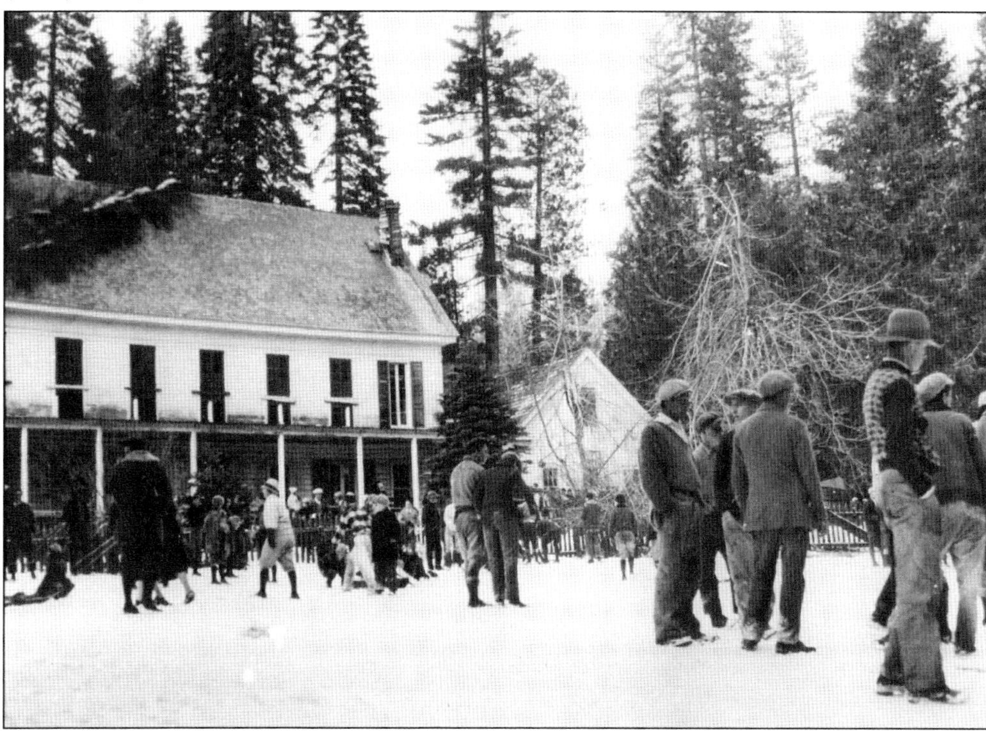

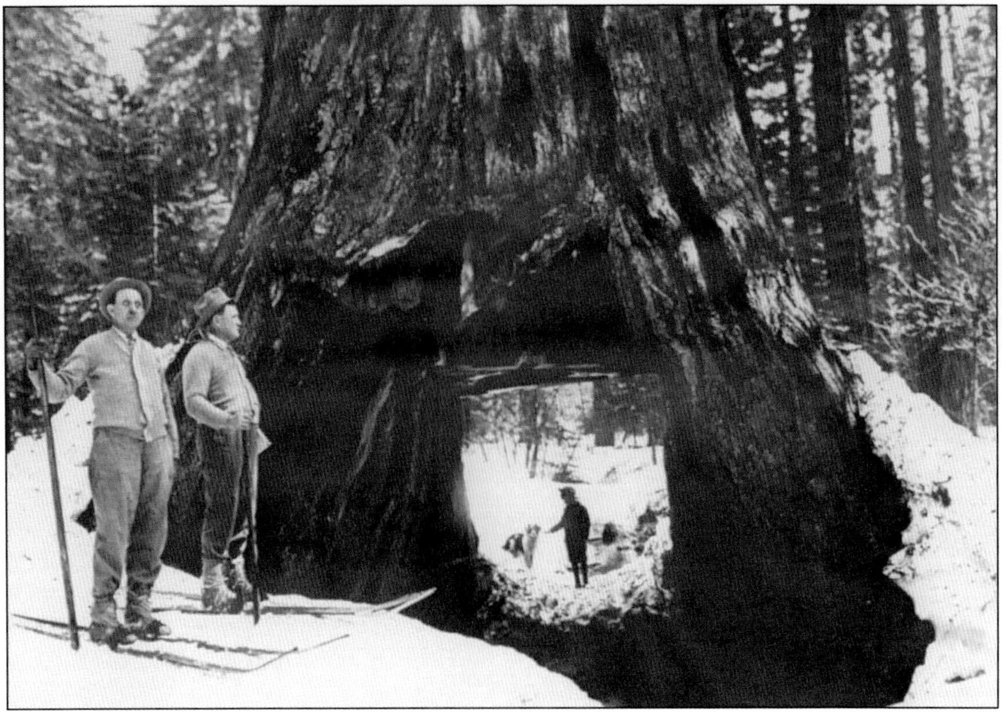

Two skiers marvel at the winter sights in the North Grove as they pause beside the Pioneer's Cabin Tree (above) in the late 1920s. Rather than ski poles, both men appear to be using walking sticks to aid their travel. A boy and dog play beyond the opening. Another group of hardy souls (below) trudged through the snow-covered grove to pose in the tree's opening in the late 1920s. (Above, BOS; below, CCA.)

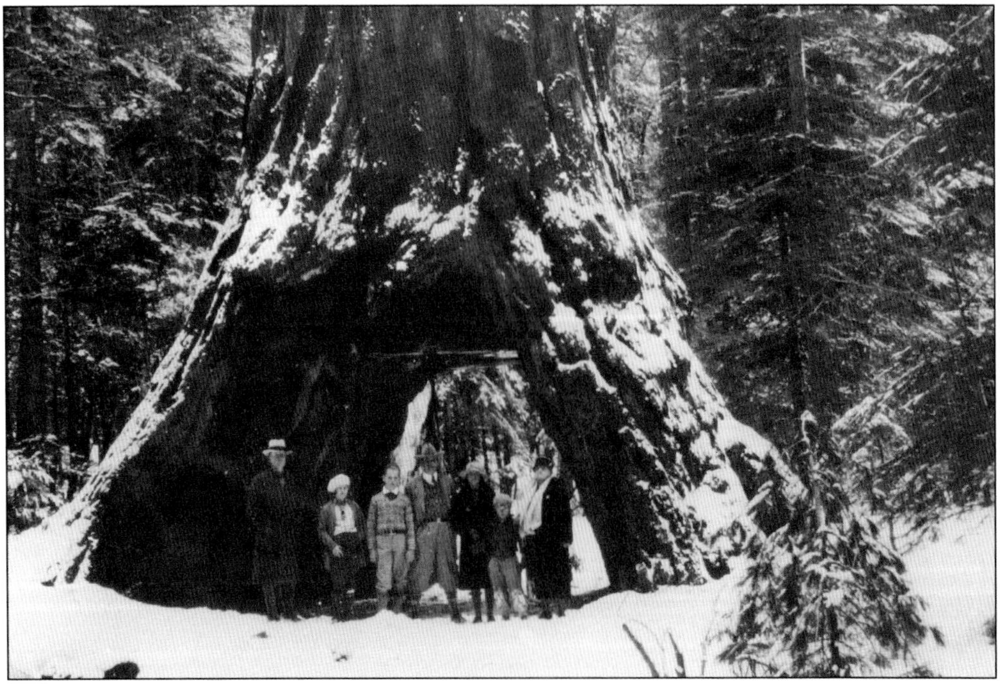

Five

A State Park is Born

For 26 years, activities at the Calaveras Big Trees went on much as they had before Robert B. Whiteside became owner. A whisper of change in the summer of 1926 became a roar when people learned that Whiteside was thinking of selling to a local lumber company. Fears about the trees falling to the lumberman's ax were reignited. Whiteside was negotiating with W. R. Pickering Lumber Company to sell 12,000 acres south of the Stanislaus River, including the 1,300-acre South Grove of big trees. Pickering was reportedly also seeking the 1,760 acres north of the river that included the North Grove and hotel. Businessman Désiré Fricot, president of the Calaveras County Chamber of Commerce, took up the banner of preservation this time. He obtained a 90-day option from Whiteside to buy the North Grove with a plan to sell it to the state or federal government. Unfortunately, he could not raise the needed funds in time. However, he successfully persuaded Whiteside to hold the North Grove property a little longer.

In the meantime, Fricot formed the nonprofit Calaveras Grove Association to preserve "primeval redwood and other forests of California." Harriet West Jackson of Stockton was its first president. Notable among the directors were James L. Sperry's son, James C., and his niece, Ethel Sperry Crocker, as well as local businessman Fred G. Stevenot, *Stockton Record* editor G. Elmer Reynolds, and Alexander T. Vogelsang, former assistant secretary of the interior. On January 5, 1927, the land south of the river was sold to Pickering for $1,804,400. This catastrophic turn of events galvanized people from all quarters into saving the North Grove, and beyond that, creating a statewide system of parks. In November 1928, Californians voted overwhelmingly in favor of the state park concept and to allocate $6 million for land acquisition. The Calaveras Grove Association then set about raising matching funds as prescribed by the new law to buy the big trees acreage. The association faced a series of obstacles, not the least of which was the Great Depression. Ultimately, they succeeded in saving the North Grove, which passed into state hands on June 24, 1931. The South Grove was finally acquired and added to the park in 1954.

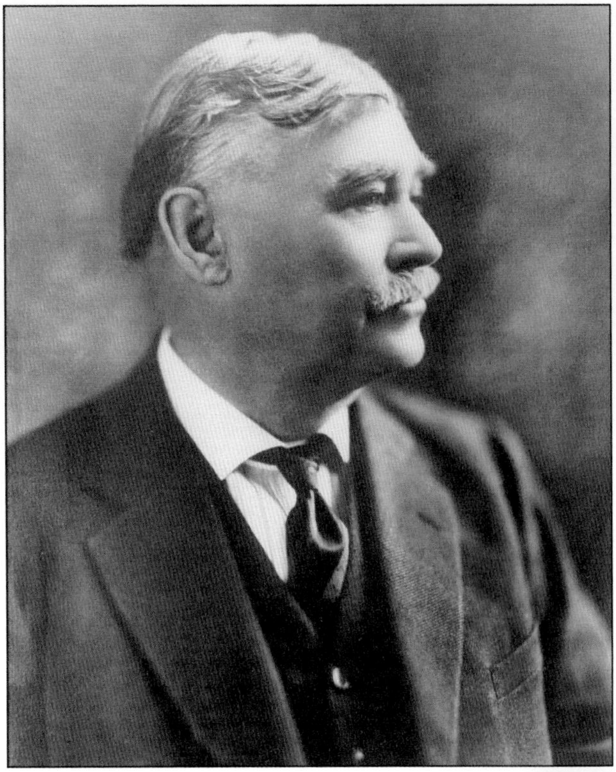

The Great Depression forced Robert Whiteside to slash the price of the North Grove, but the economic free fall also made it nearly impossible for the Grove Association to raise its half of the $275,000 asking price. Trying to speed things along, Whiteside set a deadline of March 15, 1931. Whiteside died in September 1932. (Ely-Winton Historical Society.)

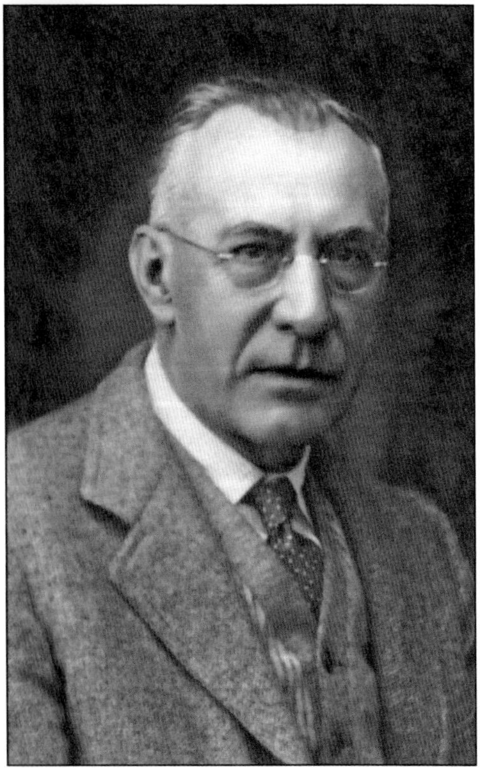

Désiré Fricot was the force behind the final push to save Calaveras' mammoth trees. After Whiteside extended the fund-raising deadline, a donation of $68,750 from John D. Rockefeller Jr. through the Save the Redwoods League was a turning point. His contribution was the single largest to the cause, followed by Eliza Sperry Crocker's of $25,000. (CCA.)

Frederick Law Olmsted Jr. (pictured with his wife, Sarah, in the early 1930s) was instrumental in creating California's park system. In 1928, his exhaustive survey identified the opportunities and needs for parks in California. He specifically cited the importance of the Calaveras Big Trees. In addition to his contributions in California, the famous landscape architect had a lifetime commitment to national parks and a devotion to the Save the Redwoods League. (CBTSP.)

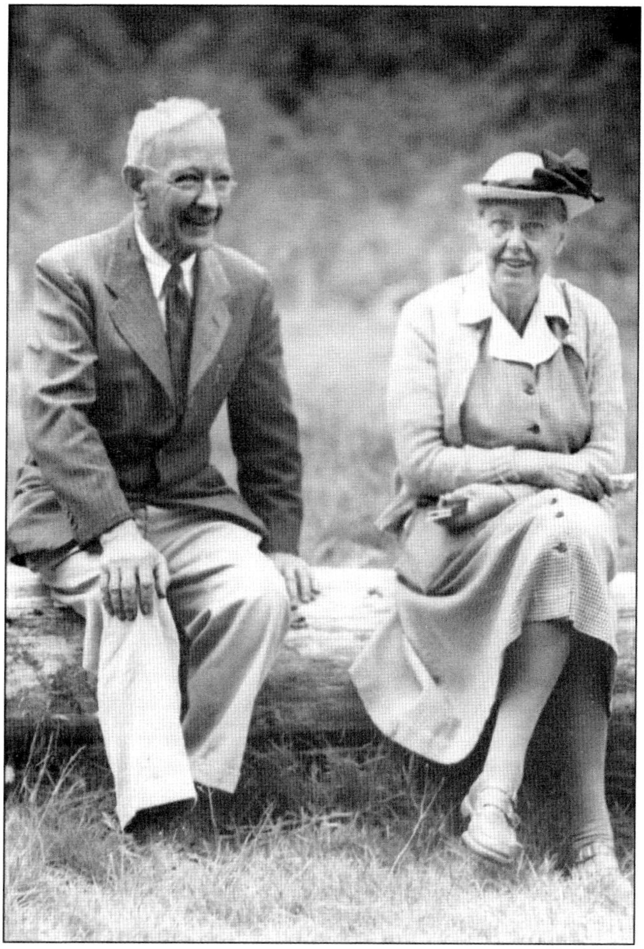

On July 5, 1931, the formal dedication of Calaveras Big Trees State Park was held following its transfer to the state on June 24. California governor James Rolph Jr. flew in to Angels Airport for the occasion. Other speakers included Col. C. W. Wing, chief of the state division of parks; William Colby, president of the state park commission; and Désiré Fricot. (CCA.)

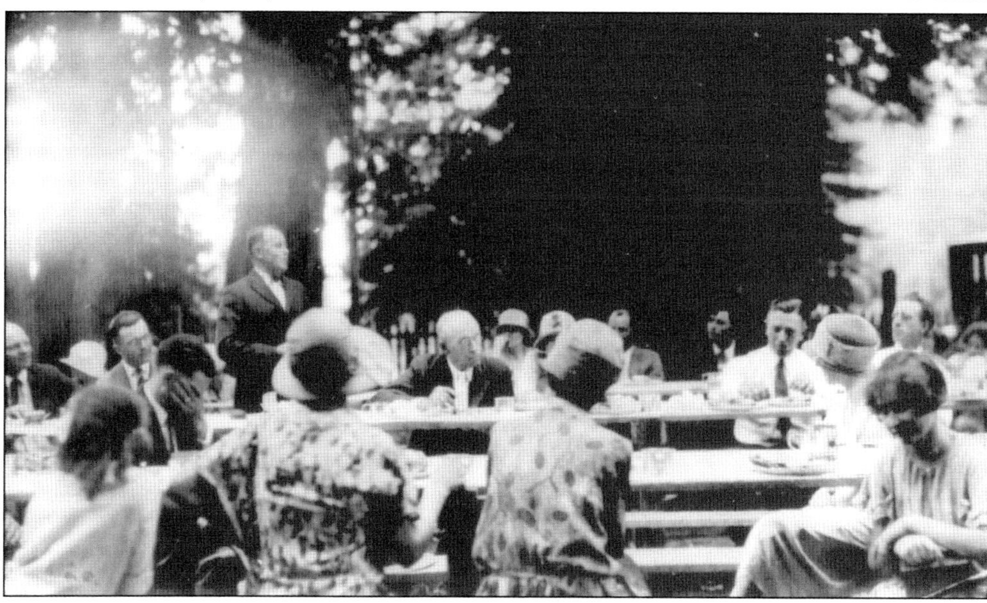

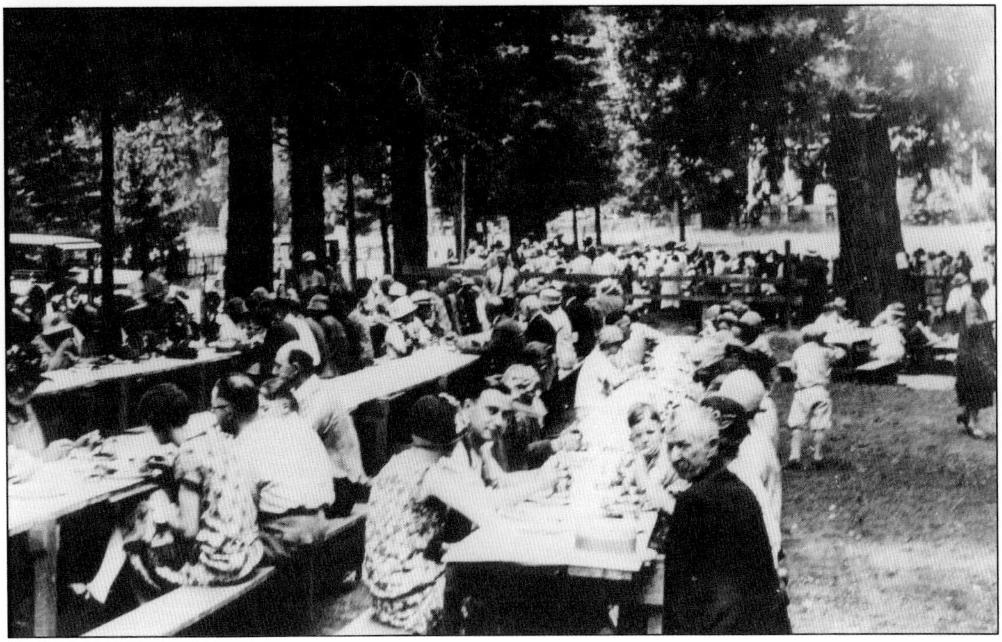

A prominent attorney, judge, and president of the Stockton Chamber of Commerce, Warren Atherton served as master of ceremonies. Hundreds of people attended the dedication, which also included special musical and singing performances, as well as a barbecue. Fricot paid tribute to all those who for the previous 30 years had tried to preserve the big trees. He urged all to now take up the banner for the South Grove. (Both, CCA.)

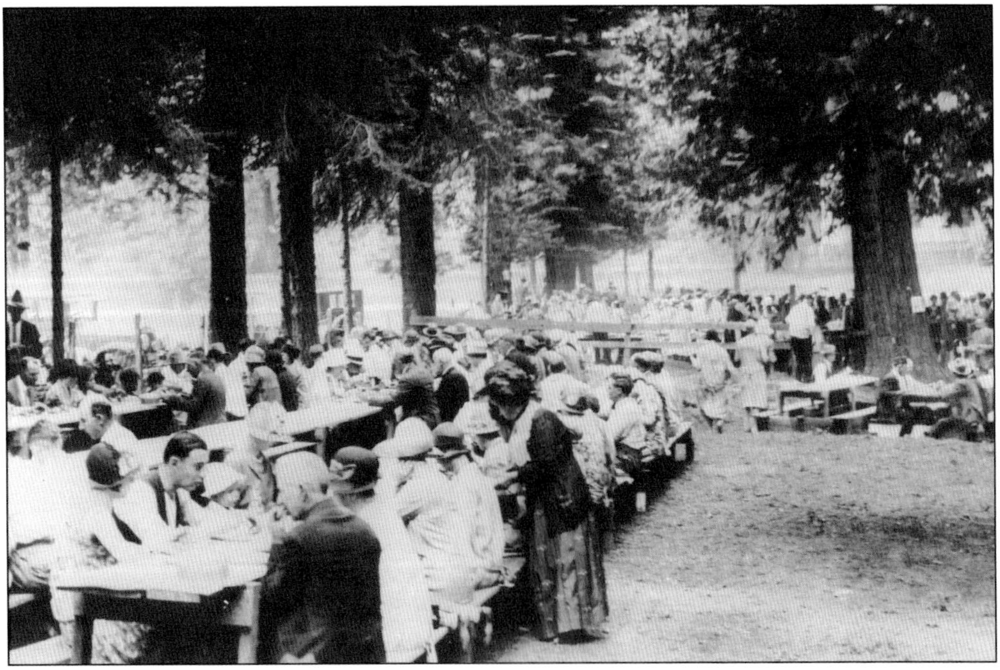

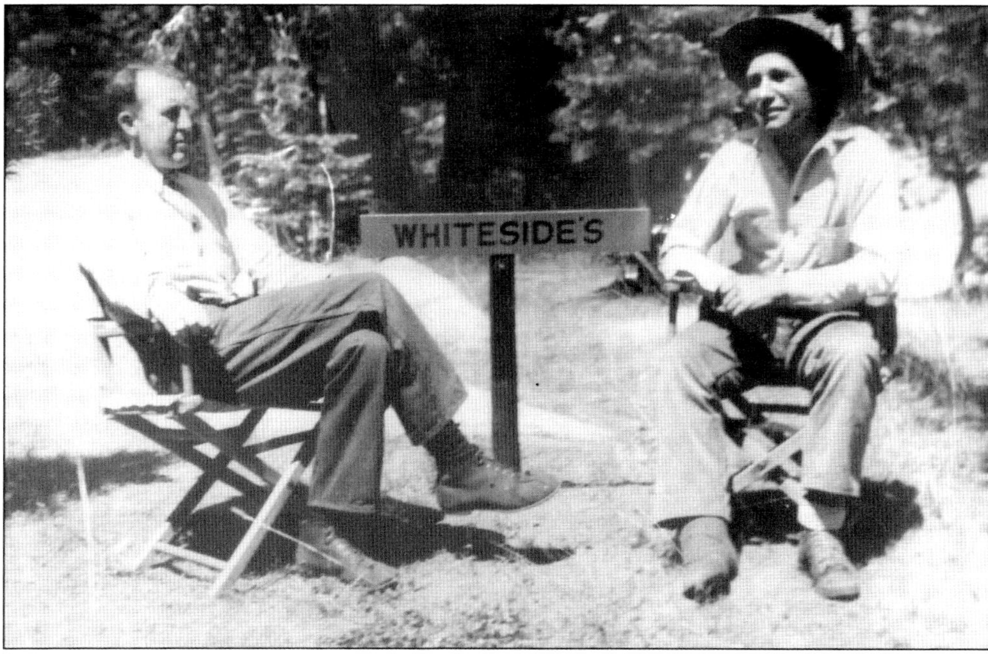

Edgar Whiteside (left) was named the first warden of Calaveras Big Trees State Park, serving in that role until December 1933. He is shown here at his mother's cabin in nearby Tamarack in the 1930s with local legend Monte Wolfe. Whiteside later served as San Joaquin County assessor in Stockton. (CBTSP.)

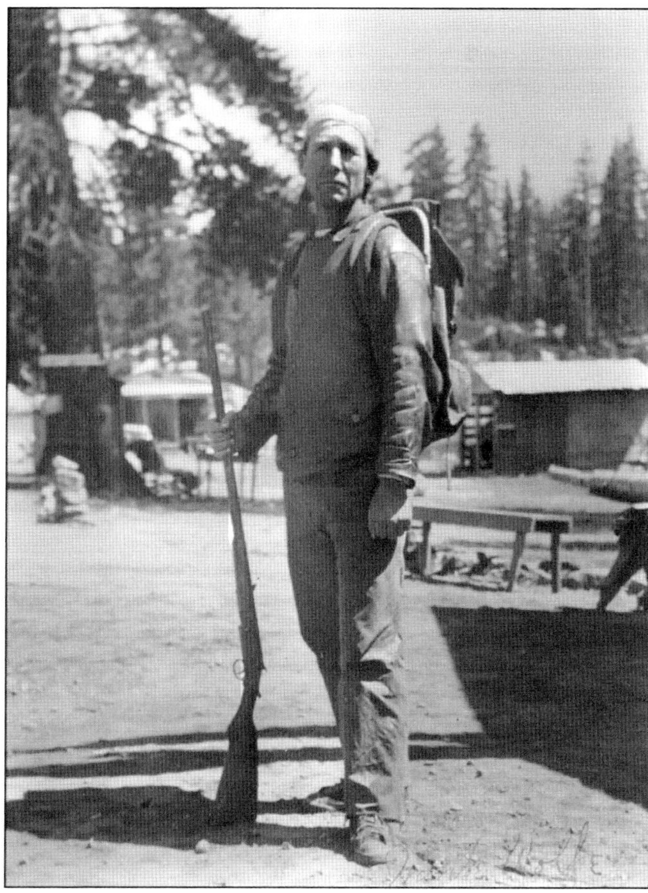

Monte Wolfe, seen in this undated photograph, was the last of the legendary mountain men who used his hunting and trapping skills to survive in the high country. Wolfe's real identity was as mysterious as his disappearance in April 1940. Even today, the Monte Wolfe Society is committed to maintaining his legend and one of his hand-built cabins. (CBTSP.)

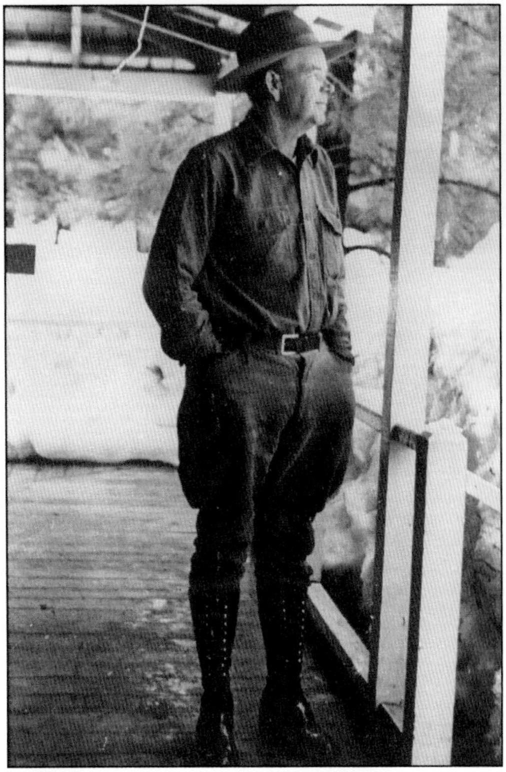

Carey "Pop" Traylor, seen in a 1939 photograph, was the warden of Calaveras Big Trees State Park from 1935 to 1941. Traylor had access to the largest workforce in the park's history when the Civilian Conservation Corps (CCC) assigned various companies to the park during the Great Depression. The CCC camp at Calaveras Big Trees State Park was the first officially approved camp in the state park system. (CBTSP.)

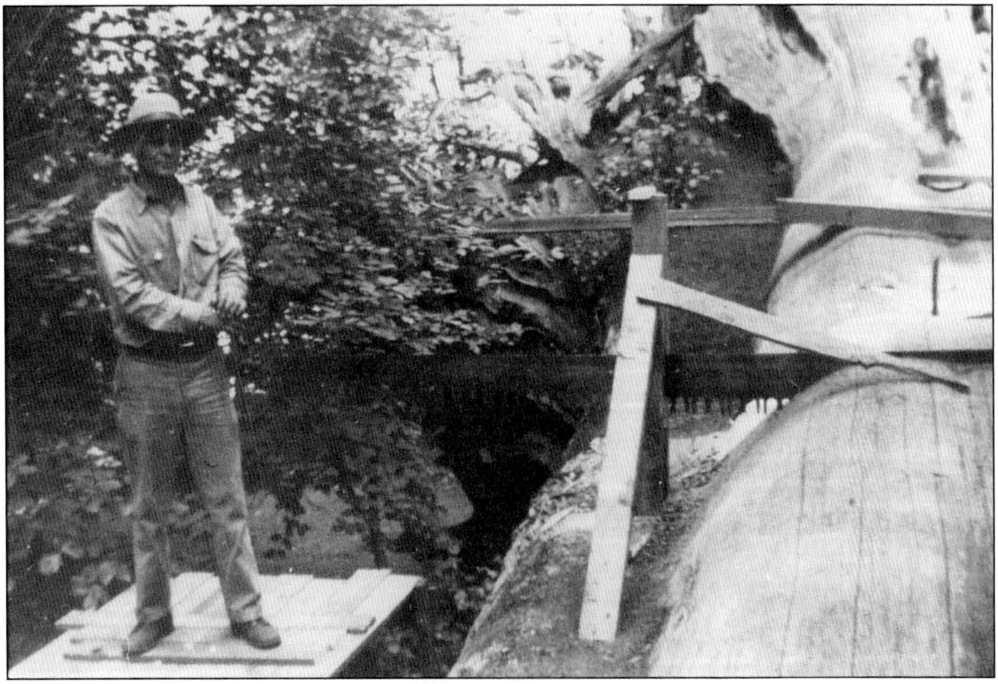

Pop Traylor cuts a slab from a fallen giant sequoia for the 1937 California State Fair. A crew of young men from the CCC spent two weeks building the platform, cutting the slab, and finishing it for the fair. (CBTSP.)

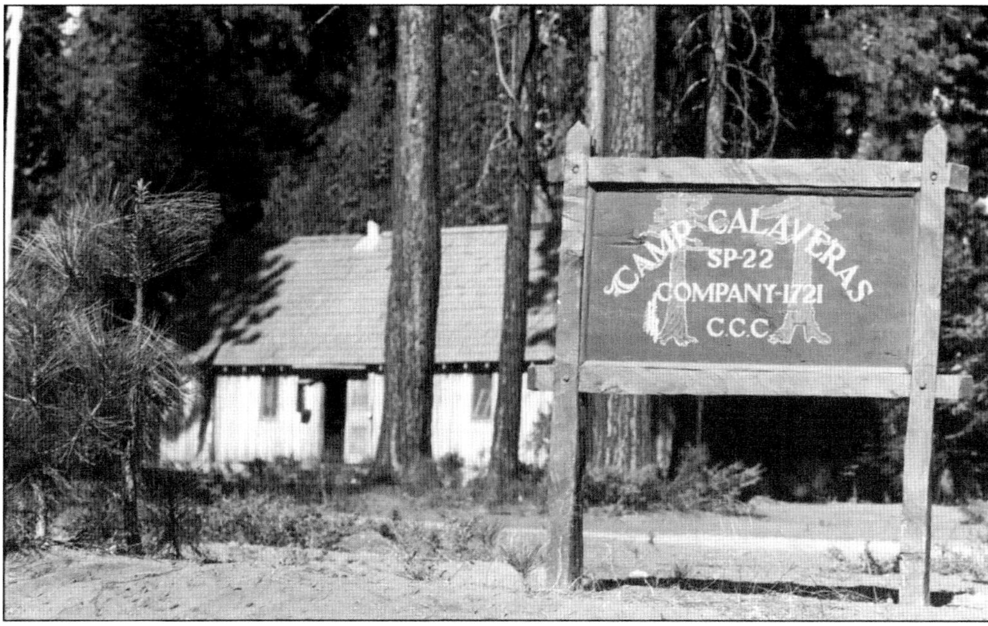

The Civilian Conservation Corps was a New Deal program under Pres. Franklin D. Roosevelt that put millions of young men to work from 1933 to 1942 in the country's national and state parks. In California, the CCC was key to developing the infrastructure for a park system in its infancy. CCC Camp Calaveras, SP-22, Company 1721, located in Big Trees State Park, initially operated only in summer. (CBTSP.)

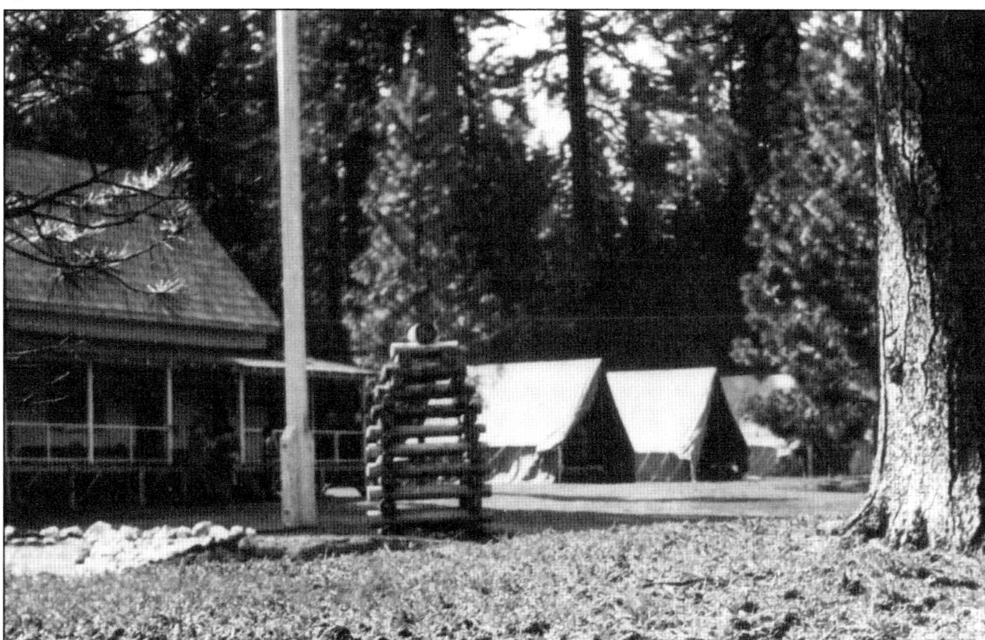

During the 1930s, young men roamed the country by the hundreds of thousands looking for work. The CCC program not only gave them jobs but a sense of dignity and a place to live, even if it was a tent in the woods. These CCC tents in 1936 were beside the White House, which had been converted into CCC company headquarters. (CBTSP.)

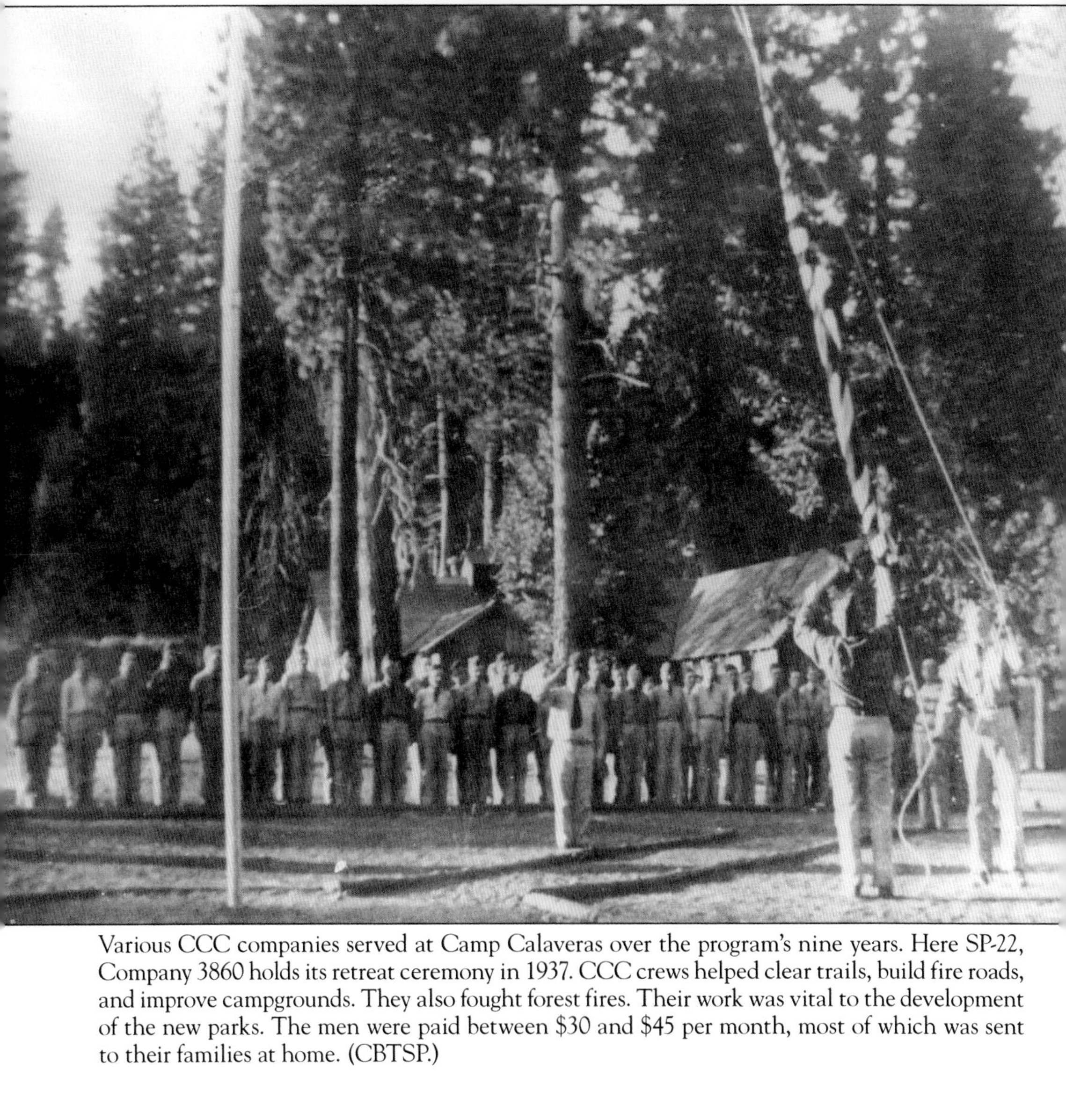

Various CCC companies served at Camp Calaveras over the program's nine years. Here SP-22, Company 3860 holds its retreat ceremony in 1937. CCC crews helped clear trails, build fire roads, and improve campgrounds. They also fought forest fires. Their work was vital to the development of the new parks. The men were paid between $30 and $45 per month, most of which was sent to their families at home. (CBTSP.)

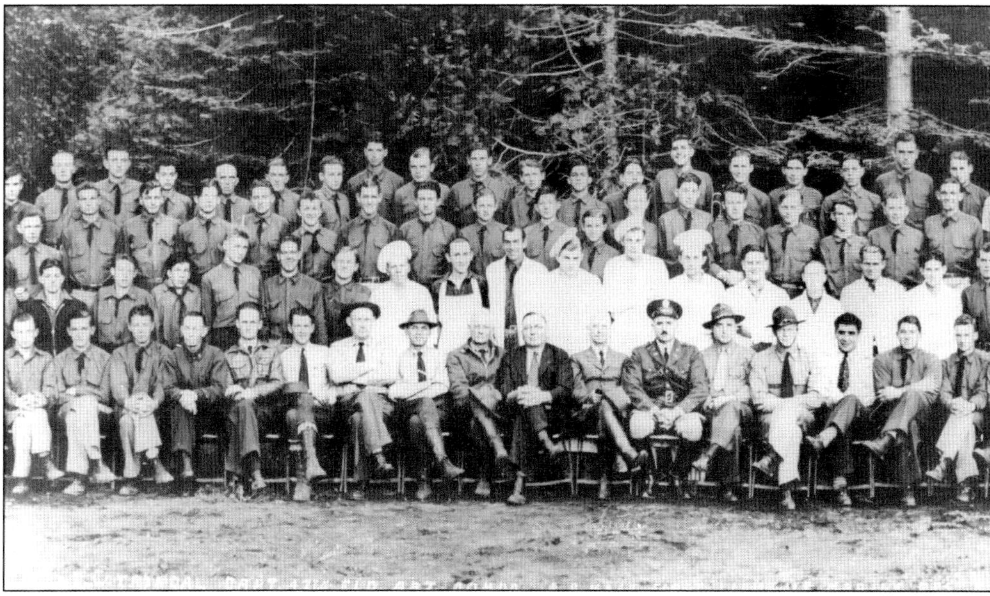

After a two-week conditioning program, CCC recruits were sent to work camps around the country. Although the forest and park services supervised the projects, the army operated the camps and supervised the men. In just four months, the CCC recruited more than 300,000 enrollees. These are some of the men and their commanders who served at Big Trees. (CBTSP.)

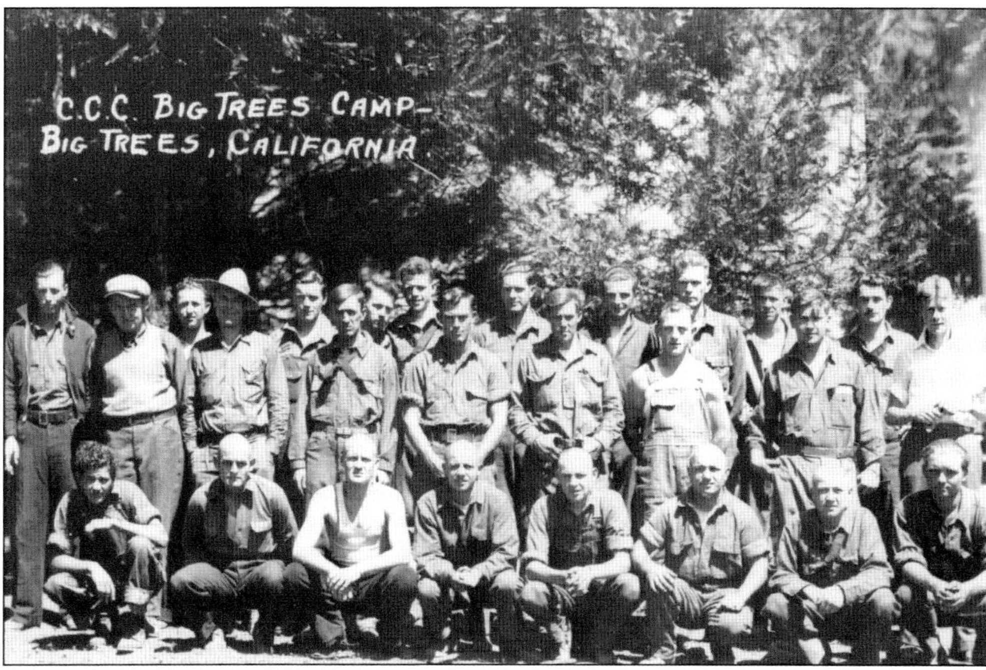

CCC crews improved the campground and day-use picnic areas at Big Trees, including constructing stone stoves. The rock bridge over the creek near the fallen Sentinel Tree was hand built by CCC crews. Their biggest legacy may be the construction of Big Trees Hall in 1937. Now called Jack Knight Hall, the one-story structure features a covered porch, massive rock fireplace, and hand-forged hardware. (CBTSP.)

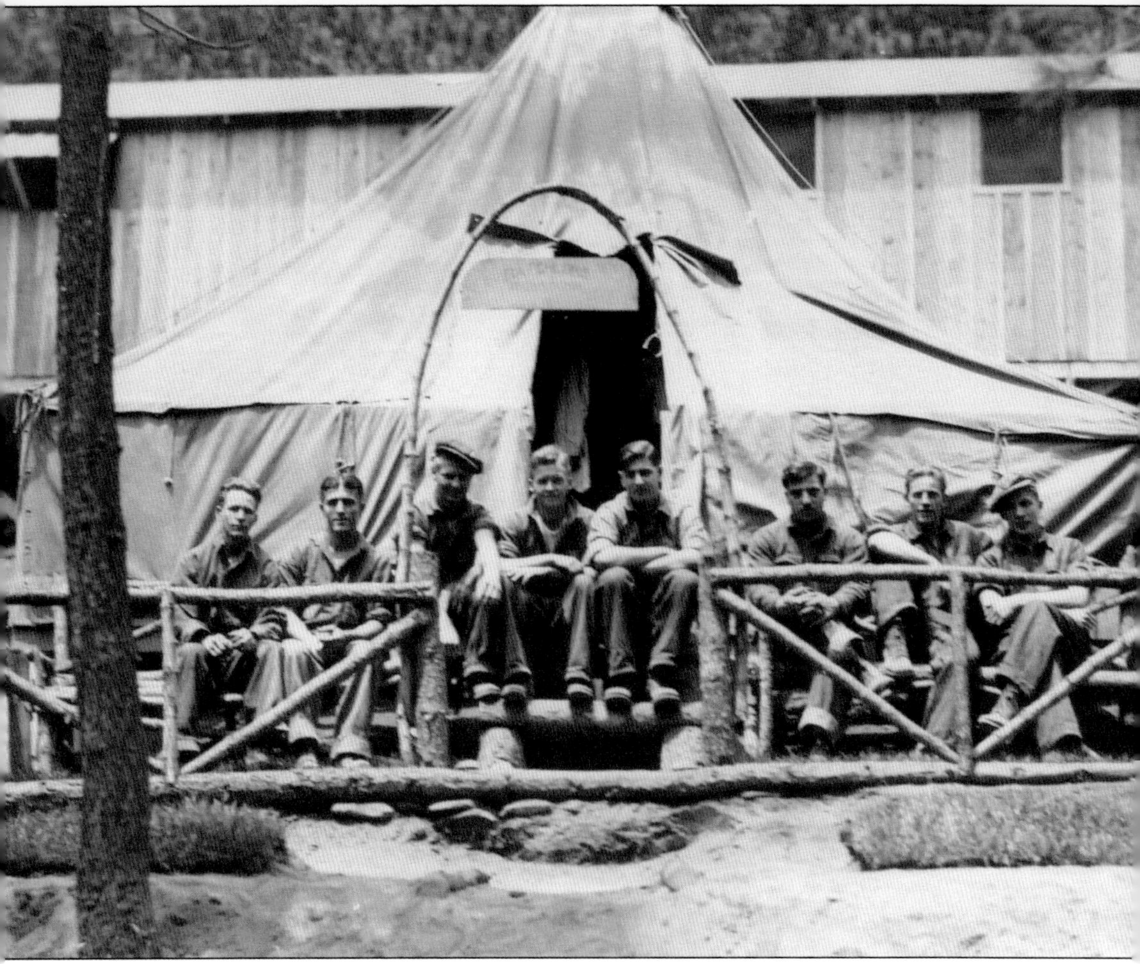

The sign above this CCC tent at Camp Calaveras reads "Batchlors Paradise." The men implemented much-needed park improvement projects. They built an entrance station, renovated the old hotel, put up perimeter fencing, cut firebreaks, and made log benches and picnic tables. After snow collapsed the pavilion on the stump in 1934, CCC crews shaved off the damaged surface and planed it smooth. (CBTSP.)

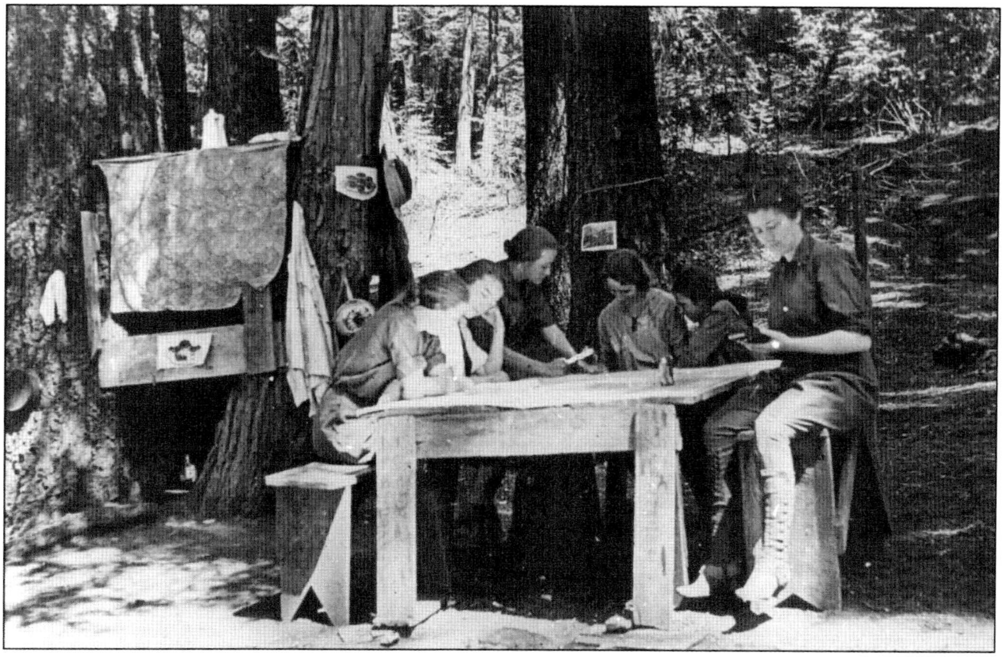

A group of female campers appears to be planning a hiking route at Big Trees State Park in their rustic campsite. The rudimentary camping table and benches dates this photograph to the early 1930s, before the CCC improved the campsites. (CCA.)

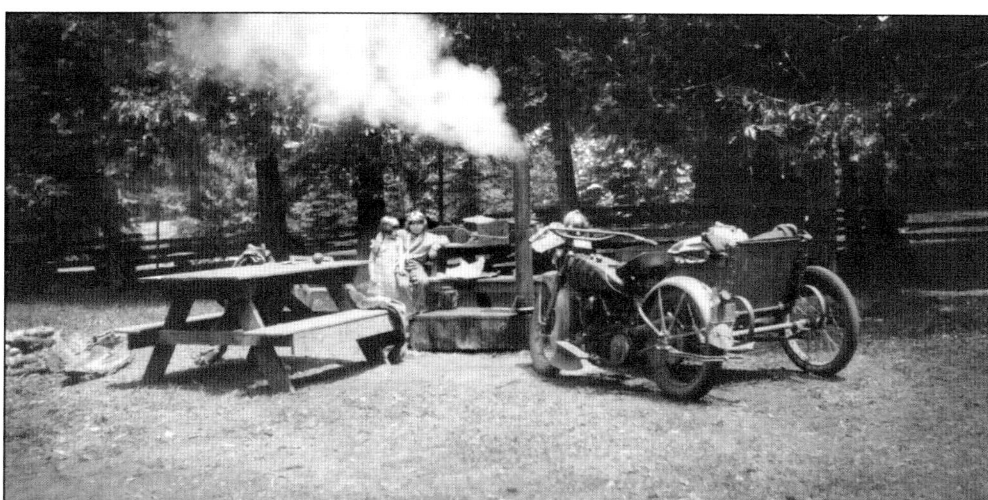

A unique camping vehicle, a motorcycle with sidecar, is parked in a campsite with a couple of youngsters in the 1930s. The new-looking picnic table was likely among those built by the CCC. (CBTSP.)

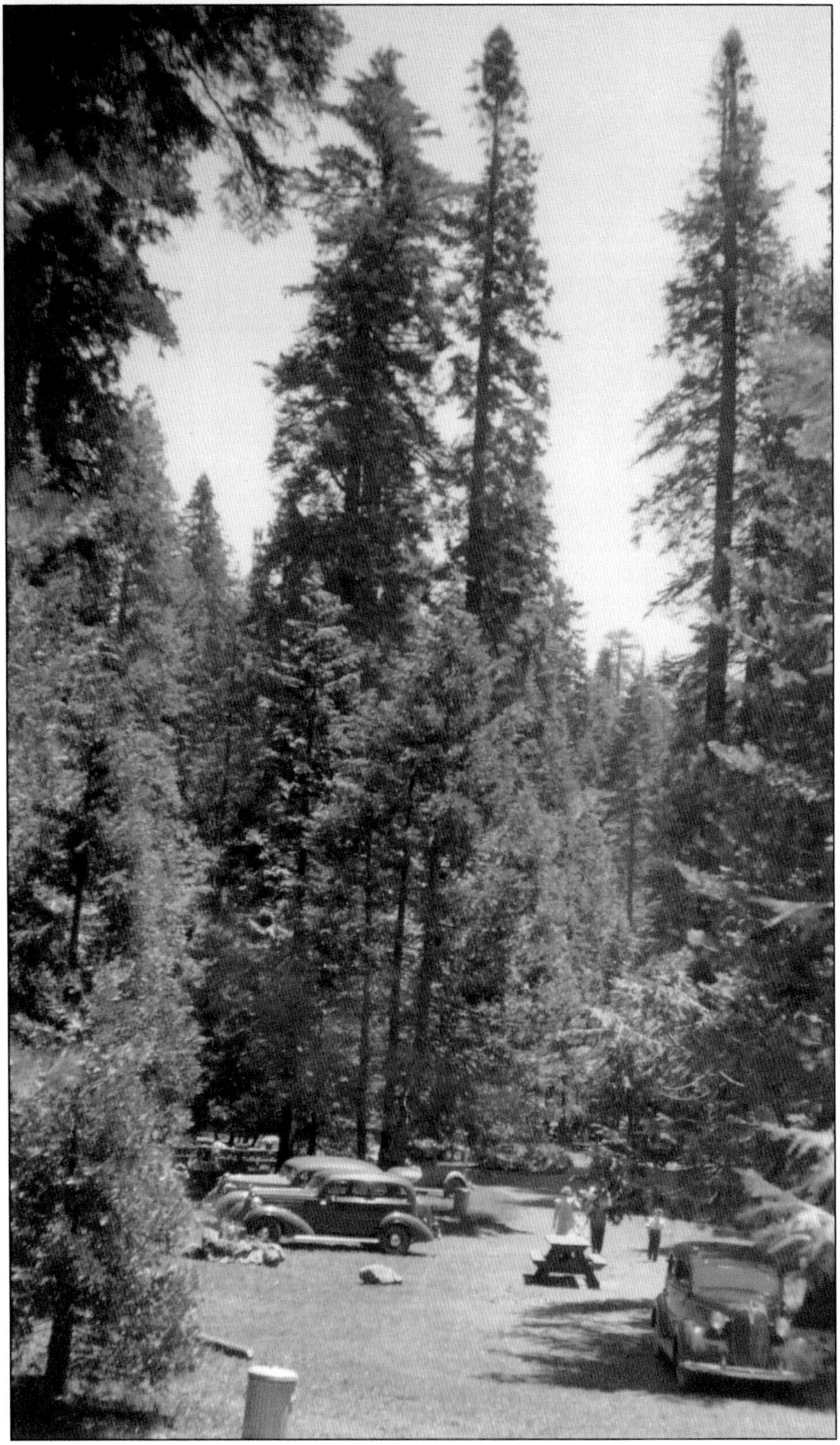

The campground area within the North Grove in the 1930s was among the pine trees neighboring the giant sequoias. The camping area, much in the same place today, has many mature trees that provide welcome shade. (CBTSP)

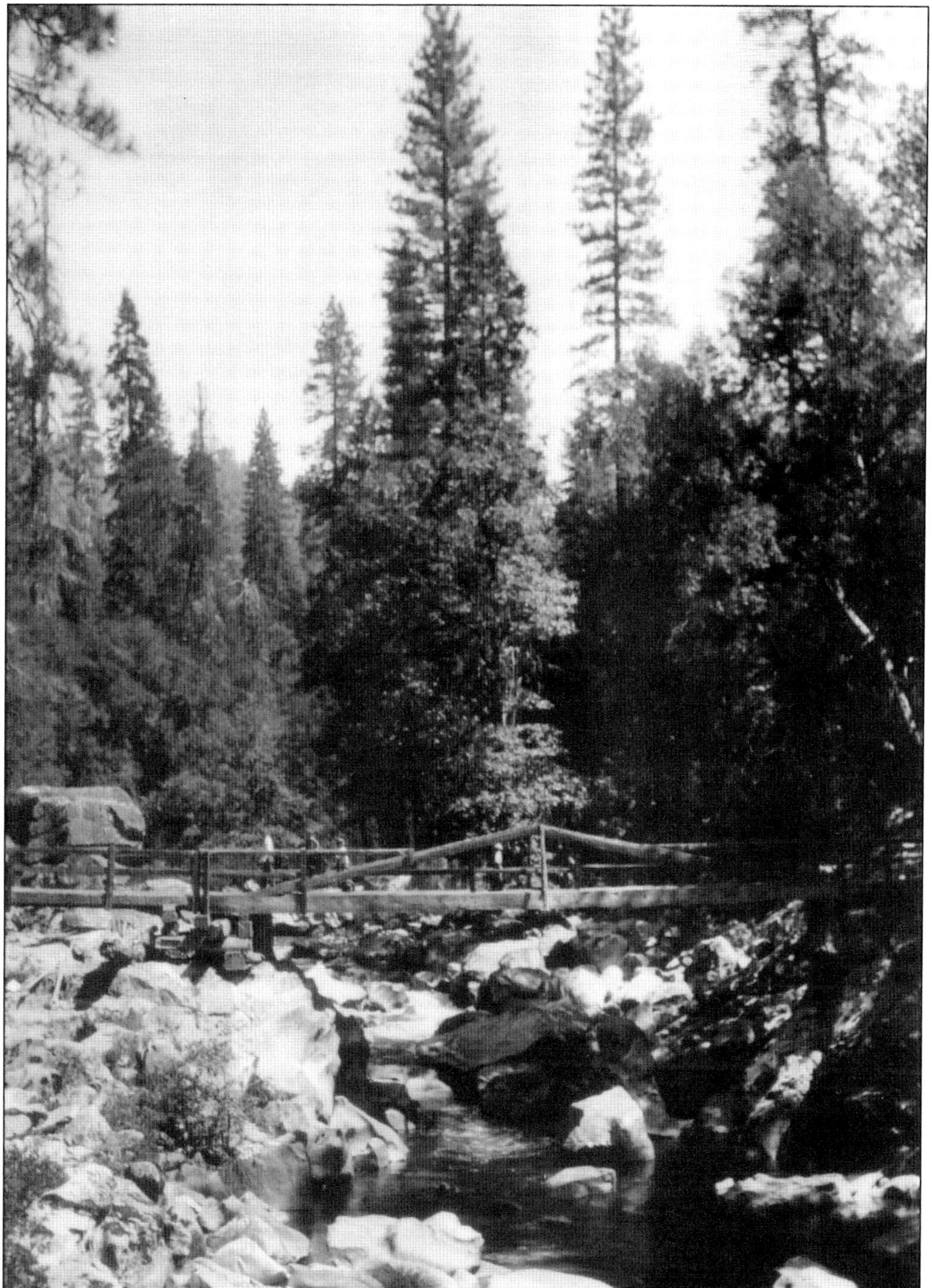

This bridge provided a path across the Stanislaus River for hikers and possibly horseback riders in the late 1930s and early 1940s. People also could cross the river at Board's Crossing near present-day Dorrington. Even though the South Grove was not yet part of the state park, people continued to explore it. (CBTSP.)

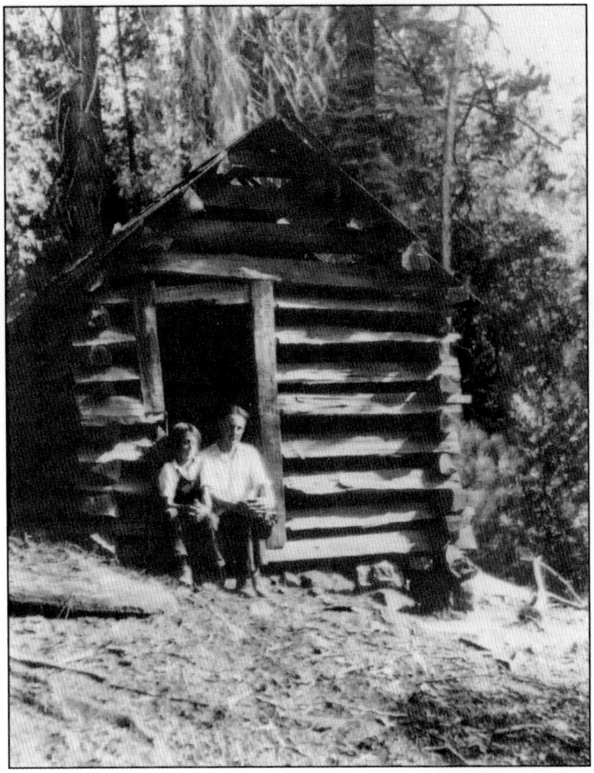

This log cabin, identified as the Overholger "shake" cabin, was still standing in Oak Hollow in the 1930s. The date 1891 was carved into one of the logs. Shake makers had moved into Oak Hollow alongside Native American residents around the 1860s. They made their living by hand-chopping cedar shakes from the trees and selling them. (CCHS.)

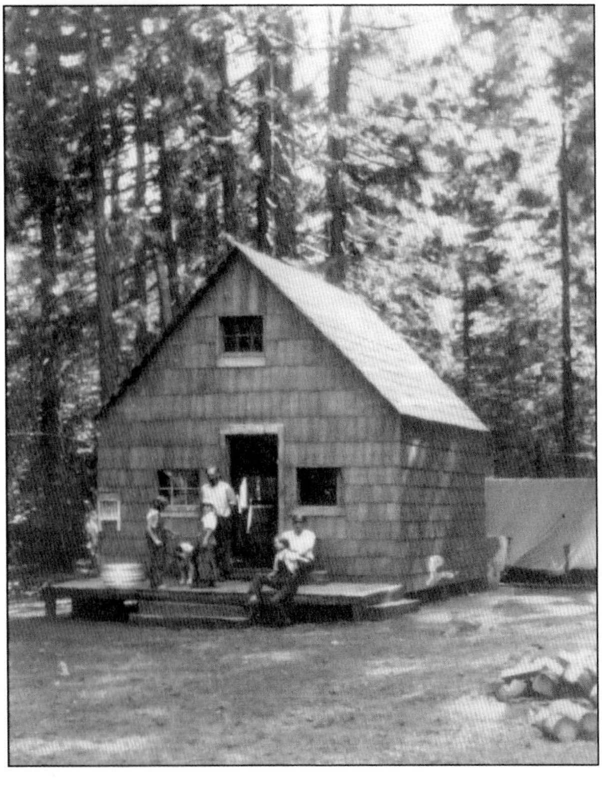

This cabin, believed to be in the South Grove in the early 1950s, was most likely housing for employees of an "honor camp" for inmates in the Beaver Creek area. Such camps, now called conservation camps, continue to be operated by the California Department of Forestry and Fire Protection and the California Department of Corrections and Rehabilitation. (CBTSP.)

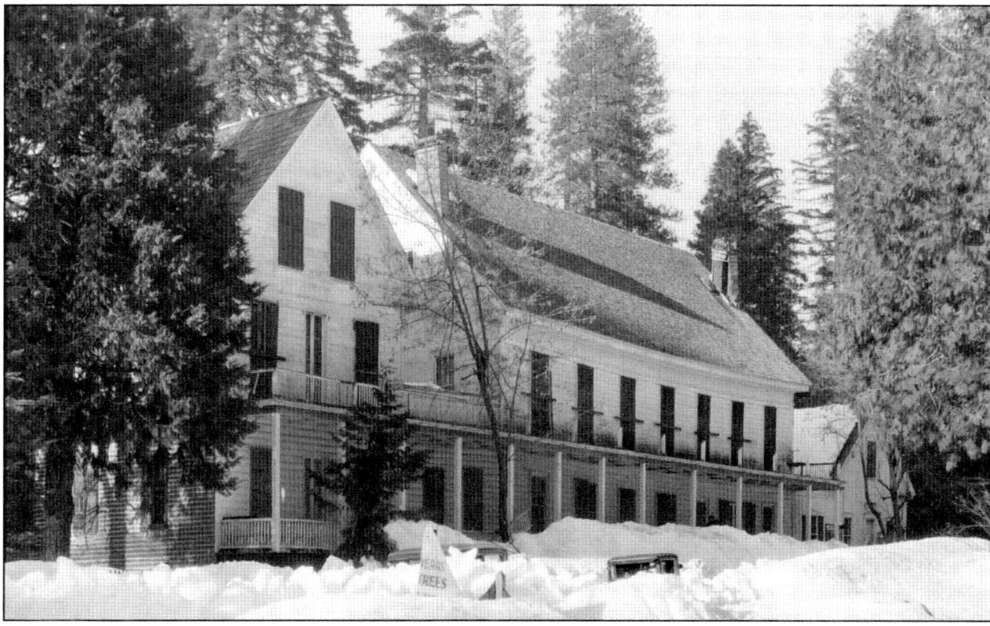

Heavy snowfall created ongoing problems in the 1930s and 1940s, while also opening the park for winter sports. The tops of cars parked in front of the hotel are barely visible above the snow in the 1932 photograph above. In February 1934, the far right portion of the hotel, which housed the lobby, was crushed by a heavy snowfall. The 1939 view of the hotel below shows that the original lobby on the right side of the building is missing. (Both, CBTSP.)

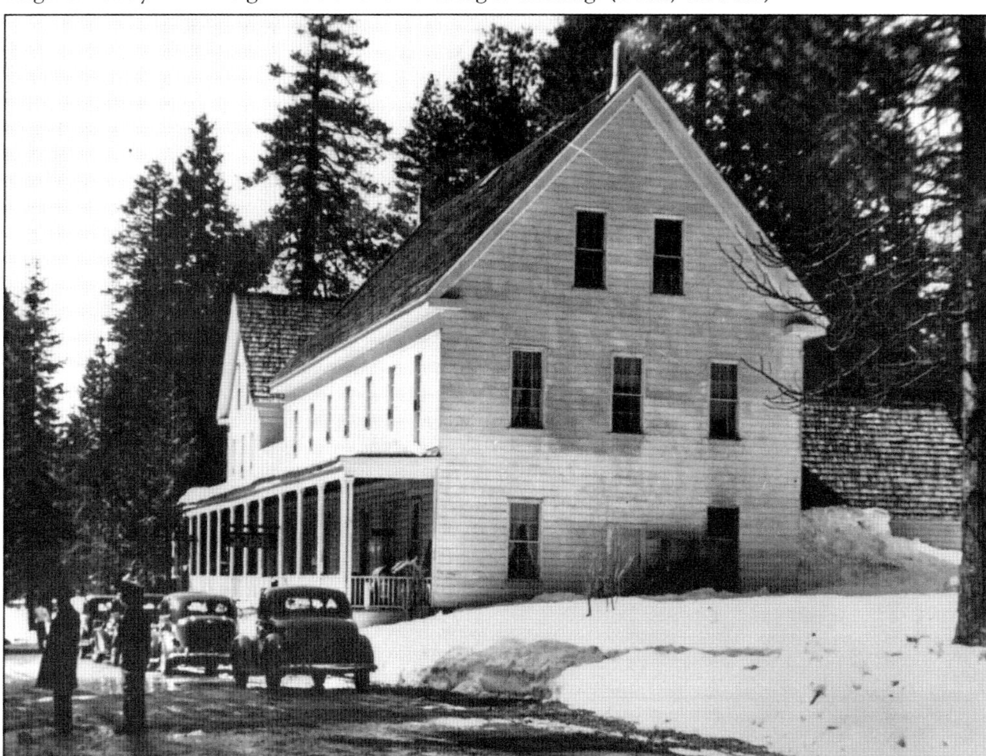

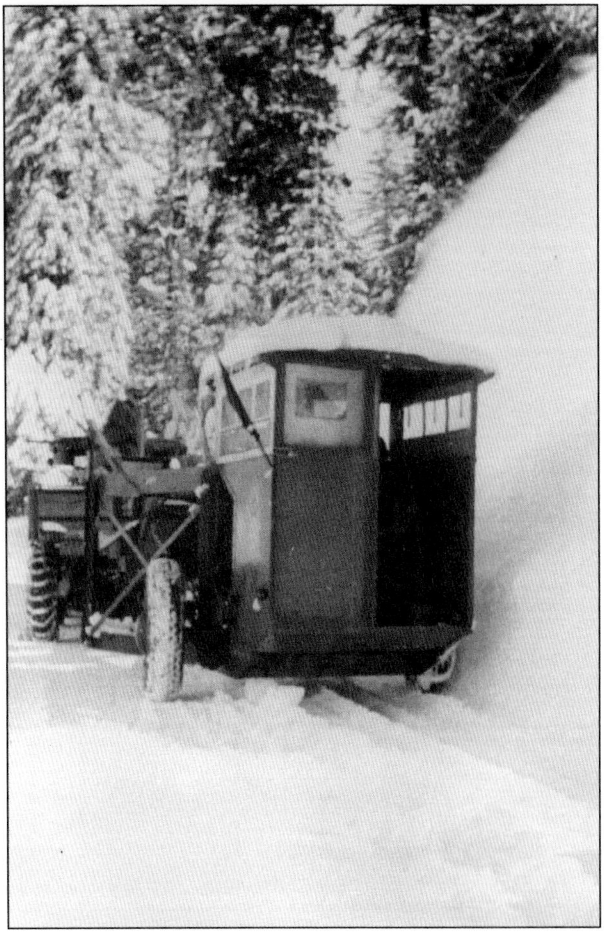

This one-of-a-kind piece of snow removal equipment, powered by steam, was built by park service personnel and the CCC in 1939 to clear the roads in Big Trees Park, which now was welcoming winter visitors. Thanks in part to the CCC, the park boasted a ski run with a rope tow and a warming hut. (CBTSP.)

A deer pulls a young boy on a toboggan in this postcard advertising winter activities at Calaveras Big Trees in 1940. (CBTSP.)

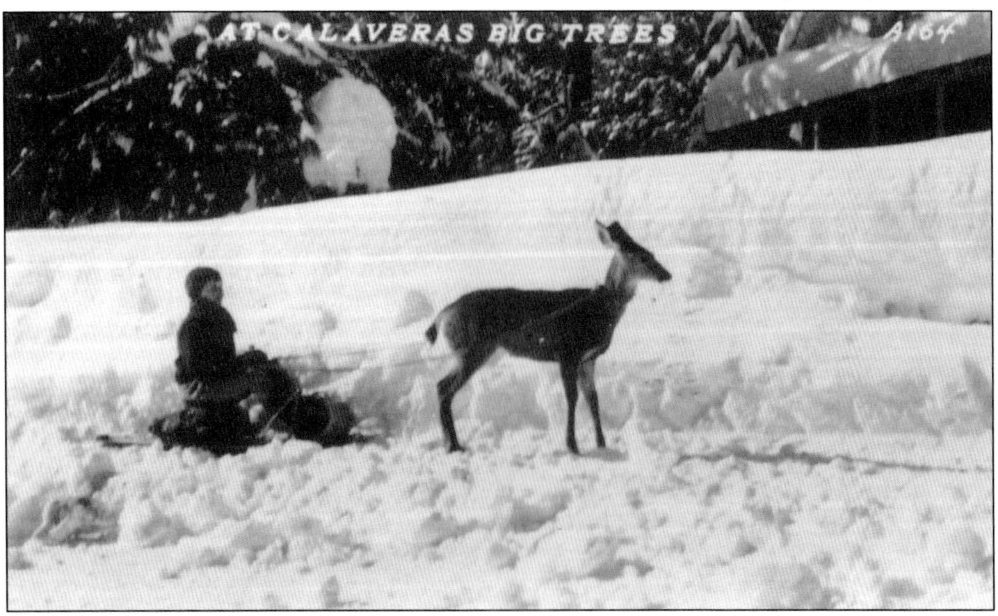

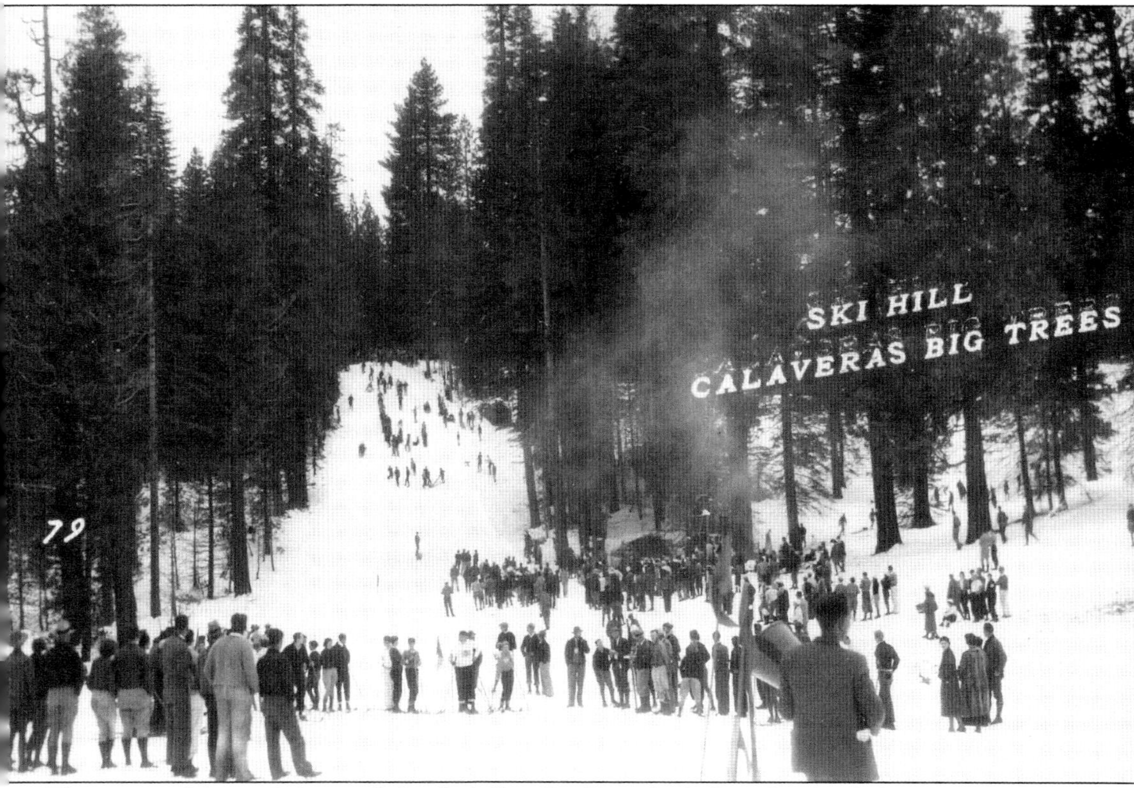

This postcard from 1940 touted the ski hill at Big Trees Park. In 1931, the Calaveras County Chamber of Commerce was awarded a lease and concession for staging winter sports at the park. The Angel's Boosters Club and the chamber worked with CCC crews to clear a slope for skiing and tobogganing. A small entrance fee included all activities, as well as free coffee, hot dogs, and beans. Besides skiing, people could engage in snowshoeing and skijoring (where a person on skis is pulled by a horse or dogs). People would come from as far away as Stockton and San Francisco to play in the snow among the big trees. (CBTSP.)

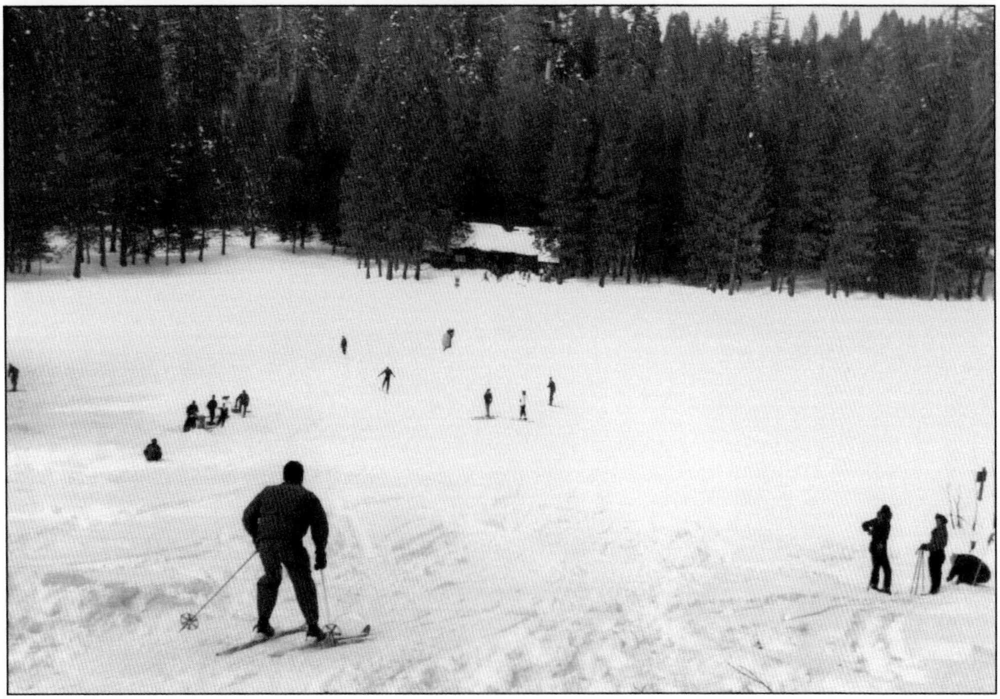

The hardy souls on the slope (above) were at the forefront of a sport gaining popularity in the United States. A sled pulled by dogs crosses below the ski run at Big Trees Park (below), one of the winter activities available in the 1930s and 1940s. (Both, CBTSP.)

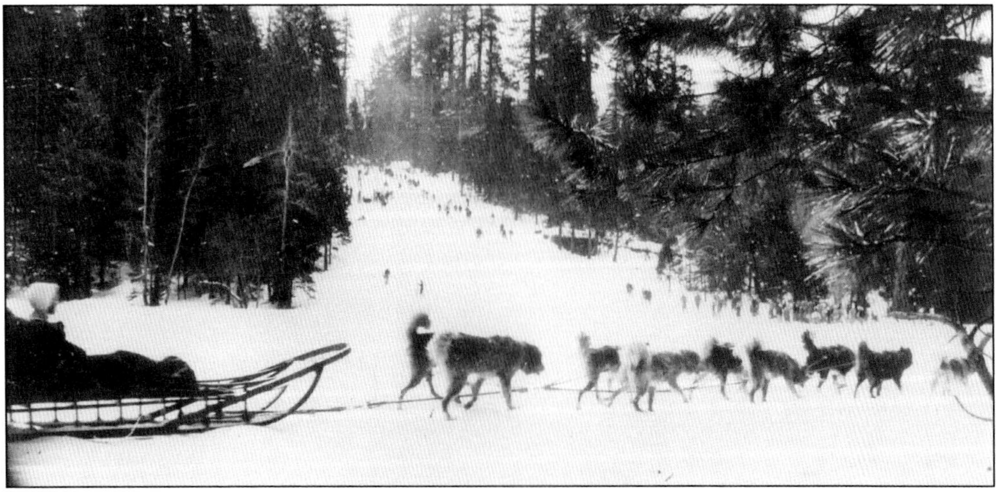

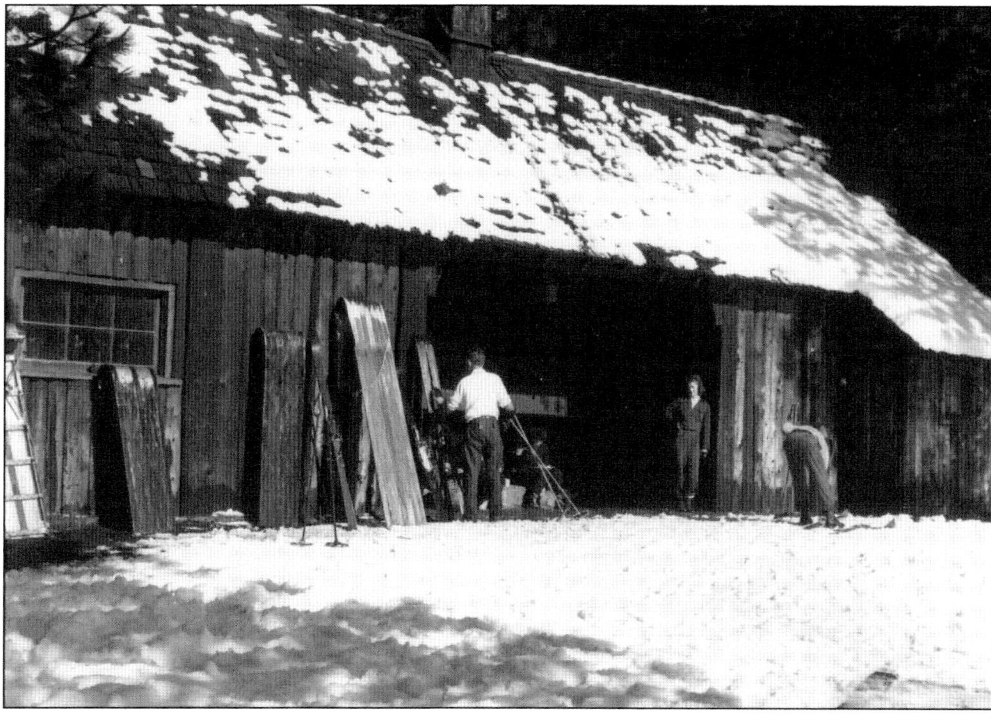

The warming hut provided a place to warm up between ski runs and relax with friends. The structure, pictured here in 1941, was open on one side (above) and featured a huge four-sided fire pit covered with an enormous hand-forged hood (below) with seating along the edge. Visitors enjoy the coffee, hot dogs, and beans that were included in the entrance fee. (Both, CBTSP.)

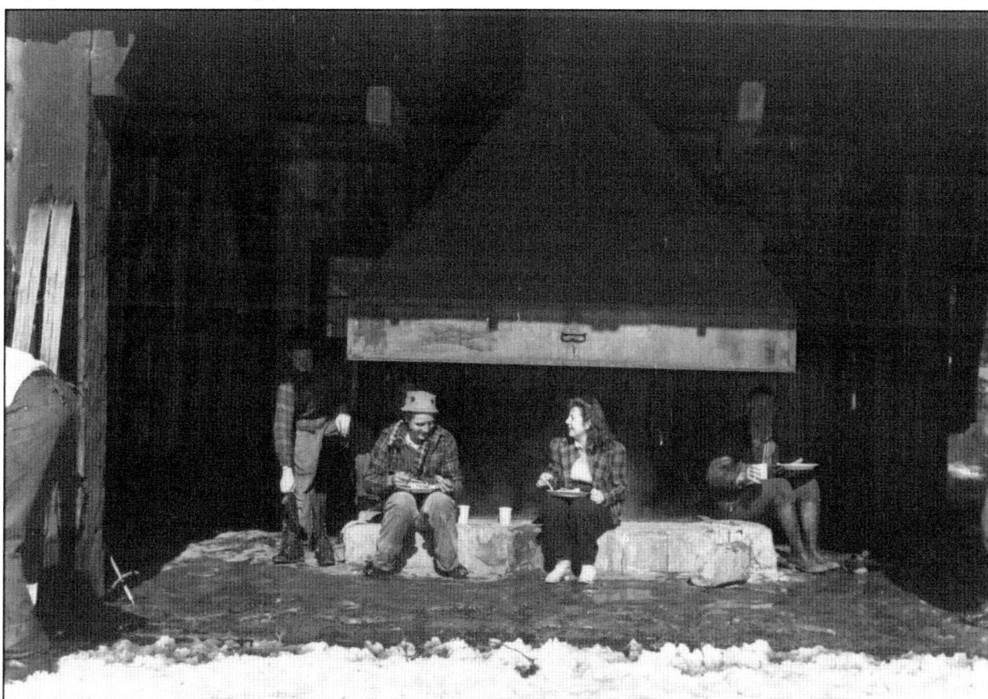

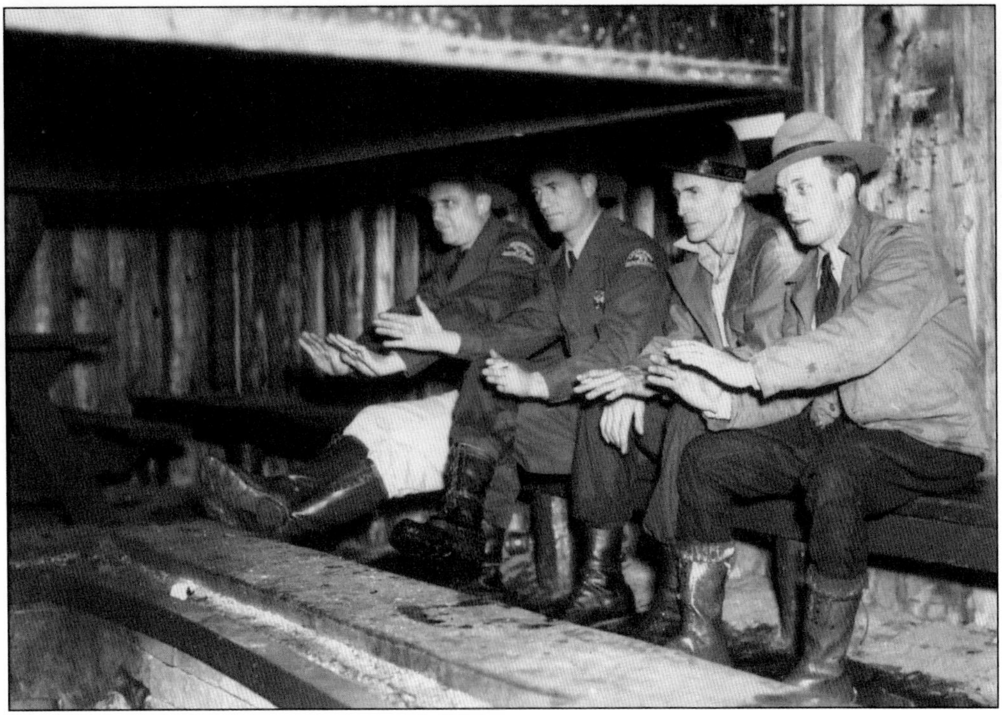

In 1948, park rangers take advantage of the benches that were added along the walls in the warming hut to sit for a moment and warm their hands and feet (above). Ranger George Lynn (below) monitors the towrope motor for the ski slope in 1949. (Both, CBTSP.)

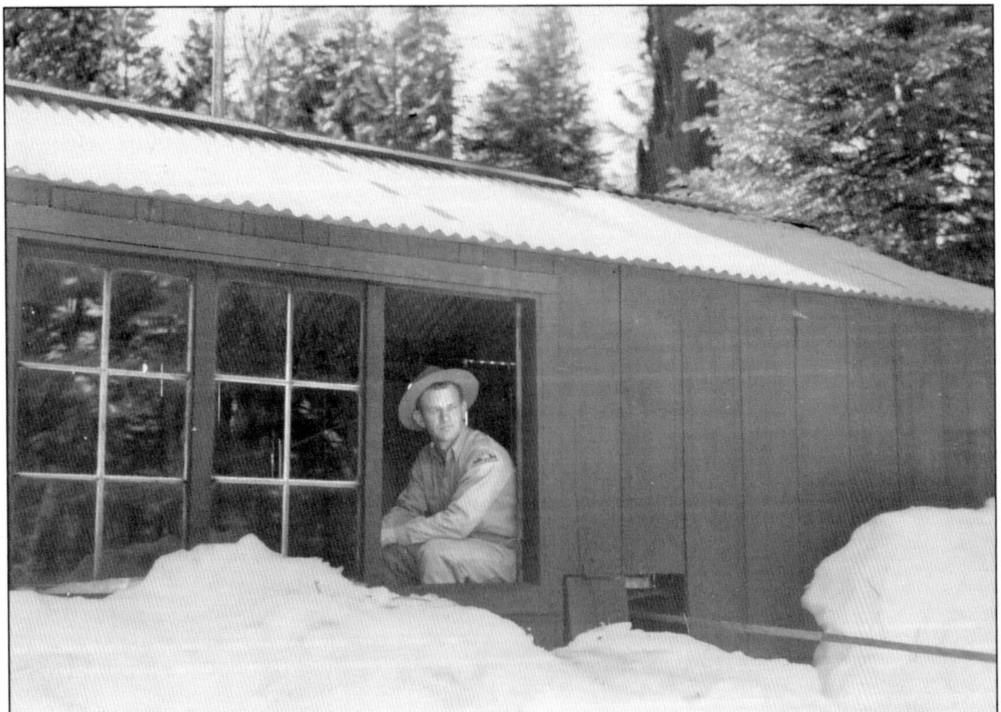

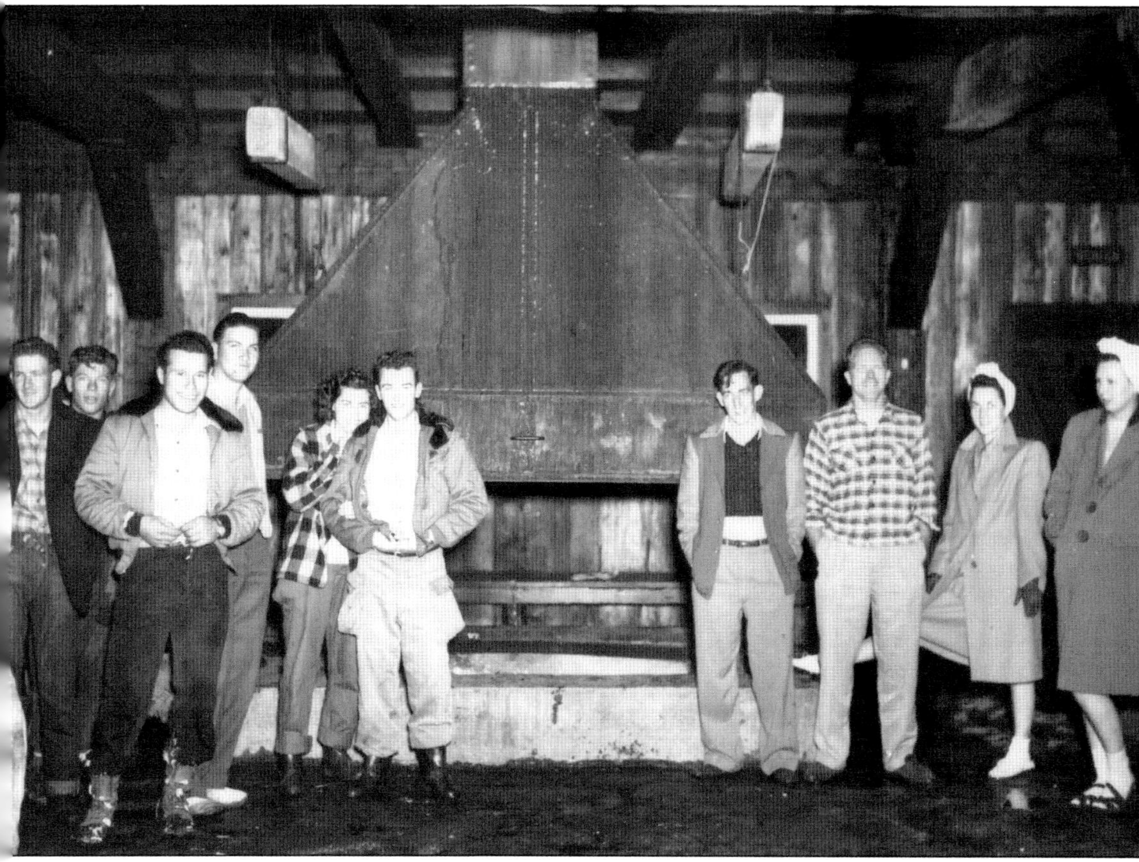

Teens and young adults gather in the warming hut in 1948. Based on their lightweight attire, particularly the barelegged women on the right, the weather must have been mild. (CBTSP.)

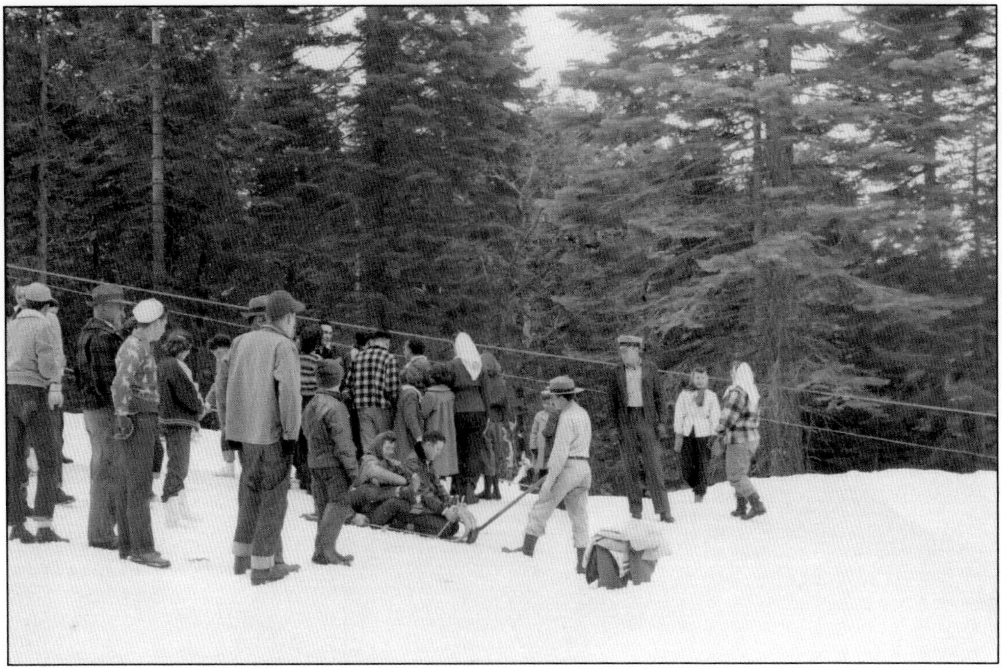

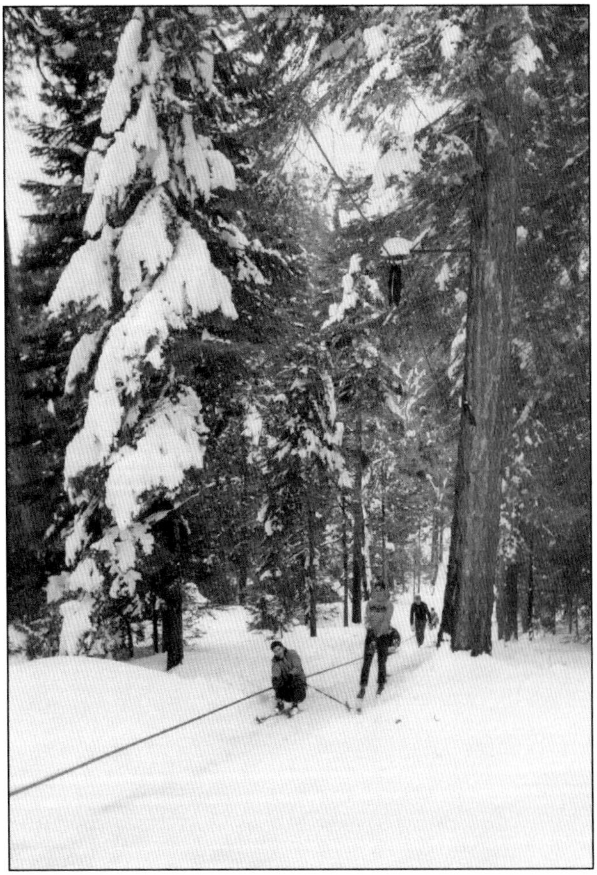

The towrope for the ski run passes behind people on the toboggan run in 1949. A ranger is assisting the couple on a toboggan, holding it in place with a shovel until they get situated for their downhill run (above). Skiers squat to grab the primitive rope tow (left) for their express ride to the top of the ski slope. (Both, CBTSP.)

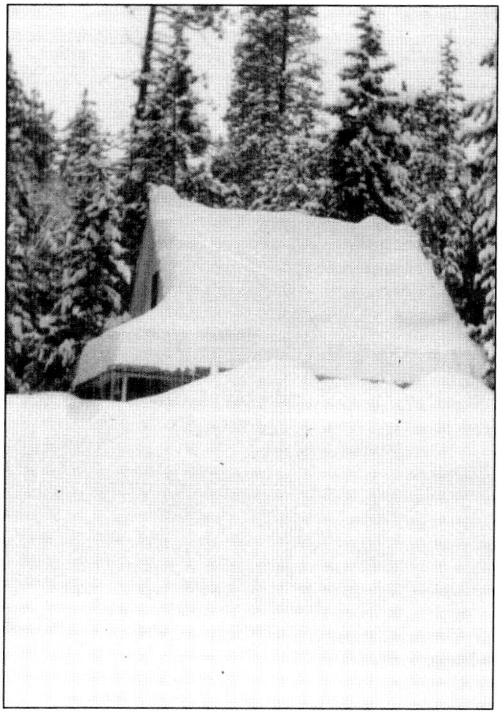

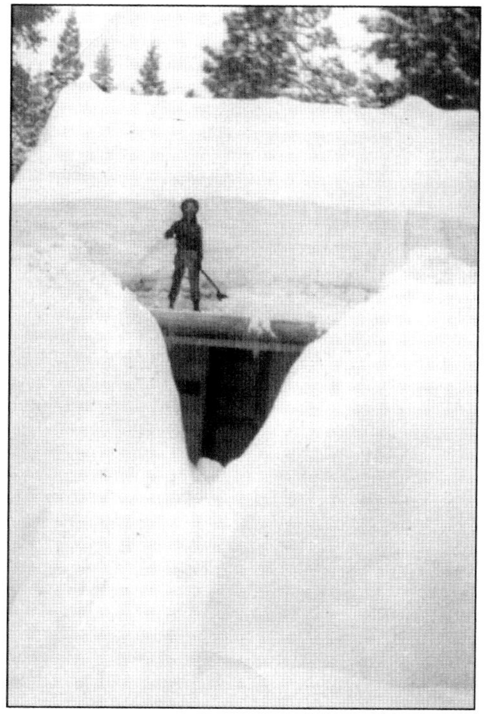

Snow nearly reaches the eaves of the White House after a 1948 snowstorm. The only way into the house was through the back door, and windows on the first floor were obscured by snow. By this time, the White House was a residence for park staff and their families. Above right, Ranger Gordon T. Kishbaugh shovels snow off the roof of the White House in 1949. A ranger at Tahoe's D. L. Bliss State Park in summer, Kishbaugh moved his family to Calaveras Big Trees, where he worked during the winter months. (Both, CBTSP.)

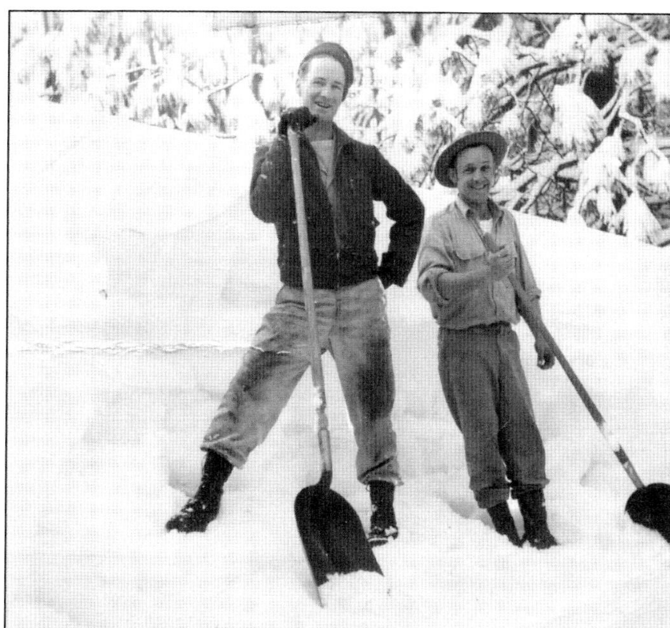

Rangers shovel snow from the roof of Big Trees Hall in 1949 to prevent its collapse. Heavy snowfall had taken a toll over the years, collapsing the pavilion on the stump and the one-story lobby of the hotel. (CBTSP.)

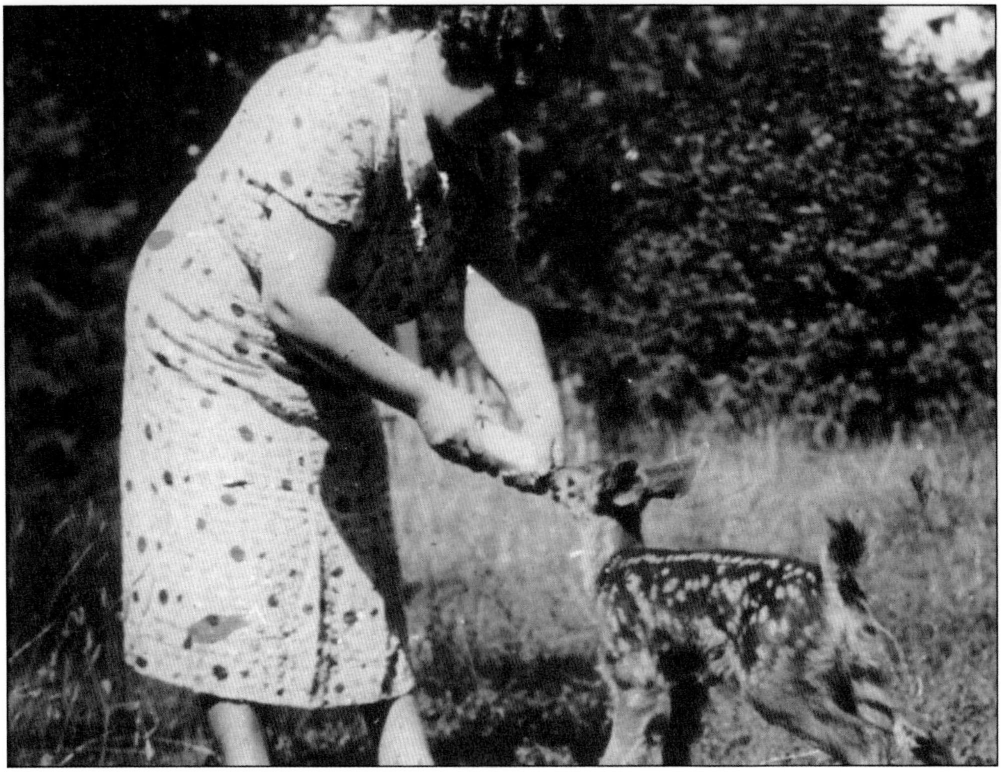

Contrary to today's long-standing state park policy prohibiting the feeding of wildlife, beginning in the 1930s a series of fawns became pets at Calaveras Big Trees State Park. Most had likely been orphaned by a hunter's shot. One, named G. I., was in residence during Carey Traylor's time. The fawn being bottle fed in the undated photograph above may be Nancy. The woman may be Waneta Gianelli, who with her husband, B. R., took over the hotel lease in 1932. She hand-raised Nancy, who lived in the hotel along with Ladybelle, the Gianelli's German shepherd (below). Nancy, who lived to be six years old, often could be seen curled up beside Waneta on the hotel's porch swing. (Both, CBTSP.)

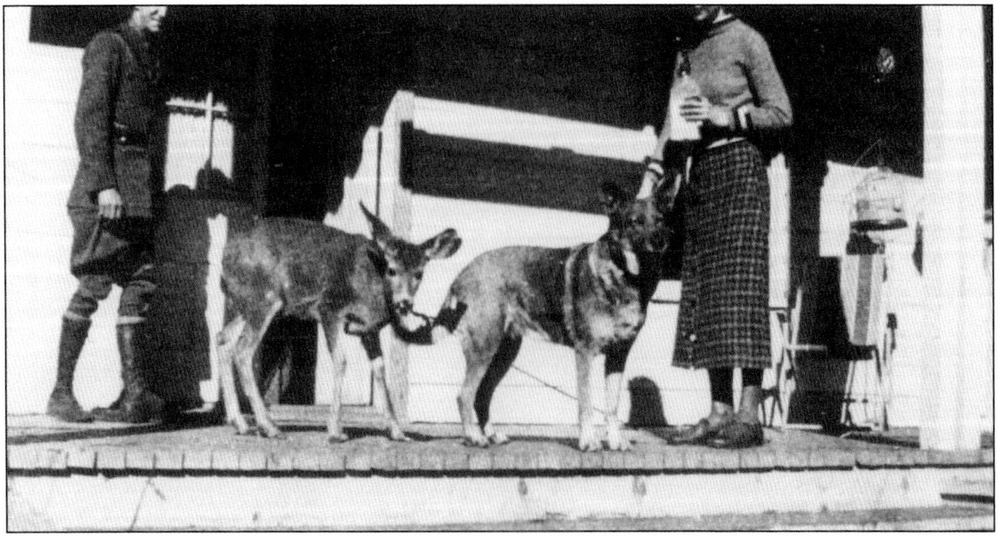

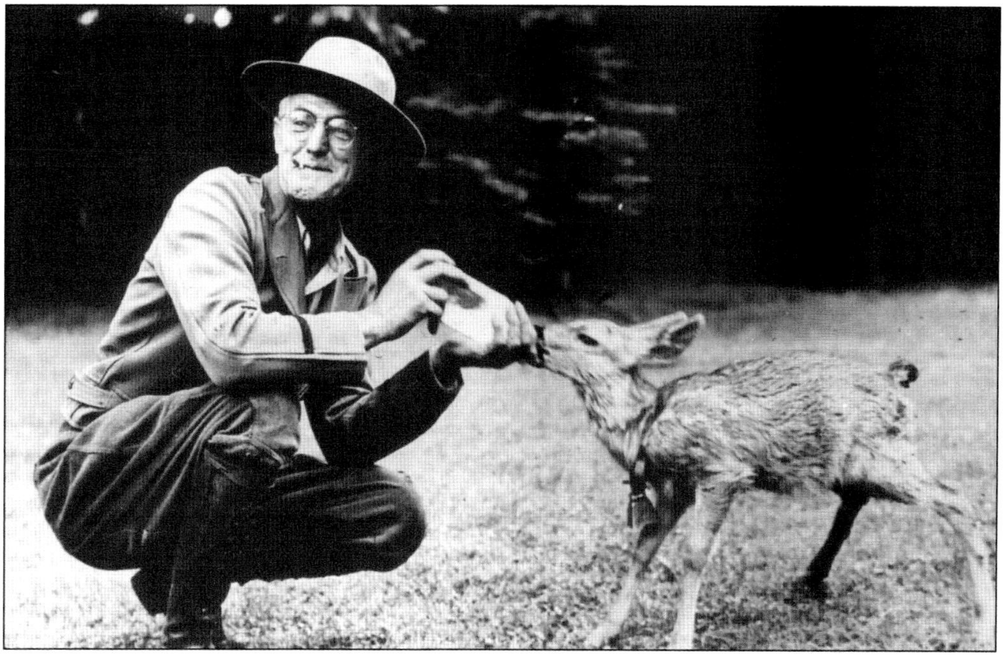

Mickey, an orphaned fawn, is bottle fed by park warden Albert A. Beck in 1943. Beck was assigned to Calaveras Big Trees for about five years before being promoted to a post at Columbia State Historic Park. Then as today, rangers were responsible for overseeing all aspects of the state park, including its wildlife. (CBTSP.)

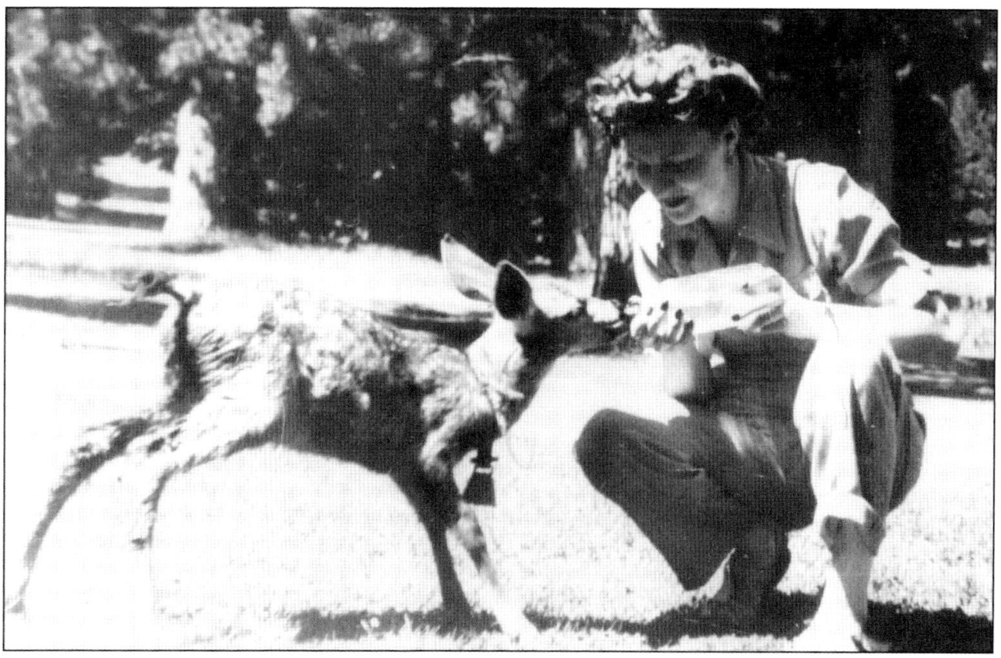

Ranger Beck's wife, Marion, takes a turn bottle-feeding Mickey in the 1940s. The park also boasted a pet bear in this era. The cub, which was small enough to fit in an orange crate, was raised by hand and kept on a 200-foot chain until about a year old. By then, he was tame enough to freely roam the park. Unfortunately, he was killed by a hunter. (CBTSP.)

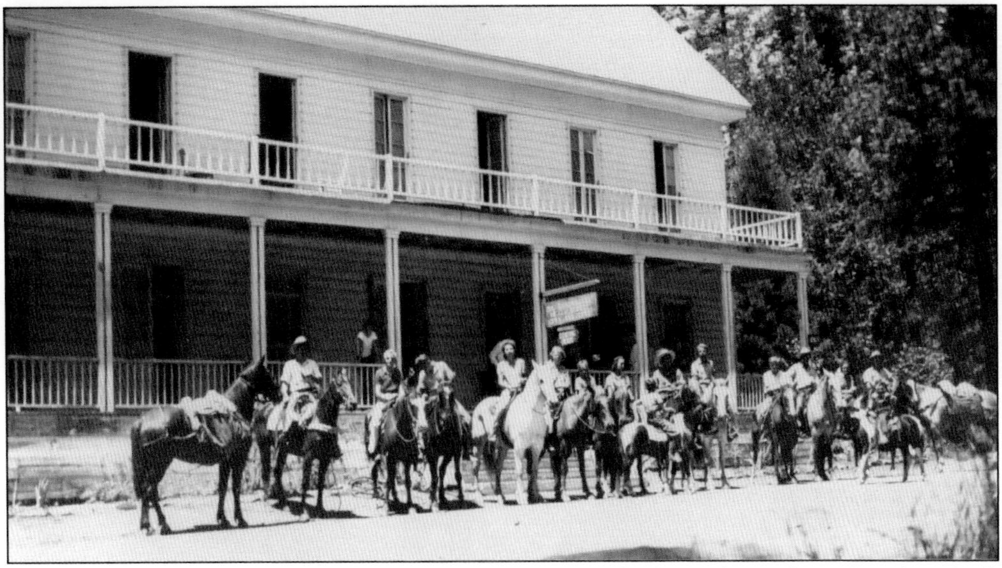

A group of riders in front of the hotel prepares to leave for a trail ride. Exploring the park on horseback was a popular summer activity and had been since the early days of discovery. (CBTSP.)

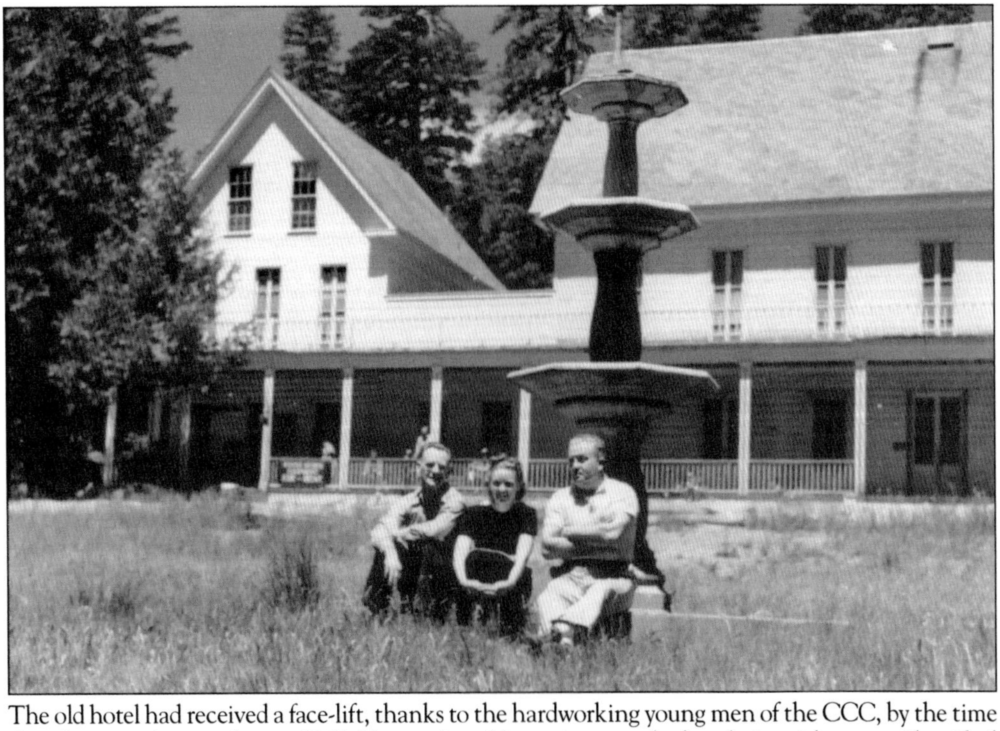

The old hotel had received a face-lift, thanks to the hardworking young men of the CCC, by the time this photograph was taken in 1940. Naomi Arnold, a waitress at the hotel, sits with two unidentified men by the old fountain installed by James Sperry during the hotel's heyday. (CBTSP.)

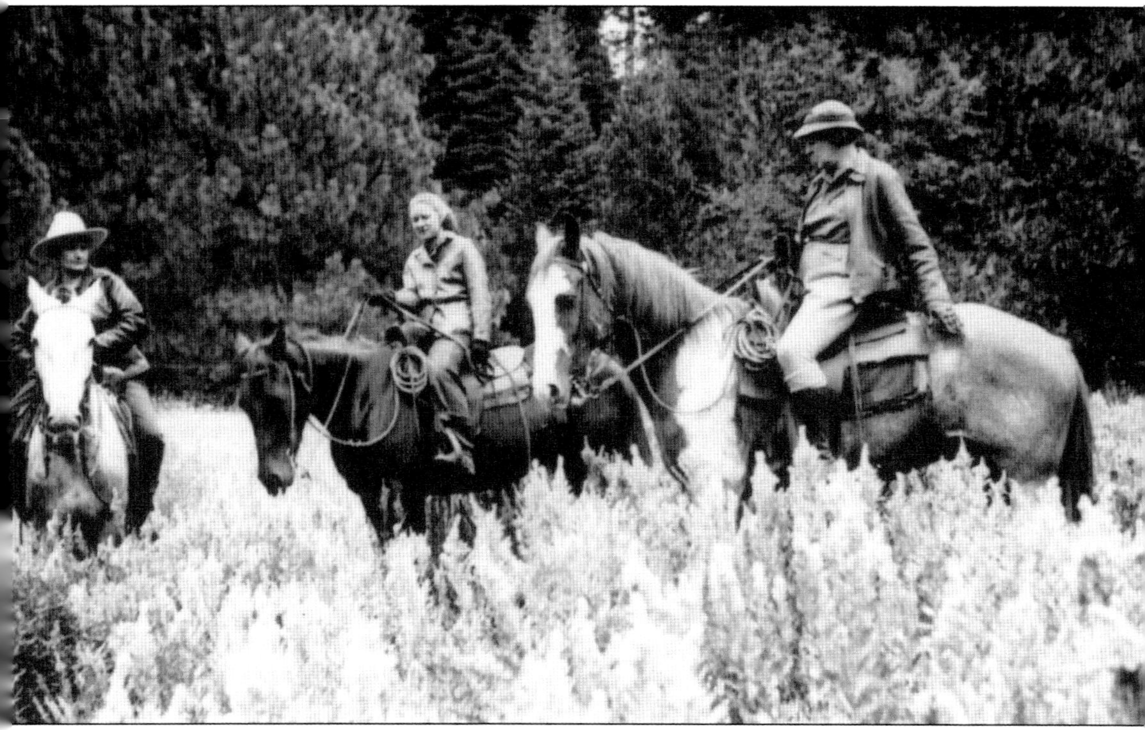

Milton and Elizabeth McGinnis, with their two children, took over the hotel lease and operated it from 1938 to 1941. Elizabeth McGinnis (right) explores the South Grove with Naomi Arnold (center) and an unidentified rider in 1940. Although the South Grove was not yet part of the state park, people would explore it by foot or on horseback. (CBTSP.)

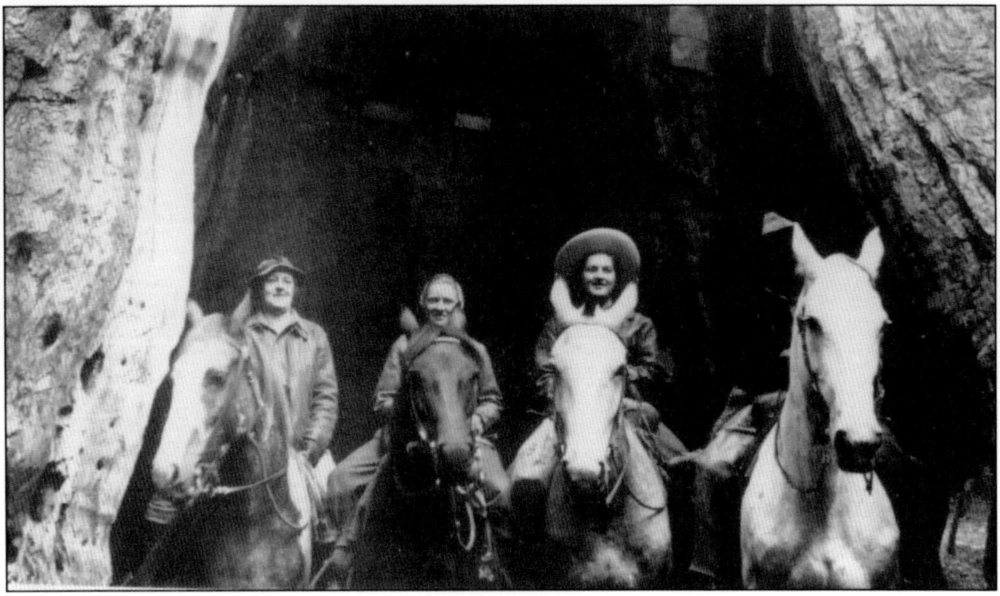

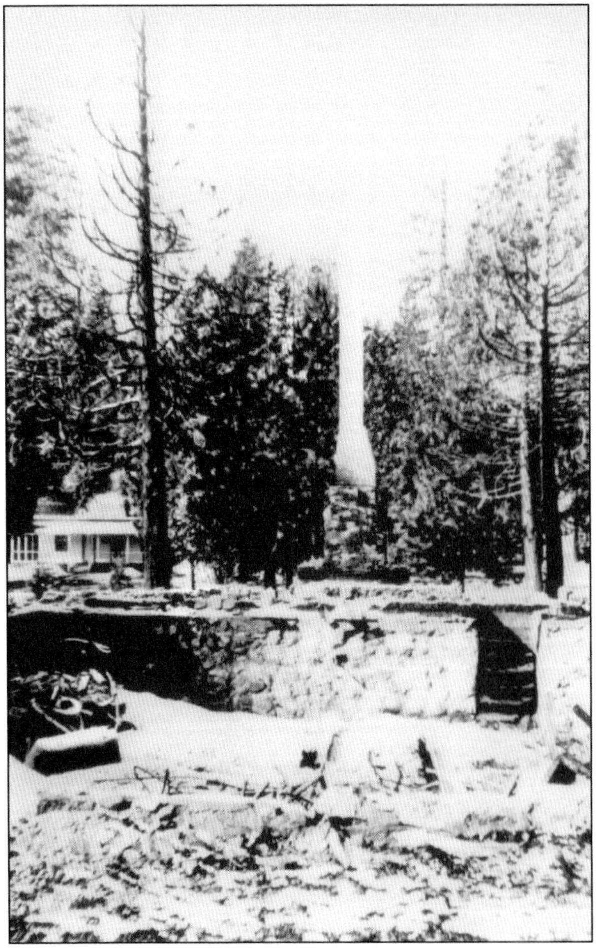

Elizabeth McGinnis (left), Naomi Arnold (center), and an unidentified rider pose on horseback inside the Palace Hotel Tree in the South Grove. In early 1941, partners Alvin Pecchenino and Ernest "Barney" Bernasconi took over the hotel lease. Pecchinino joined the military after World War II was declared and sold out to his partner. Bernasconi was the hotel's last lessee. (CBTSP.)

At 1:00 a.m. on August 19, 1943, a fire of unknown origin broke out in the historic hotel. Despite the heroic firefighting efforts of Warden Beck, 25 California Youth Authority camp boys, and a crew from Avery station, the 82-year-old hotel and barn burned to the ground within an hour, ending an era. The men also battled 25 spot fires ignited by shakes exploding off the hotel's roof. (CBTSP.)

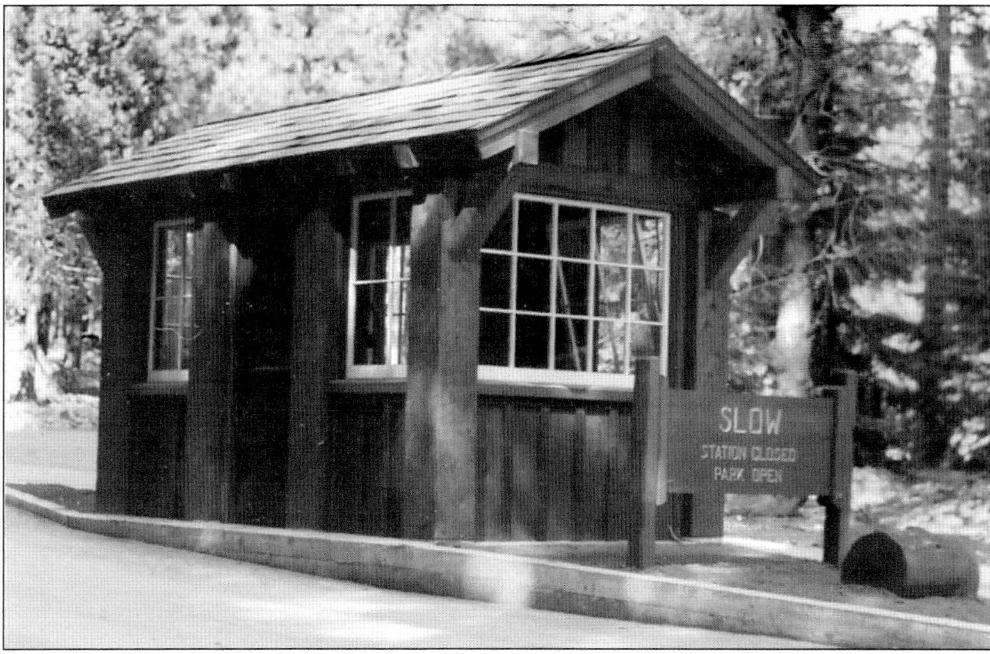

By the time this new entrance station to the North Grove was opened in 1949, interest had picked up again in acquiring the South Grove. Pickering Lumber had offered to sell to the state after it declared bankruptcy during the Depression, but state funds were in short supply, and with the start of the war, state priorities lay elsewhere. (CBTSP.)

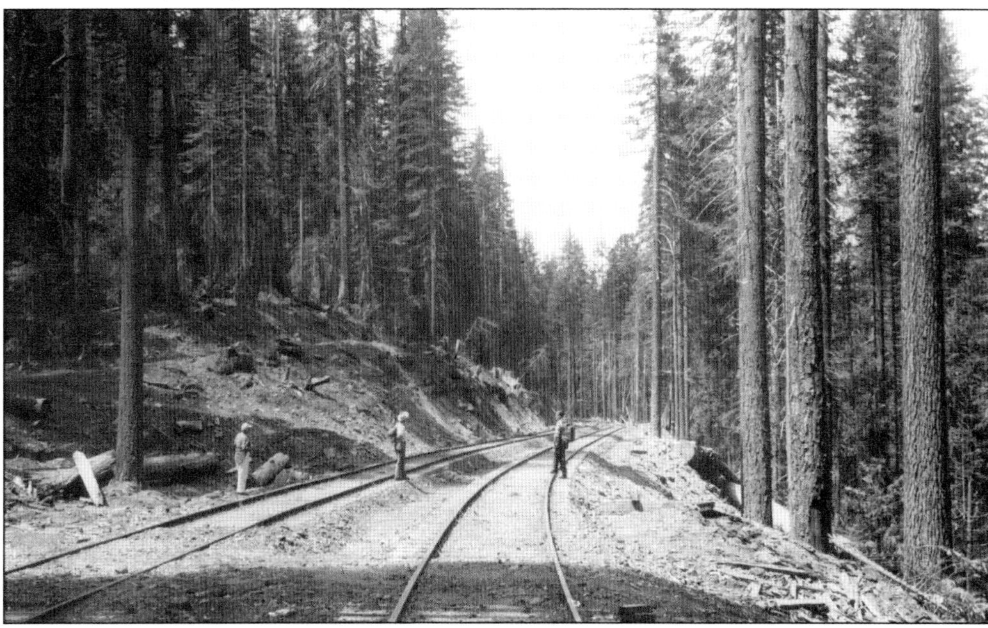

By 1945, Pickering had revived lumbering activities near the South Grove. It completed a rail line into the pristine wilderness, shown here in 1951. It stopped short of the South Grove only because of the persuasive efforts of Frederick Law Olmstead Jr. He negotiated with Pickering on behalf of the State Park Commission, which was again acquiring land for state parks. In the meantime, logging was creating a wasteland along Beaver Creek. (CBTSP.)

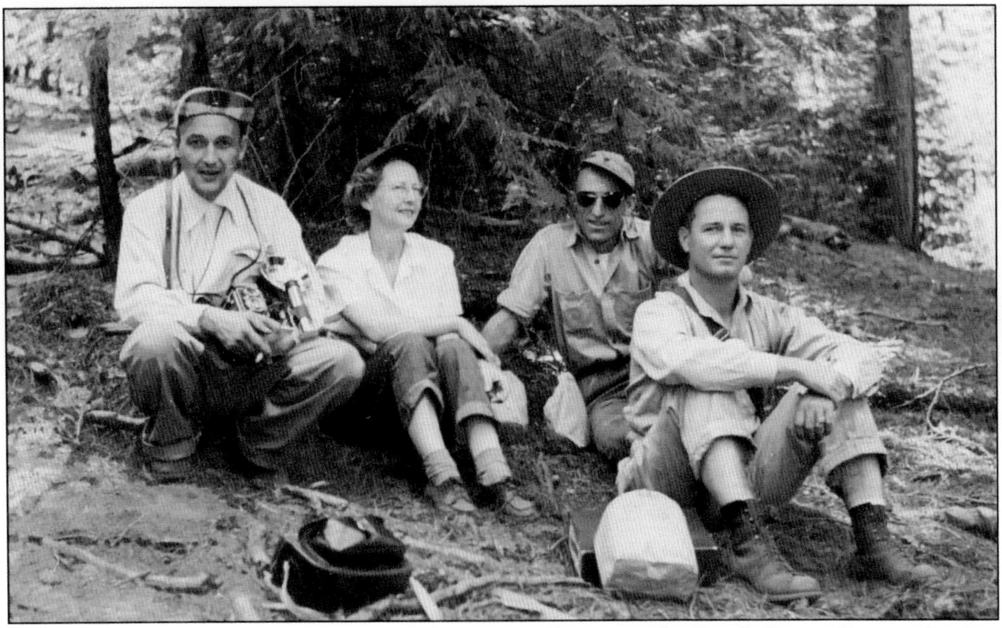

Despite imminent threat of logging, people continued to enjoy the South Grove. Ranger Gordon Kishbaugh (right), with companions John Reese (left) and Imogene and Bud Campbell, takes a break there in 1950. Among the explorers were Adrienne and Owen Bradley of Modesto. After visiting the majestic South Grove in 1947, they launched a homegrown preservation campaign that began with single-handedly reviving the Calaveras Grove Association. (CBTSP.)

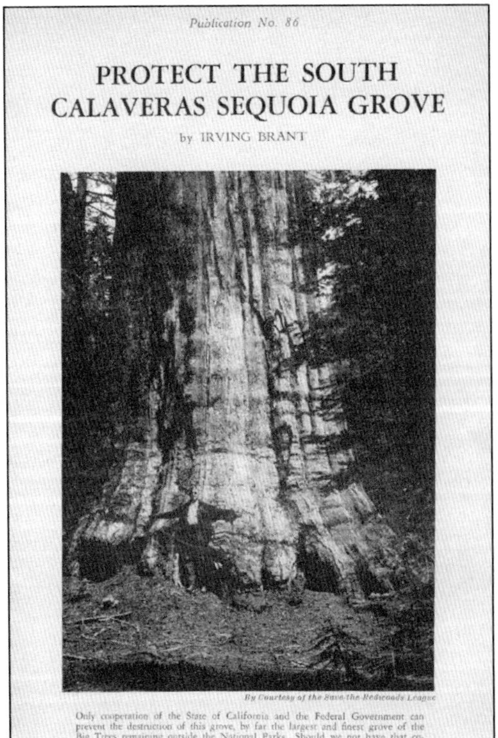

Publication No. 86

PROTECT THE SOUTH CALAVERAS SEQUOIA GROVE

by IRVING BRANT

By Courtesy of the Save-the-Redwoods League

Only cooperation of the State of California and the Federal Government can prevent the destruction of this grove, by far the largest and finest grove of the Big Trees remaining outside the National Parks. Should we not have that co-operation?

In July 1948, Stockton businessman Stuart Gibbons became association president. As executive secretary, Adrienne Bradley traveled the state talking up preservation supported by slides of the grove's beauty. Brochures such as this and a new 28-minute color film assisted with fund-raising. Hundreds of people joined the association and many more donated, but meeting the matching fund requirement of the state proved daunting. The fund grew, but all too slowly. (CBTSP.)

Former National Park Service director Newton Drury wrote in 1952 that saving the South Grove is "the most important piece of unfinished nature protection business in America." Ultimately it was made possible by a $1 million donation from John D. Rockefeller Jr. through the Save the Redwoods League. In April 1954, one of the longest park acquisition campaigns in history ended when Pickering Lumber agreed to sell 2,155 acres, including the South Grove, to the state of California for $2.8 million. In 1959, workers construct a federally funded bridge to the South Grove (right). State senator Stephen Teale (fifth from left) and other dignitaries dedicate the new bridge (below) in November 1959. (Both, CBTSP.)

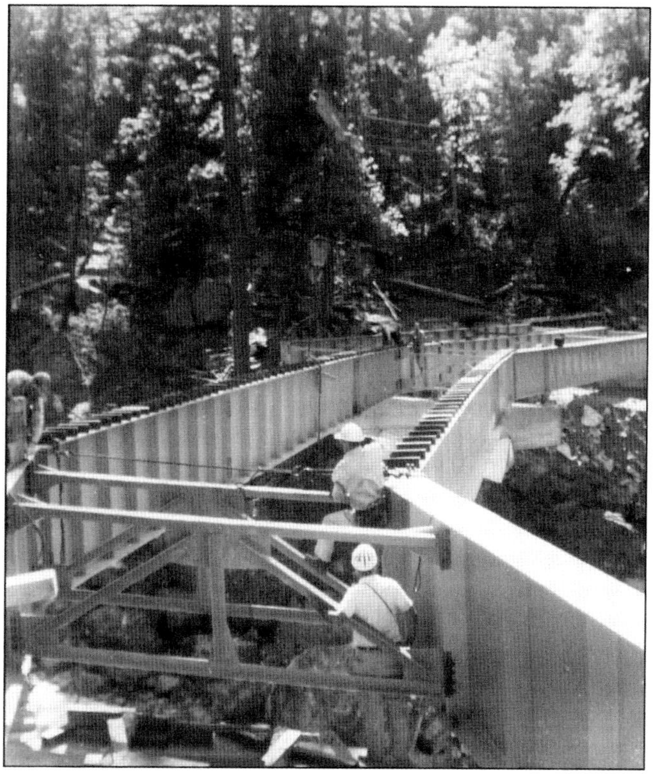

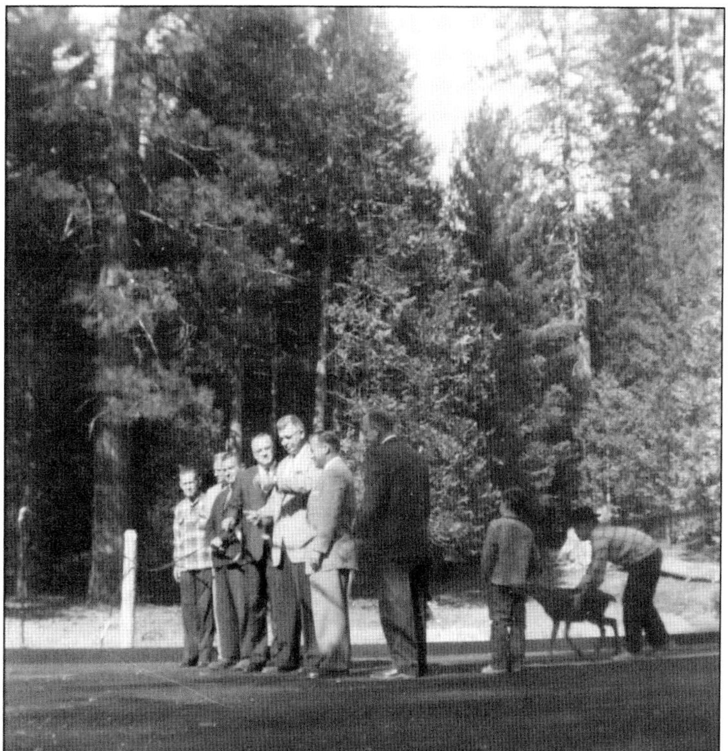

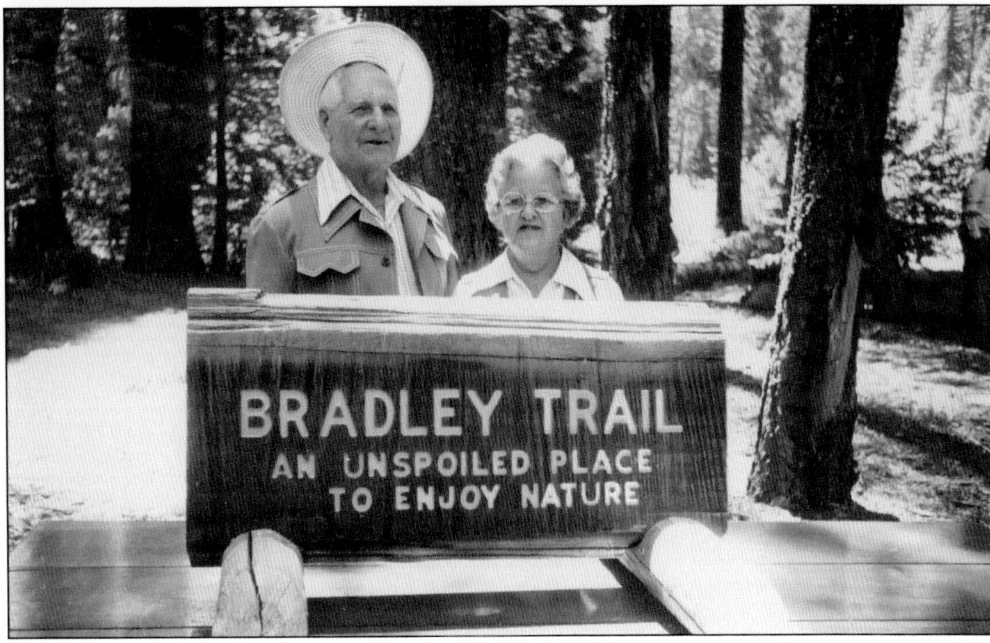

Owen and Adrienne Bradley were vital to the successful acquisition and preservation of the South Grove. As executive secretary of the Calaveras Grove Association, Adrienne helped raise $73,000 for the grove's purchase. Owen planted giant sequoia seedlings along Beaver Creek as a state park employee in the mid-1950s. In the undated photograph above, the Bradleys pose with the marker for the Bradley Trail, named in their honor. The South Grove (below) was formally dedicated on September 9, 1967, finally completing the preservation of the historic groves of giant sequoias. More than 115 years after their discovery, the North and South Groves were at last united in Calaveras Big Trees State Park, protecting the sacred trees for generations to come. (Both, CBTSP.)

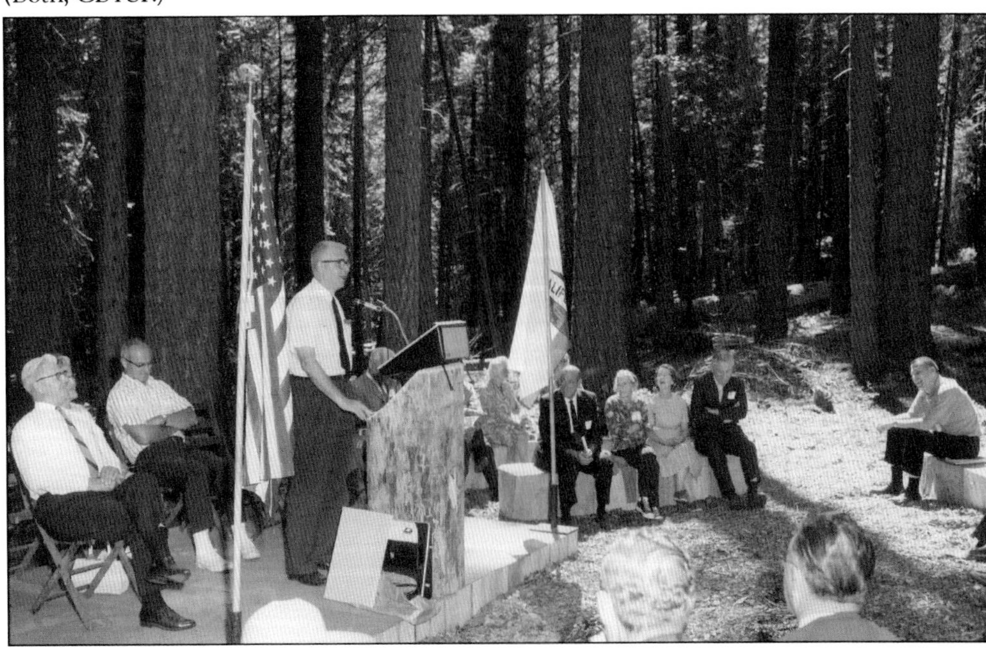

Six

Big Trees State Park Today

Of course, the story of Calaveras Big Trees State Park does not end with the acquisition of the South Grove. It was another two years after the South Grove's formal dedication before a roadway was completed from the Stanislaus River to the South Grove trailhead. Visitors could at last more easily explore one of the most pristine forest areas in the state. The lack of human influence is the South Grove's most outstanding feature. Frederick Law Olmstead Jr., when surveying for new parklands in the 1940s, described it as "one of the most important and beautiful examples of the great primeval forest of California yet remaining unspoiled." And it remains so today. In 1984, the state designated the South Grove as a natural preserve, the highest level of protection within California State Parks.

An interesting side note to the South Grove was the creation of Calaveras Big Tree National Forest on May 11, 1954. It was set aside to protect 390 acres of exceptionally large, old growth sugar pine. Authorized by the 1909 legislation drafted during initial grove preservation efforts, it was the smallest unit in the National Forest System before it was combined administratively with the Stanislaus National Forest, within which it sat. In the mid-1990s, the 390 acres was conveyed to and made part of Calaveras Big Trees State Park.

As part of the California State Parks, and with the aid of numerous volunteers and supporters (such as the Calaveras Big Trees Association), the park offers a wide range of activities within a unique setting of giant sequoia and conifer trees. There are activities for everyone, including miles of established hiking trails, two campgrounds with 129 campsites, six picnic areas, bird watching, cross-country skiing, snowshoeing, evening ranger talks, Junior Ranger programs, and numerous interpretive and educational programs. Thanks to the preservationists, a quarter of a million people from all over the world are able to visit the North and South Groves of Calaveras Big Trees State Park every year. Like generations of visitors before them, they walk among these forest giants, marveling at nature's wonder.

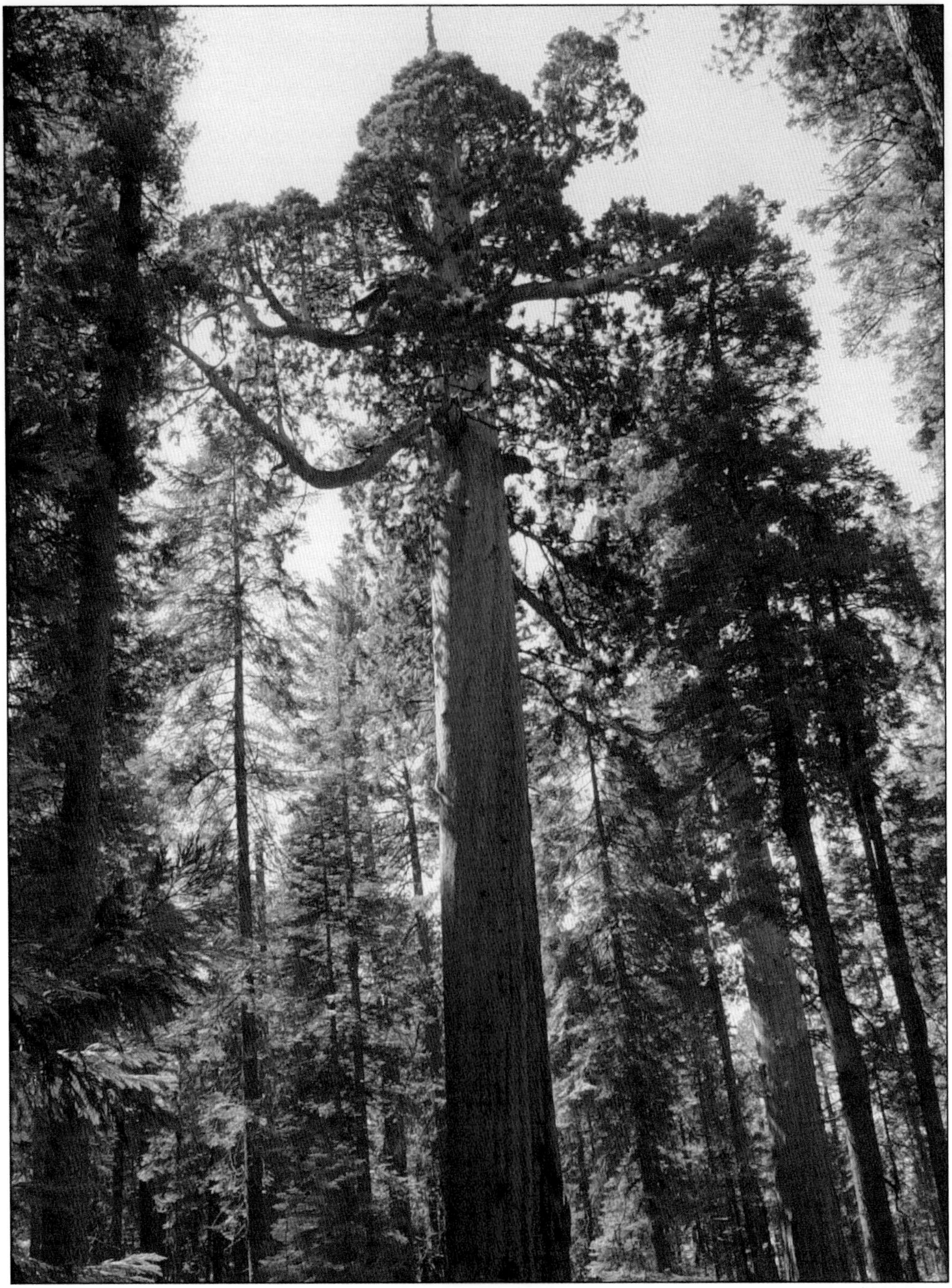

"No description can give any adequate idea of the singular majesty, much less of their beauty," John Muir said of the giant sequoia, such as this beauty in the North Grove of Calaveras Big Trees State Park. (Photograph by Carol Kramer.)

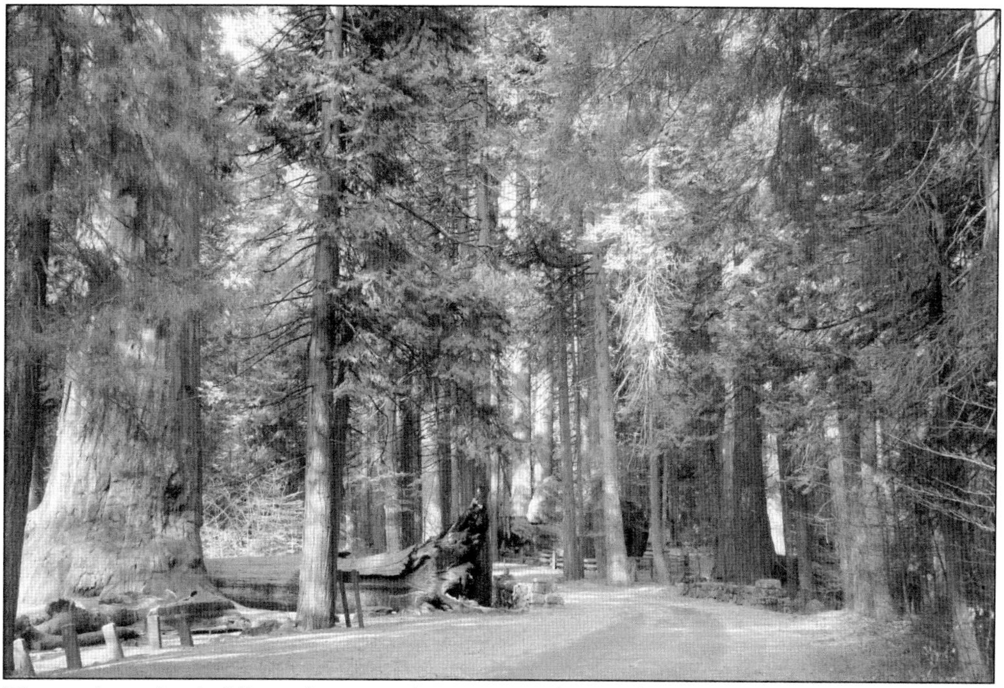

This roadway closely follows the original entrance to the North Grove of giant sequoia. The road passed between the still standing Sentinel Tree (left) and the one that is fallen at its base. The stone bridge over the creek was built by CCC crews in the 1930s. (Photograph by Carol Kramer.)

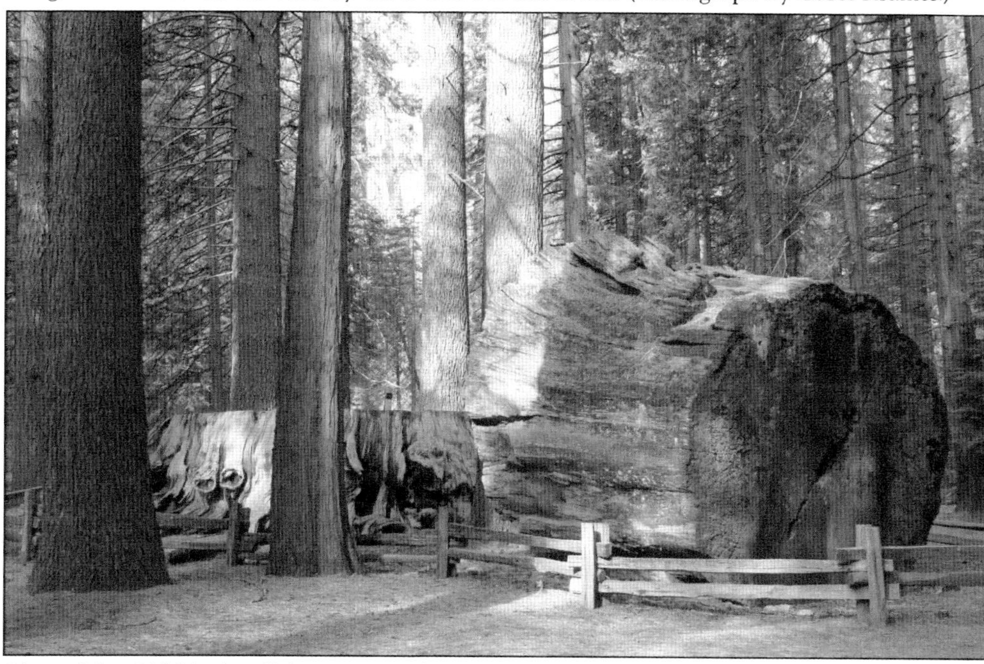

Chip of the Old Block still lies next to the Discovery Stump, just as it has since 1853 when the tree was cut down by men greedy to exploit the trees for their own financial gain. Today pine trees are growing in close proximity to the Discovery Stump and Chip, including one large sugar pine growing between them. (Photograph by Carol Kramer.)

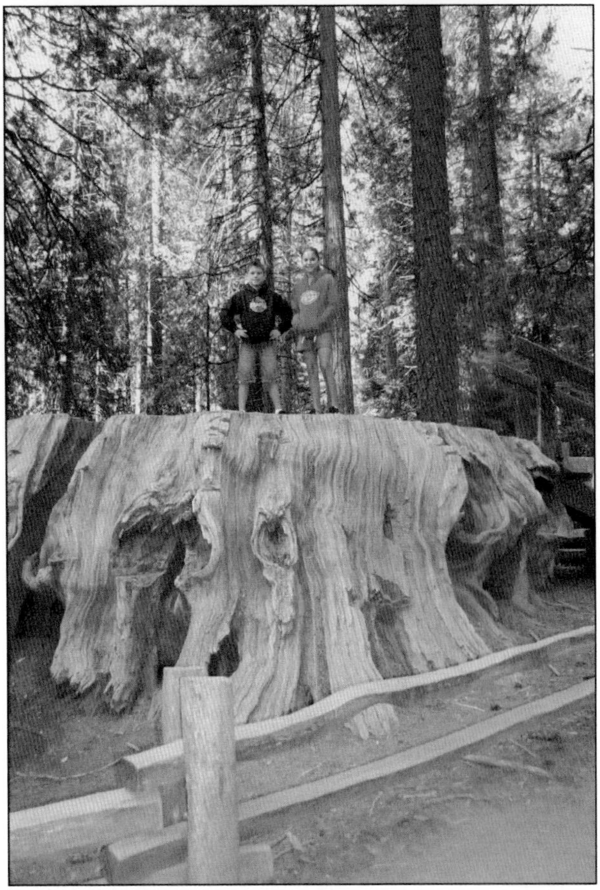

Stairs enable visitors to climb to the Discovery Stump, where park docents share the history of the tree and its fate. Two young visitors, Tanner and Tanya Gallagher, provide a perspective on the stump's size. (Photograph by Dawn Gallagher.)

Nearly 160 years after it was felled by a crew of five men using pump augers, the drill marks from the augers are still visible on Chip, a testament to the slow decay of giant sequoias. The stump itself has become whitened from weathering, and Chip has grown smaller as it has settled into the soft forest floor. (Photograph by Carol Kramer.)

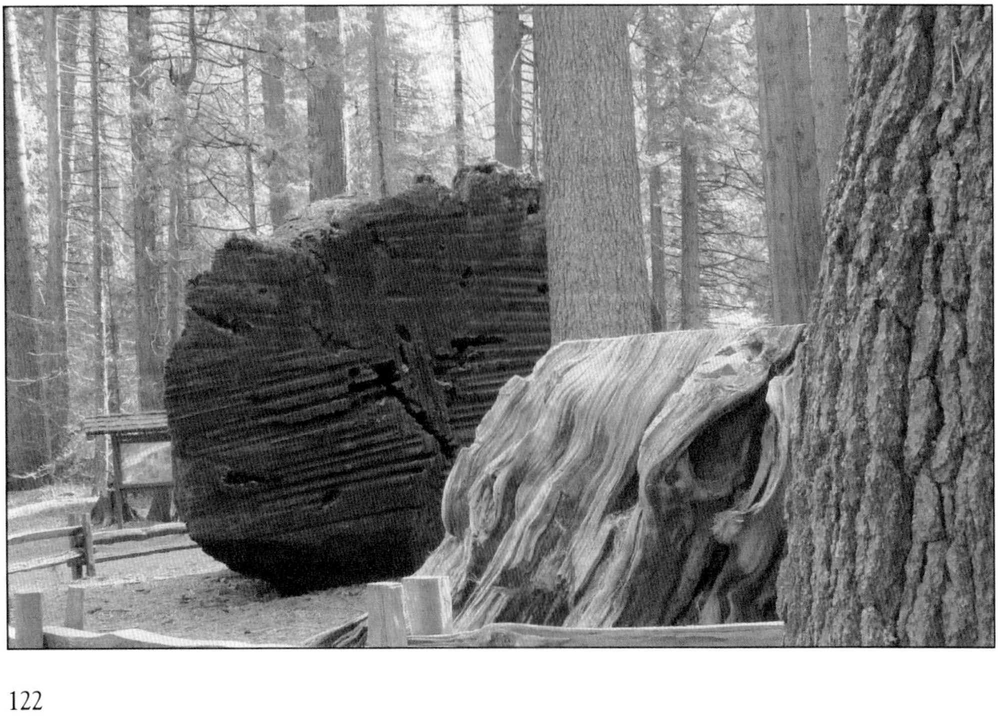

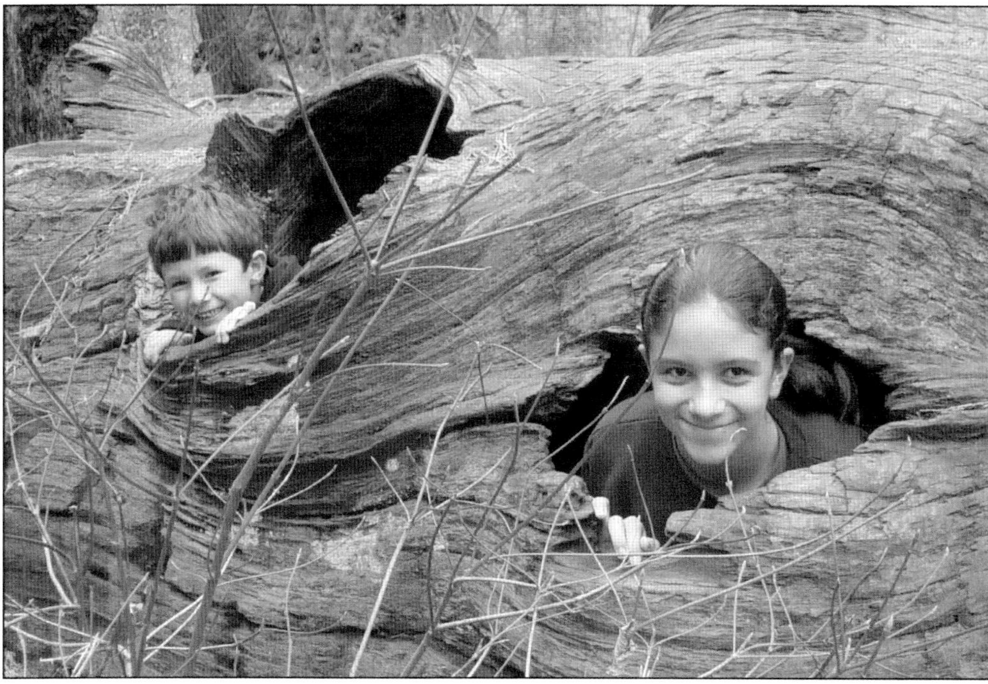

Visitors to Calaveras Big Trees State Park still delight in poking their heads out of the knotholes in fallen giant sequoia. Here Christopher Kramer and Irene Diaz strike a pose similar to those of visitors from the early 1900s. (Photograph by Carol Kramer.)

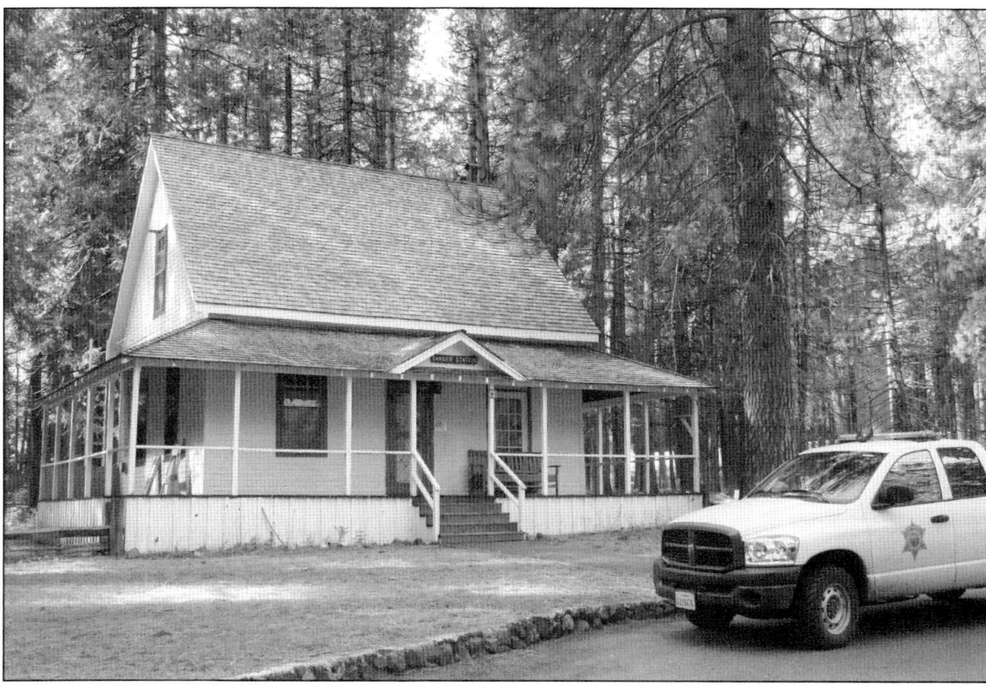

This cottage was originally built in 1865 for John and Eliza Perry. Over the years it has served as camp headquarters for the CCC and as housing for park rangers and their families. Today it is the ranger station, and everyone calls it the White House. (Photograph by Carol Kramer.)

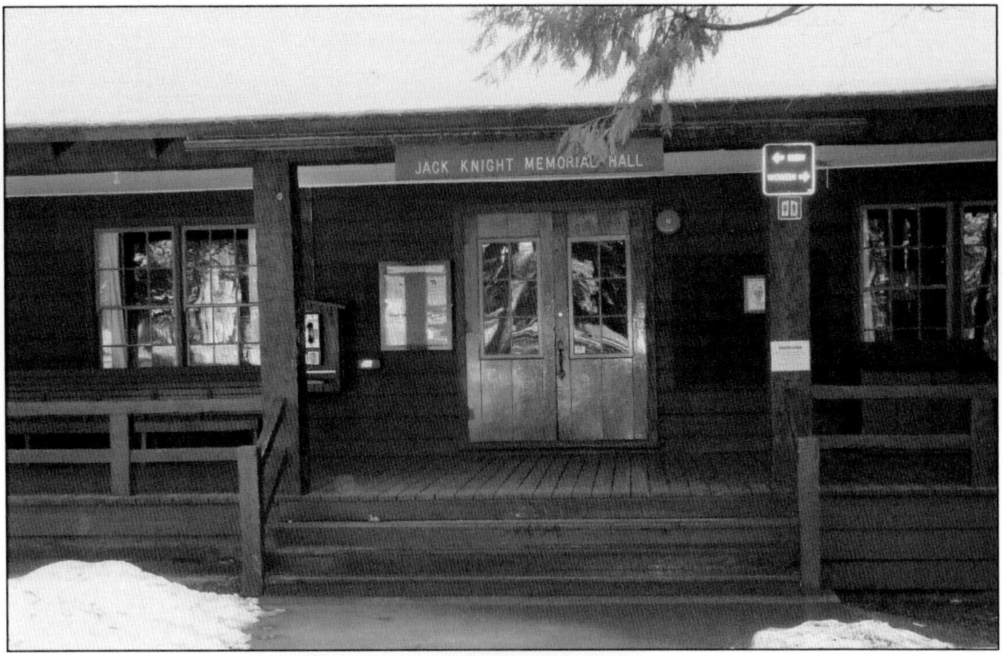

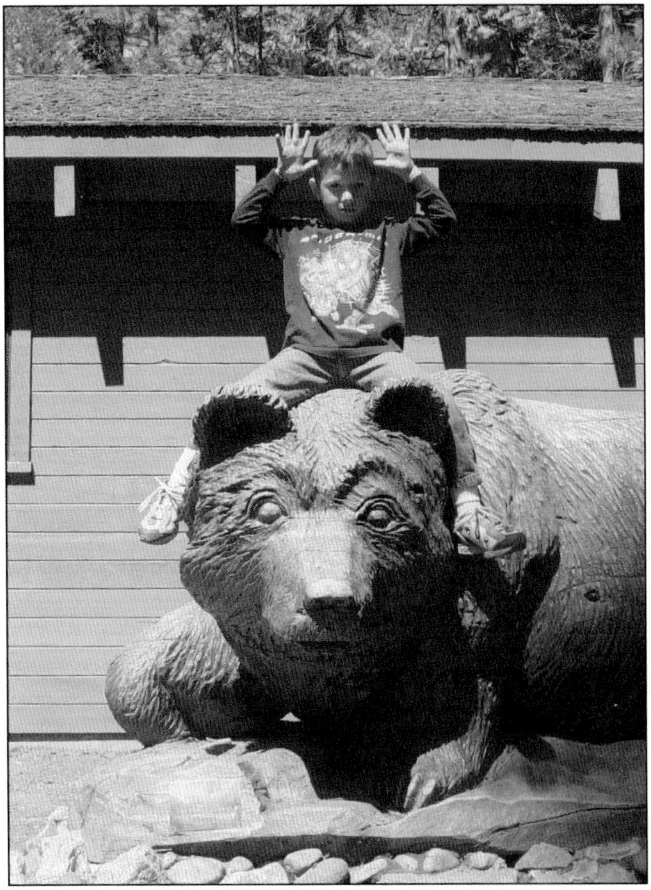

The CCC built the Big Trees Recreation Hall in 1937. The name was changed to Jack Knight Hall to honor John H. "Jack" Knight, a park ranger at Big Trees in the 1940s. Knight began as a seasonal employee in 1937 and spent 40 years with the park service. He retired in 1980 as associate director of operations for the park system. (Photograph by Carol Kramer.)

This carved bear graces the entrance to the Calaveras Big Trees State Park Visitor Center, which is funded by the Calaveras Big Trees Association and operated by the park. (Photograph by Carol Kramer.)

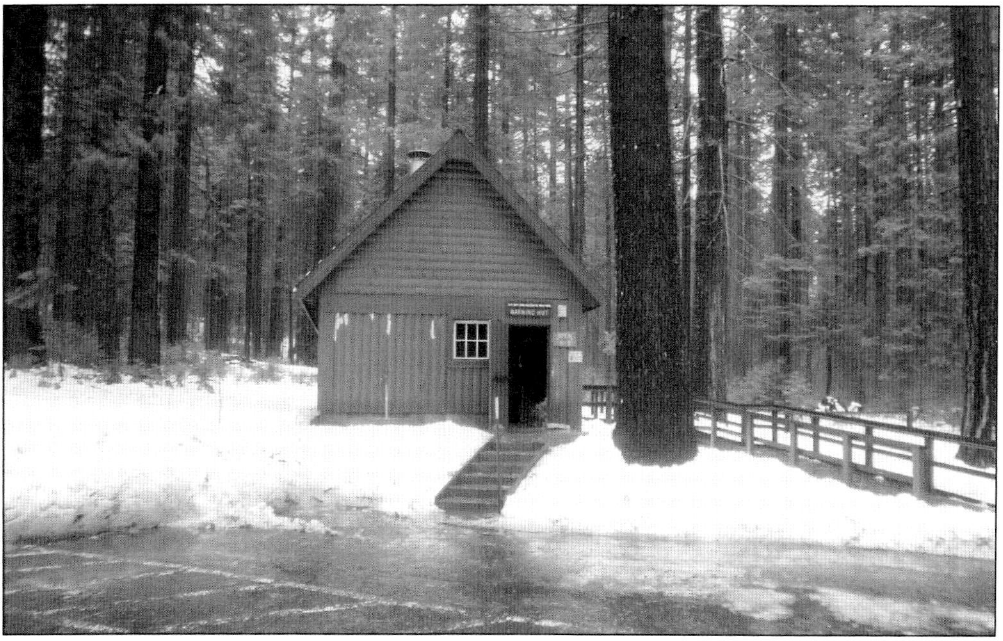

The original warming hut at Big Trees was removed in 1977 in order to restore the natural environment. In 2002, the park used state bond funds to construct a new warming hut adjacent to the visitor parking lot. It generally follows the original's floor plan and includes a similar hand-forged hood over the fire pit. (Photograph by Cathy Fitzpatrick.)

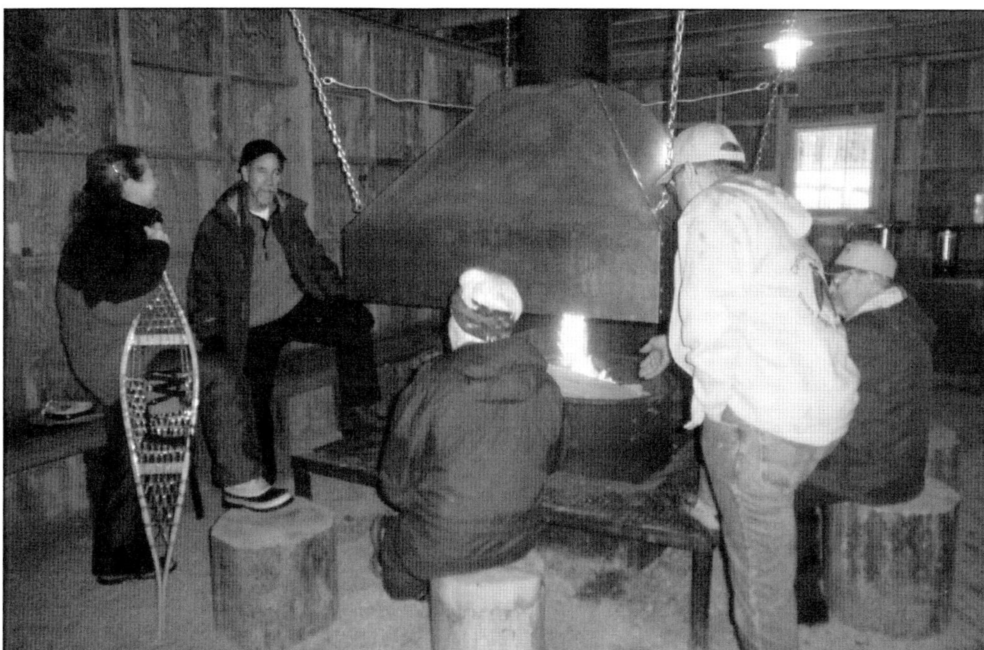

Most Saturdays during snow season, state volunteers (also called docents) staff the hut and lead snowshoe hikes through the North Grove. The snowshoes and refreshments are funded by the Calaveras Big Trees Association as part of its support of interpretive programs at the park. (Photograph by Cathy Fitzpatrick.)

About Calaveras Big Trees Association

In 1974, a group of individuals created a new nonprofit association, Calaveras Big Trees Association (CBTA). Building on the legacy of the historical Calaveras Grove Association formed in 1926, CBTA has a different purpose—supporting the delivery of high quality educational and interpretive programs at Calaveras Big Trees State Park. Membership is open to individuals, families, and businesses. The board members are all volunteers.

CBTA's vision is that each and every visitor experience inspires awe and appreciation for the natural, cultural, and recreational resources at Calaveras Big Trees State Park. CBTA uses membership fees, donations, and fund-raising to accomplish this mission.

CBTA funds programs including Junior Ranger Cubs, school tours, the warming hut and snowshoe walks, seminars, campfire programs, summer interns, scholarships, interpretive staff and printed materials, park publications, trail maps, book store operation and maintenance, and the Visitor Center Library. The association also sponsors special projects and the annual Family Day, which attracts thousands of visitors every August.

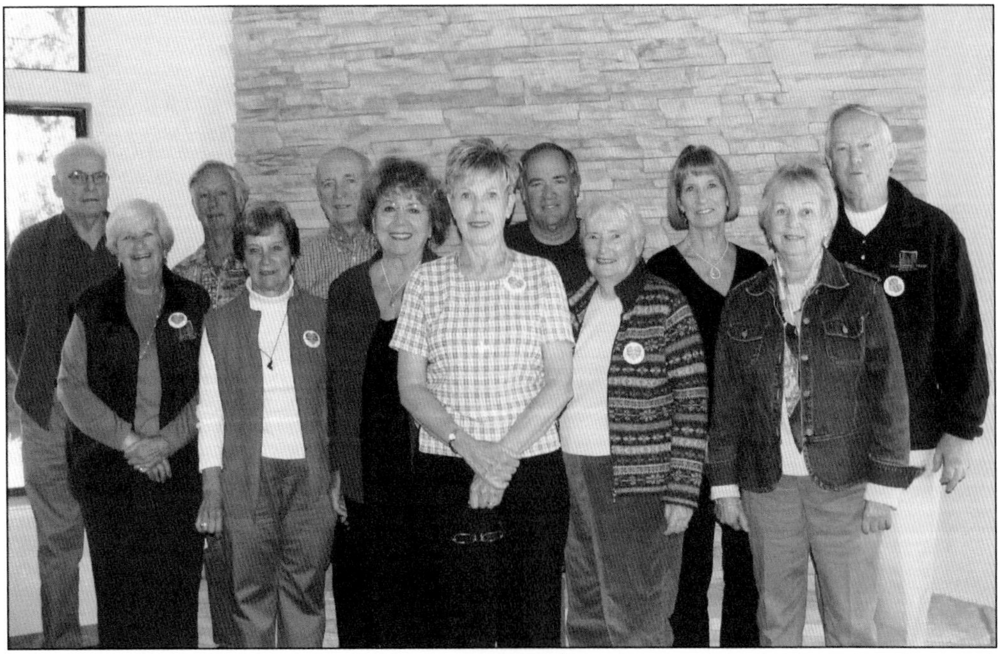

The 2010 Calaveras Big Trees Association board of directors are, from left to right, (first row) Bunny Firebaugh, Marilyn Regan, Marcy Crawford, Margaret Bell, Betty Ann Prescott, and Anne Saunders; (second row) Richard Szukalski, Dick Watson, John Woodward, Bruce Thomsen, Charlotte Hunt, and Steve Stocking. (Photograph by Tami Rakstad-Schaner.)

Bibliography

Bishop, Frances E. "The Big Trees Story." Unpublished manuscript, 1988.

———. *A Brief History of the Big Tree and the Big Tree Stump*. Angel's Camp, CA: Calaveras Big Trees Association, 1985.

Brewer, William H. *Up and Down California in 1860–1864*. Berkeley, CA: University of California Press, 2003.

Engbeck, Joseph H. Jr. *The Enduring Giants*. Sacramento, CA: California Department of Parks and Recreation, 1988.

———. *By the People, For the People: The Work of the Civilian Conservation Corps in California State Parks, 1933–1941*. Sacramento, CA: California State Parks, 2002.

Farquhar, Francis P. *History of the Sierra Nevada*. Berkeley, CA: University of California Press, 2007.

Hutchings, James M. *Scenes of Wonder and Curiosity in California*. San Francisco: J. M. Hutchings, 1862.

———. *In the Heart of the Sierras*. Oakland, CA: Pacific Press Publishing House, 1888.

Lowe, Gary D. *The Big Tree Exhibits of 1870–1871 and the Roots of the Giant Sequoia Preservation Movement*. Livermore, CA: Lowebros Publishing, 2004.

Lynch, Michael G. *California State Park Rangers*. San Francisco: Arcadia Publishing, 2009.

Muir, John. *Our National Parks*. San Francisco: Sierra Club Books, 1991.

Wood, Richard Coke. *Murphys Queen of the Sierra*. Lodi, CA: Abrahamson Printing, 1982.

———. *Big Tree-Carson Valley Turnpike, Ebbetts Pass, and Highway Four*. Murphys, CA: Old Timers Museum, 1985.

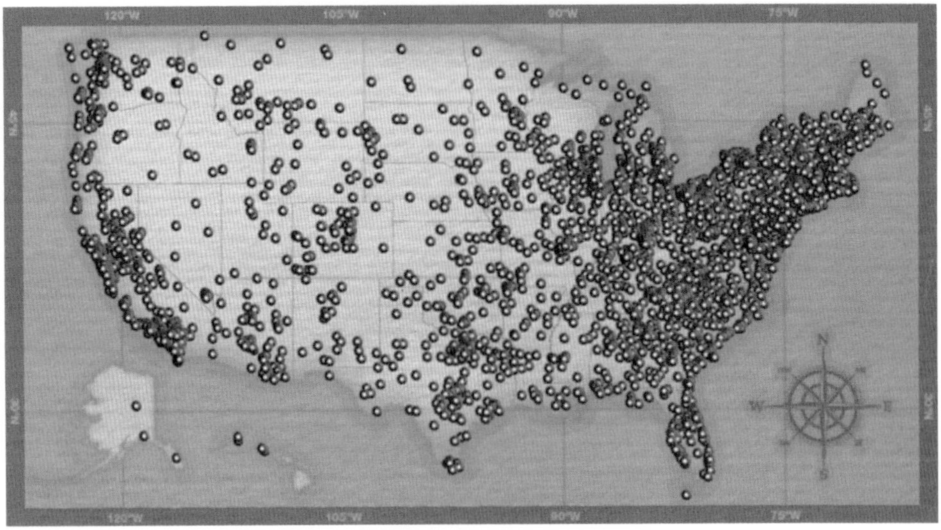